*it*SMF International
The IT Service Management Forum

AN IMPLEMENTATION GUIDE

CONTAINING CD with templates

Implementing Metrics For IT Service Management

ITSM LIBRARY

About the ITSM Library

The publications in the ITSM Library cover best practice in IT management and are published on behalf of itSMF International.

The IT Service Management Forum (itSMF) is the association for IT service organizations, and for customers of IT services. itSMF's goal is to promote innovation and support of IT management. Suppliers and customers are equally represented within the itSMF. The Forum's main focus is exchange of peer knowledge and experience. Our authors are global experts.

The following publications are, or soon will be, available.

Introduction, Foundations and Practitioners books
- Foundations of IT Service Management based on ITIL® (V2, Arabic, Chinese, German, English, French, Italian, Japanese, Korean, Dutch, Brazilian Portuguese, and Russian; Danish and Spanish)
- Foundations of IT Service Management based on ITIL® ((V3, English, Dutch, German, Spanish, Italian))
- IT Service Management – An Introduction (V2, being replaced by V3, only a few languages left)
- IT Service Management – An Introduction (V3, English, Dutch)
- IT Services Procurement based on ISPL – An Introduction (Dutch)
- Project Management based on PRINCE2™ 2005 Edition (Dutch, English, German)
- Release & Control for IT Service Management, based on ITIL® - A Practitioner Guide (English)
- ISO/IEC 20000 - An Introduction (English)

IT Service Management – best practices
- IT Service Management – best practices, part 1 (Dutch)
- IT Service Management – best practices, part 2 (Dutch)
- IT Service Management – best practices, part 3 (Dutch)
- IT Service Management – best practices, part 4 (Dutch)
- IT Service Management - Global Best Practices, Volume 1

Topics & Management instruments
- Metrics for IT Service Management (English)
- Six Sigma for IT Management (English)
- The RfP for IT Outsourcing – A Management Guide (Dutch)
- Service Agreements – A Management Guide (English)
- Frameworks for IT Management (English, German, Japanese)
- Implementing ISO/IEC 20000 Certification - The Roadmap (English)
- IT Governance based on CobiT® – A Management Guide (English, German)

Pocket guides
- IT Service Management – A summary based on ITIL® (V2, Dutch)
- IT Service Management - A Pocket Guide (V3, English, Dutch)
- IT Service Management based on ITIL - A Pocket Guide (V3, English, Dutch)
- IT Service Management from Hell!! (V2, English)
- IT Service Management from Hell. Based on Not-ITIL (V3, English)
- ISO/IEC 20000 – A Pocket Guide (English, German, Japanese, Italian, Spanish, formerly BS 15000 – A Pocket Guide)
- IT Services Procurement based on ISPL – A Pocket Guide (English)
- IT Service CMM – A Pocket Guide (English)
- Six Sigma for IT Management – A Pocket Guide (English)
- Frameworks for IT Management - A Pocket Guide (English, Dutch)

For any further enquiries about ITSM Library, please visit www.itsmfbooks.com, http://en.itsmportal.net/en/books/itsm_library or www.vanharen.net.

Implementing Metrics for IT Service Management

A measurement framework that helps align IT with the business objectives and create value through continual improvements.

A data warehouse model for ITSM.

*it*SMF **International**
The IT Service Management Forum

A publication of itSMF International

Van Haren
PUBLISHING

Colophon

Title:	Implementing Metrics for IT Service Management
Author	David A. Smith
A publication of:	itSMF International
Editors:	Jan van Bon (chief editor) Arjen de Jong (editor)
Publisher:	Van Haren Publishing, Zaltbommel, www.vanharen.net
ISBN-13:	978-90-87531-14-0
Edition:	First edition, first impression, July 2008
Design & Layout:	CO2 Premedia bv - Amersfoort - NL
Printer:	Wilco, Amersfoort -NL

For any further enquiries about Van Haren Publishing, please send an e-mail to: info@vanharen.net

© 2008
All rights reserved. No part of this publication may be reproduced in any form by print, photo print, microfilm or any other means without written permission by the publisher.

Although this publication has been composed with much care, neither author, nor editor, nor publisher can accept any liability for damage caused by possible errors and/or incompleteness in this publication.

Foreword

The IT Service Management community is fast becoming the authoritative body of knowledge and practical advice for businesses wishing to make the best and most efficient use of its IT systems & implementation. For many companies this is an entirely new field of management science that needs careful exploration and exploitation. Other companies have been successfully implementing excellent IT Service Management for longer periods but the level of expertise varies tremendously.

itSMFI sees the spreading of best practice and the further production of material highlighting best practice as essential to leveling the playing field and making sure that as a fledgling industry, the movement goes forward united. We believe that the material in this title helps organizations to get up to speed on what is good IT Service Management practice is all about, helping them to achieve more from what they have within their operations. Greater efficiency means greater profitability!

This title looks practical implementation of Metrics within our Industry. It has received the benefits of a full global peer review and I believe there is real valuable material in here. The sister publication in the series: *Metrics for IT Service Management* makes the point that this activity is only useful if it communicates to the business as well as to the Service area. In addition, measurements are there to ensure the business runs smoothly, hits its objectives and that problems are ironed out even before they arise. My itSMF USA colleague Ken Wendle makes the point more succinctly:

"Yesterday's hero is today's suspect. If you could fix it at 3 am when it broke, chances are you could have prevented it from breaking in the first place."

I'm sure that this guidance will prove invaluable to those addressing these two key points.

Many individuals and organizations have contributed to the development of this book. At itSMF we are indeed very fortunate to have so many people willing to put in time and effort to support our aims of spreading Best Practice throughout the world. I would like to thank all these people and especially those who have spent so much of their own time working on this particular title. They have a lot to be proud of.

Keith Aldis
Interim Chief Editor, ITSM Library

Acknowledgements

We owe author David Smith, President of Micromation Canada, huge thanks for generously sharing his knowledge, best practice and valuable time to develop the contents for this book.

An important role was played by the review team. This team was composed of a wide variety of professionals from all over the world:
- Pierre Bernard, Pink Elephant Inc
- Charles Betz, erp4it
- Peter H.M. Brooks, Phmb Consulting, itSMF South Africa
- William Carruthers, Micromation Inc.
- Janaki Chakravarthy, Infosys Technologies Limited
- Nicole Conboy, CGI Inc.
- Deirdre Conniss, Fujitsu Services
- Greg Danyluk, Danyluk Consulting Inc.
- Karen Ferris, itSMF Australia
- Peter van Gijn, Logica, Netherlands
- Carolien Glasbergen
- Rosario Fondacaro, Quint Wellington Redwood Italy
- Oscar Halfhide, EquaTerra, incorporating Morgan Chambers
- Matiss Horodishtiano, Amdocs, itSMF Israel
- Jim Janes, JBC Enterprises
- Patrick L. Musto
- Brian Shipston, Micromation Inc.
- Rui Soares, GFI Portugal
- Steve Tremblay, Excelsa Technologies Consulting Inc.
- Antonio Valle, G2, Gobierno y Gestión de TI, SLU

Together, they raised a good nine hundred issues that were all taken into account by the editor and the author. In this way, we hope we have achieved best practice in the truest sense of the word, having lots of experts contributing their 'private best practice' experiences, and merging these into a consistent whole.

Given the desire for a broad consensus in the field of IT Service Management, new developments, additional material and other contribution from IT Service Management professionals are welcome to extend and further improve this publication. Any forwarded material will be discussed by the editorial team and where appropriate incorporated into new editions. Comments can be sent to the chief editor, email: j.van.bon@inform-it.org.

Jan van Bon

Table of Contents

Foreword V
Acknowledgements VI

1 Introduction 1

2 What this book is about 3
   2.1   Goals & objectives 3
   2.2   What you will learn 4
   2.3   Scope 4
   2.4   Who should read this book 5

3 How to implement ITSM metrics - overview 7
   3.1   What metrics are all about 7
   3.2   Why implement metrics 7
   3.3   Steering towards value creation 10
   3.4   Who should use metrics 10
   3.5   Implementing metrics 11

4 Basic concepts 13
   4.1   Measurement framework 13
   4.2   Measurement lifecycle 15
   4.3   Determine what is of value 15
   4.4   IT and business alignment 17
   4.5   Defining goals, objectives & metrics 18
   4.6   Core elements of a metric 19

5 Reporting techniques 27
   5.1   Trending 27
   5.2   Aggregation of measures 27
   5.3   Classification of measures 29
   5.4   Alignment of key measures 29
   5.5   Dashboards 30
   5.6   Role based dashboards 31
   5.7   Balanced scorecards 32
   5.8   General scorecards 32
   5.9   Cascading of scorecards 34
   5.10 Strategy maps 34
   5.11 Process scorecards 35
   5.12 Analysis techniques 37
   5.13 Tuning 39

6 The measurement process 41
   6.1 Inputs 42
   6.2 Activities 42
   6.3 Outputs 43
   6.4 Measurement activities 43
   6.5 Administration of metrics data 46
   6.6 Monitoring the metrics 63
   6.7 Analysis of metrics 66
   6.8 Tuning the process 81
   6.9 Implement process initiatives 88
   6.10 Measurement reporting 91

7 ITSM metrics – case study example 103
   7.1 Background 103
   7.2 Planning for implementation 104
   7.3 Implementation 104
   7.4 Monitoring 107
   7.5 Analysis 108
   7.6 Tuning 112
   7.7 Implementation 112
   7.8 Results 112

8 Implementing a measurement program 115
   8.1 Planning and implementation overview 115
   8.2 The 7-Step improvement process 117
   8.3 Planning the process 118
   8.4 Implementation of the measurement process 132
   8.5 Optimizing the measurement process 137
   8.6 Review and audit 139

9 Costs, benefits and possible problems 141
   9.1 Costs 141
   9.2 Benefits 141
   9.3 Possible Problems 142
   9.4 Reduce total cost of ownership 144

10 Conclusions 147

11 User instructions for itSMF KPI Scorecard© metrics template 149
   11.1 Overview 149
   11.2 System requirements 150
   11.3 Installation instructions 150
   11.4 Navigation & structure 151
   11.5 itSMF KPI Scorecard v 1.533 - Metrics MDB template 152

11.6 Process templates.. 157
11.7 Getting Started.. 178
11.8 Printing 180

List of tables and figures 181

References 185

x

Chapter 1
Introduction

Even though we are often too busy to ask for directions, implementing a measurement framework should help align IT with the business objectives and create value through continuous improvements because it helps us create a roadmap and keeps us from getting lost.

It's often been said that "you can't manage what you don't measure" which is still true to this day. Without purpose and a course to follow, the destination is uncertain and almost always unpredictable. Many management books have been written on this subject ranging from personal development to organizational leadership. They all agree in principle that a purpose, goal or destination must be determined in order to chart a course and path to achieve them. Once the path or road map has been defined, the journey must be carefully planned to guide safely the traveller to the desired destination in the prescribed time within planned costs.

Measurements are like navigational aids. They help identify the destination, the road-map to follow, hazards to avoid, mile-stones to reach, fuel consumption, constraints or limitations, expected time of arrival, and so-on. Without navigational aids, one could get lost, end up anywhere, get stranded, fall off a cliff, run out of fuel, get in an accident or fall asleep at the wheel.

The challenge for Information Technology (IT) providers is that the destination can change quickly, frequently and without notice. The information age fuelled by IT has made it possible to accelerate the pace of business. Product and service lifecycles have been reduced from years to days in extreme cases. The business must now lead the market-place, stay close behind or it will vanish as a result of heightened global competition. This has resulted in a run-away feedback loop, IT enables the business to evolve more quickly; competition requires IT to change more rapidly, efficiently and effectively. It's "the nature of the beast".

IT is quickly becoming one of business's most costly, critical and strategic assets. Of late, the money spent on IT is in question, business leaders are continually asking for proof of value delivered. This has put more strain on IT leaders to demonstrate value, reduce costs and improve services or else be outsourced.

IT providers need navigational aids, more so than ever. This presents somewhat of a conundrum. Most IT providers are too busy to figure out how to implement measurements let alone become experts in their use to control and manage the business of IT.

The purpose of this book is to endow IT providers with a flexible and scaleable measurement framework which is easy to learn, implement, manage and improve. It provides methods, concepts, examples, techniques, check lists and metrics templates to accelerate adoption through a "how to" based approach.

Chapter 2
What this book is about

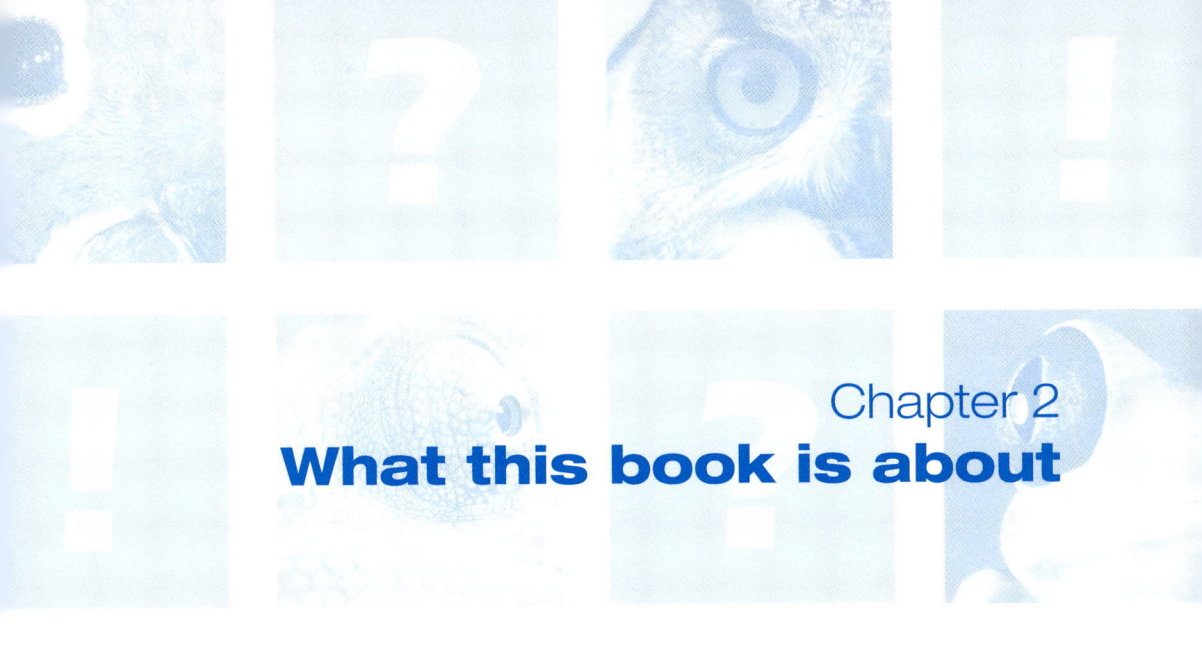

This book "Implementing Metrics for IT Service Management" provides a measurement framework which is based on a continual improvement lifecycle. The measurement framework is aligned with the IT Infrastructure Library (ITIL®)[1] set of best practices. The framework is compatible with the Control Objectives for IT (CobiT®)[2] framework and supports ISO/IEC 20000 standard for IT service management[3].

This book also provides the basic concepts around measurements for business/IT alignment, achieving compliance and driving operational efficiency, effectiveness and quality. Where possible, examples, case studies and check lists have been included along with a scorecard accelerator metrics templates to further improve the learning experience and accelerate the adoption of measurements.

2.1 Goals & objectives

The goal of this book is to provide the reader with a measurement framework that helps align IT with the business objectives and create value through continual improvements; making processes and services more efficient and effective'. This book is complimentary to the book "Metrics for IT Service Management" published by Van Haren Publishing[4].

The objectives of the measurement framework are to help the reader determine ways to:
- help align IT with business objectives and verify results
- maintain compliance requirements for business operations
- drive operational efficiencies, effectiveness and quality

The measurement framework can be implemented as a comprehensive measurement program for all processes and services or selectively for individual process or services.

2.2 What you will learn

By reading this book, the reader will learn:
- Information Technology Service Management (ITSM) metrics overview
- basic measurement framework concepts, core elements, analysis and reporting techniques
- implementing ITSM metrics design approach for operational, tactical and strategic services
- measurement lifecycle of monitoring, analysis, tuning and process improvement
- costs, benefits and common problems
- implementing and optimizing the measurement system

By using the scorecard accelerator metrics templates included with this book, the reader will learn how to:
- conceptualize and apply many of the ideas presented in this book through visualization and practice creating scorecards
- plan the application of a measurement framework for IT service management processes
- personalize and test scorecards and dashboards using predefined metrics and templates
- implement a basic measurement framework pilot
- complete a measurement lifecycle of monitoring, analysis, tuning and process improvement
- report and verify performance improvements; and report value realized over time
- justify the adoption, continuance, customization, expansion, investment and optimization of the measurement framework (fit-for-purpose)

2.3 Scope

Although this measurement framework can be applied to any technology, process or service, the scope of this book is primarily about strategic, tactical and operational processes from the IT Infrastructure Library ITIL®[1] set of best practices. Examples of specific metrics for ITIL® processes can be found in the book "Metrics for IT Service Management"[4] and in the scorecard metrics templates include with this book. Table 2.1 provides an example of strategic, tactical and operational processes:

Strategic	Tactical	Operational
Business Perspective	Service Level Management	Service Desk
Service Improvement Program	Problem Management	Incident Management
Risk Management	Financial Management	Configuration Management
Document Management	Availability Management	Change Management
Competence, Awareness & Training	Capacity Management	Release Management
Program and Project Management	Service Continuity Management	Application Development
	Security Management	Application Support
		Operations Management

Table 2.1 Strategic, tactical and operational processes

2.4 Who should read this book

This book is intended for all levels of IT Management. Specific interest by role includes:
- IT Executive Management
- process/service owners and managers
- CSI owner/manager
- measurement process owner/manager
- IT team leaders
- Service quality professionals
- service level managers

Chapter 3
How to implement ITSM metrics - overview

3.1 What metrics are all about

Based on the book "Metrics for IT Service Management"[5], a 'metric' is just another term for a measure. Metrics provide the feedback mechanism allowing management to steer and control and guide IT toward strategic objectives. The book further explains that metrics help to:
- Align business/IT objectives
  - accounting of IT processes & deliverables
  - inform stakeholders
  - understand issues
  - influence behaviour
  - maximize value creation
- Achieve compliance
  - IT Operations Strategy
  - ISO/IEC 20000[3], CobiT®[2], service levels
  - maturity levels
  - service levels
- Establish operational excellence
  - measure, control, and manage cost effectiveness
  - improve effectiveness and quality
  - service level improvements

3.2 Why implement metrics

You can't manage what you don't measure and what you measure gets done. The ITIL® V3 CSI "Continual Service Improvement" book[6] states four very good reasons why organizations should monitor and measure:
1. to validate previous decisions
2. to set direction for activities in order measure achievements
3. to justify with factual evidence or proof that a course of action is required
4. to intervene as a result of subsequent changes or corrective actions

Today, many IT organizations are producing management reports, metrics and service level achievement statistics. Three key questions for determining value realization:
1. Who receives existing reports?
2. What is done with them?
3. To what degree do they support the goals?

1. Who receives existing reports?

2. What is done with them?

3. To what degree do they support goals?

Figure 3.1   Steering towards value realization

In many cases, today's management reports are often widely distributed and include many technical details which are not easily understood by the average reader. Most of the time they report industry standard metrics but they are not structured or aligned to support the business or IT goals and objectives. Unless there is a serious problem to solve, the reports are often filed away and quickly become 'shelf-ware'. There is very little analysis and determination of root cause done and action plans developed to improve.

Business managers are more aware of IT costs and the value of IT. The Year 2000 (Y2K) non-event started this trend, where billions of dollars were spent to fix a potential date roll-over problem, senior executives have become more aware, concerned and focused on the IT costs and value proposition. The management reports provided by IT have not been meeting the business needs to articulate the cost and value proposition very well.

Additionally, IT has evolved to become such an integral part of the business that for many companies "IT is now the business" and its success is crucial. The business is looking for a way to view the impact of IT in meeting goals and objectives and expressed in business terms.

External regulatory compliance has also elevated the role of IT to help address the business adherence requirements. For example, the Sarbanes-Oxley (SOX) Act in the United States has caused tremendous change and rigor to be applied to the financial reporting processes which are supported by IT systems and processes for any company trading on the New York Stock exchange. IT needs to report and maintain compliance requirements for business operations.

How to implement ITSM metrics - overview

Compounding this even further is that the pace of change and the increase in complexity has gone up exponentially making it very difficult to be proactive. For example, IT has enabled business cycles to become shorter; the IT processes change more frequently as a result of the shorter business cycles; software development lifecycles are quicker to keep pace with the business and IT; and finally the rapid hardware procurement lifecycles because of the advancements in processor speeds. IT needs to report and determine ways to improve operational performance to keep pace with change.

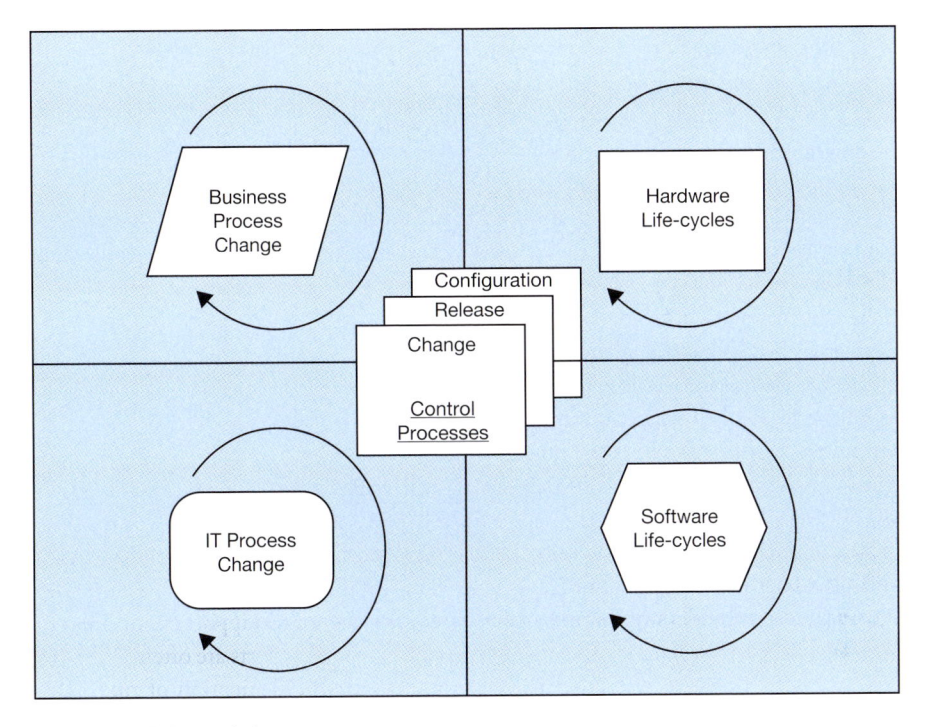

Figure 3.2 Drivers of change

An effective measurement process can help manage change more effectively by focusing on what's important. IT Managers are faced with many challenges to overcome, enabling compliance initiatives and rationalizing, improving and innovating the quality, efficiency and effectiveness of day-to-day IT operations:

- Agility, through managing the pace of change.
- Enablement, by improving IT/Business alignment.
- SOX, C198 (the Canadian version of SOX), ISO/IEC 20000 service levels, through being compliant.
- Transparent open management control through IT governance.
- Management control through error detection and corrective actions to minimize deviations from stated goals.
- Availability and performance by improving service levels.
- Customer satisfaction by improving service quality.
- Efficiency and effectiveness by improving cost/value.
- Rationalization and innovation objectives on service level, quality and cost/value.

Measurements compliment and are a requirement of many best practice frameworks. There has been great demand for IT best practices and management frameworks. Many private and public IT organizations are gravitating towards IT service management frameworks and best practices such as the Control Objectives for IT (CobiT®)[2] best known as an IT Governance model and the IT Infrastructure Library (ITIL®)[1] best known as a library of good practices for IT service management. Both frameworks compliment one another and present many methods, controls, processes, best practices and key performance metrics.

The ITIL® V3 CSI "Continual Service Improvement" Book[7] explains that a measurement framework is needed to help:
- validate the strategy and vision
- provide direction with targets and metrics
- justify with a means to gauge value realized
- intervene and provide corrective actions

Metrics can support all issues listed above when used effectively within the measurement framework, and they can help to:
- provide the instrumentation for management control
- make it easier to concentrate on what's important
- make it easier to spot danger in time to correct it
- improve morale in an organization by recognizing successes
- stimulate healthy competition between process owners
- help align IT with the business goals and objectives; verify alignment
- drive cost efficiencies and effectiveness
- improve service levels and quality of service, increasing satisfaction
- reduce the total cost of ownership (TCO)
- transforms data into information to impart knowledge and gain wisdom

3.3 Steering towards value creation

Metrics used within a measurement framework can help to steer towards value creation by keeping the following guiding principles in mind:
- Focus on metrics which demonstrate IT value either directly or indirectly.
- Use metrics to drive continual improvement strategies and tactics which have outcomes that support the organization's goals and objectives.
- Regularly communicate the successes and impact to the key stakeholders.
- Align the IT goals and objectives with the business, choose critical success factors to help meet the objectives, then formulate the key metrics required to monitor the progress against them.
- Evolve and optimize the metrics to help predict and prescribe solutions which better support the business goals and objectives.

3.4 Who should use metrics

Metrics are used by executive management, service/process owners and technical staff to gauge performance of services, processes and technologies. Executives are concerned with meeting strategic goals and objectives of the business and IT strategy. Metrics help management summarize the efficiency, effectiveness and quality of their capabilities and resources to delivery services to customers. Service and process owners are most interested in the justifying, directing and controlling services and processes. Metrics help service and process owners to measure service and process capabilities from a customer's perspective. Technical staff are focused on service delivery execution and technology management. Technology staff require metrics to measure the resources that provide the capabilities from a functional and technical perspective. Metrics provide the ability to measure performance from many perspectives.

Figure 3.3 shows that capabilities in the form of services and processes rely on resources which may span multiple functions and technologies; all of which can be measured through metrics.

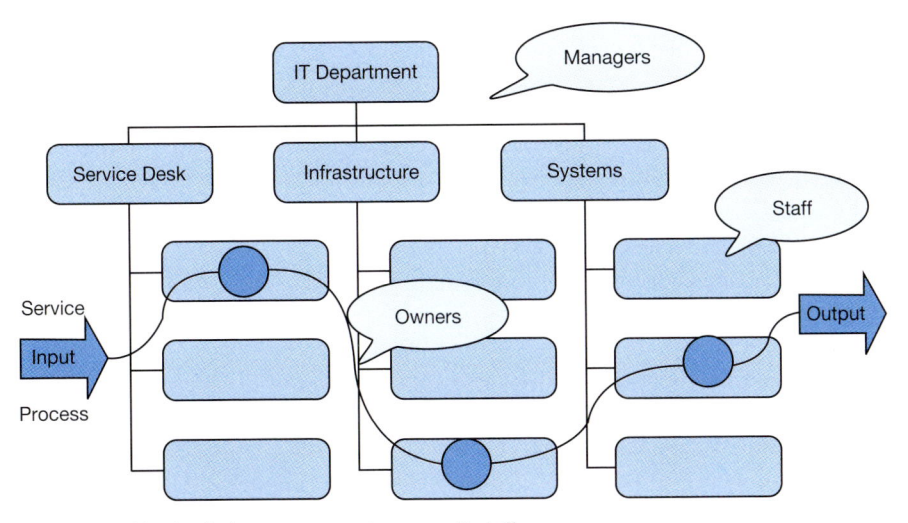

Figure 3.3   Metrics help management, owners & staff

3.5   Implementing metrics

Metrics need to be aligned with the business and IT goals and objectives. Metrics implemented in isolation of business and IT strategy, goals and objectives will quickly result in fragmented groups running in different and sometimes opposing directions. For example, implementing metrics to monitor and only reduce Service Desk costs can be at the expense of service levels; resulting in the increase of hidden costs due to shifting the burden of support to the business users. TCO studies have uncovered these scenarios where IT cost controls can increase hidden costs. The overall effect is an increase in organizational costs.

Metrics help improve process performance. Metrics in IT have traditionally been measured in functionally oriented silos like the Help Desk, Server Technical Services or the Operations Department. Information technology itself has enabled process or service centric organizational models requiring metrics which report beyond the functional boundaries to determine success. For example, the Application Development and IT Operations departments are both functionally very mature and when independently measured, appear successful. However, they don't work well with each other and together frequently fail to deliver deployments.

Metrics can be used to measure and improve end-to-end services. Metrics have been very mature for measuring system availability on a discrete component basis, but in many cases without consideration for the end-to-end user experience. For example the application server was available 99.99% of the time but the network is not measured and is frequently not available or not responsive. Therefore the measure of system availability does not match the user experience. Improving the service from the user's perspective will improve customer satisfaction.

Metrics can verify the benefits and value realized from performance improvements. Metrics have been used on many occasions to produce elaborate justifications for new projects through cost/benefit analysis then quickly forgotten once the money has arrived. For example, implementing the new change management software to reduce change costs, improve through-put and increase customer satisfaction which was never re-calculated and verified after the project implementation. Measuring results can verify the benefits and value were actually realized.

Metrics help drive continual service improvements. Metrics reports are regularly produced and widely distributed throughout the company but not used to evaluate trends or make performance improvements. In some cases they are not used at all. For example, a business compliance audit discovered that the monthly IT reports had not been produced for six months because the report administrator was given new duties. The real value that metric reports can provide is often overlooked like setting direction and targets, evaluating goal attainment, identifying trends or issues and making adjustments and corrections.

A new and improved approach for implementing metrics using a continual improvement framework is needed to align IT to the business, meet new and changing compliance requirements and provide a means to gain operational excellence. This book provides a "measurement framework" reference model which can be quickly implemented, adapted and evolved to meet the organizations needs. Some of the key features of this measurement framework reference model include:
- continual improvement, that is, W. Edward Deming's[8] Plan/Do/Check/Act cycle
- top-down design approach for aligning goals and objectives
- process and service based IT service management approach
- scalable and flexible fit-for-purpose model with hundreds of sample metrics and scorecards
- bottom-up reporting of facts, metrics, indicators, scorecards and dashboards
- aggregation of metrics to formulate key performance indicators
- accountability and roles based matrix models
- techniques for comparative, causal and predictive analysis
- method for filtering improvement initiatives and tracking performance status
- ability to report performance improvements and derived value based benefits
- multiple implementation methods and scenarios
- how- to -check lists for planning and implementing metrics
- scorecard accelerator metrics templates to demonstrate principles and techniques; and to help kick-start a measurement program implementation

Chapter 4
Basic concepts

Some basic concepts are covered to provide background and structure to building and implementing a measurement program. These include describing a measurement framework; techniques for determining what is of value to achieving business alignment; the performance measurement lifecycle; core elements of a metric and reporting, analysis and tuning techniques.

4.1 Measurement framework

The goal of the measurement framework is to provide process, metrics and techniques to help align IT with the business objectives and create value through continual improvements. The objectives of the measurement framework are to:
- help align IT with business objectives and verify results
- maintain compliance requirements for business operations
- drive operational efficiencies, effectiveness and quality

The measurement framework can be implemented as a comprehensive measurement program for all processes and services or selectively for individual process or services.

The ITIL® V3 CSI "Continual Service Improvement" book[7] suggests that the four main reasons to monitor and measure are to help validate, direct, justify and intervene when necessary to make improvements.

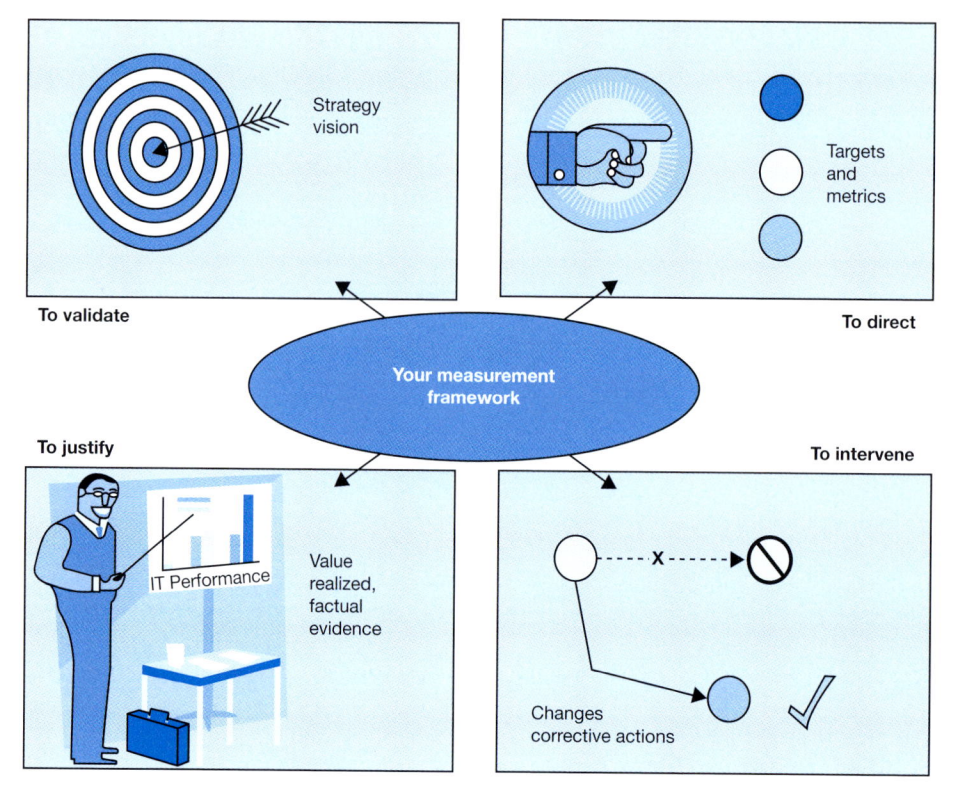

Figure 4.1 Measurement framework

There are four critical success factors for an effective measurement framework:
- Enable validation of the strategy and vision
  - aligned with the IT goals and objectives
  - validation that alignment is working
  - confirm goals and objectives are met
- Provide direction with targets and metrics
  - set targets through metrics
  - control and manage the processes
  - verify targets are being met
- Justify with a means to gauge value realized
  - justify performance improvements with a solid fact base
  - improve decision making
  - quantify benefits realized
  - communicate value realized with factual evidence
- Intervene and provide corrective actions
  - identify deviations when they occur
  - understand the root causes
  - intervene with corrective actions to minimize consequences

Basic concepts

4.2 Measurement lifecycle

The measurement lifecycle is comprised of four core processes which repeat to form a continual improvement feedback loop based on W. Edward Deming's Plan/Do/Check/Act cycle[8].

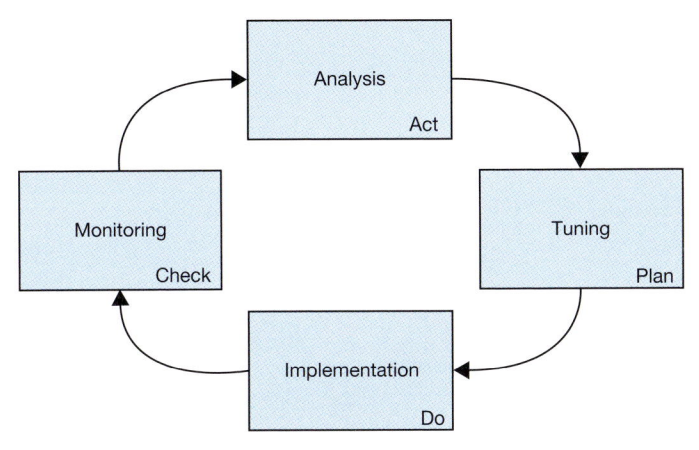

Figure 4.2 Deming Plan/Do/Check/Act Cycle

- **Tuning / Plan** - Tuning is responsible for identifying improvement opportunities and recommendations for the subject process or service which is being measured.
- **Implementation / Do** - Implementation is responsible for implementing the recommended changes through normal change management processes.
- **Monitoring / Check** - Monitoring is responsible for the data gathering, calculations and validation of the required measurements.
- **Analysis / Act** - Analysis is responsible for comparative, causal and predictive analysis of the measurements.

There are additional supporting processes "Administration of the measurements" and "Reporting the results". These supporting processes help manage and communicate information.

4.3 Determine what is of value

Determining what is of value to the organization requires regular review of the business and IT strategy and plans. What is of value to one organization may be very different from a competing organization and may change significantly over time as internal and external priorities and influences evolve. Additionally, there can be different customer groups within a business who may have a different perception of what is of value. Value could range from emphasis on the economic delivery of services; to efficient utilization of resources; through effective realization of business outcomes. For example, an Accounting Department may view reduced costs as high value but a sales department might consider improved quality as high value.

The ITIL® V3 SS "Service Strategy" book states "what the customer values is often quite different than what the IT organization believes it provides". It further suggests that to understand the customer's value of percept, a marketing mindset should be used to ask questions like:
- What is our business?
- Who are our customers?
- What do our customers value?
- Who depends on our services?
- How do they use our services?
- Why are they valuable to them?

Using the marketing mindset to understand the opportunities and challenges of the customer's business provides great insight to understand how customers perceive the positive effect of the IT services on their business outcomes. For customer, the positive effect is known as the utility of the service. The assurance of the positive effect is knows as the warranty. With review of the business and IT strategy and plans and meeting with the business, it can be determined where IT can provide the most value to the IT customer and align or adjust the IT goals, objectives and measures accordingly. The next step should be that programs are defined, agreed upon, planned and initiated to meet the "value add" objectives that have been selected. Organizing benefit management explicitly may help significantly in allocating, planning, controlling and achieving the different value themes across the organization entities.

Figure 4.3 provides an example of different value themes.

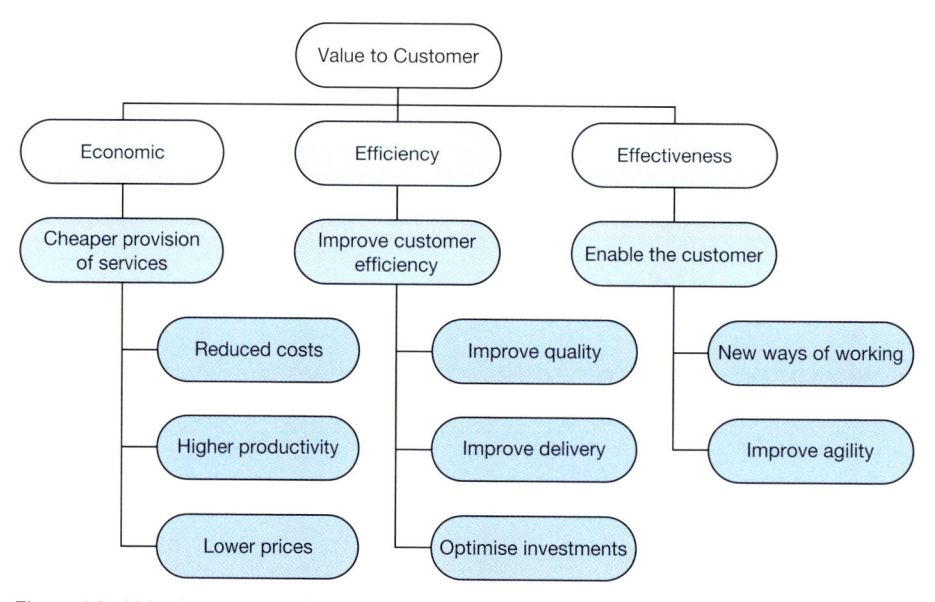

Figure 4.3   Value to customer themes

Basic concepts

4.4 IT and business alignment

Business goals are the desired medium to long-term future states to be attained. They are best expressed in measurable terms through objectives. The objectives of the business are shorter-term measurable milestones detailing how the business will achieve the goals.

Critical success factors are the essential elements or actions which are necessary to steer, control and achieve the business goals and objectives. They help provide guidance on what's important.

Key performance indicators measure the objectives success rate in enabling the goal to be reached and/or provide insight as to why business goals are not being met. This method is further propagated to the IT goals and objectives where they become critical success factors or necessary elements to steer, control and achieve the business objectives and so-on.

Objectives should be expressed in terms of how much bigger, how much faster, how much more value is aimed for. At the very least, the achievement of an objective must be demonstrable in terms of acceptance: for example, by individuals (such as sponsors) or groups (such as steering committees) who are stakeholders. Key Performance Indicators (KPIs) are the measures by which it will be determined if the objectives have been met. Key Goal Indicators (KGIs) are the measures to verify and confirm that the goal has been achieved.

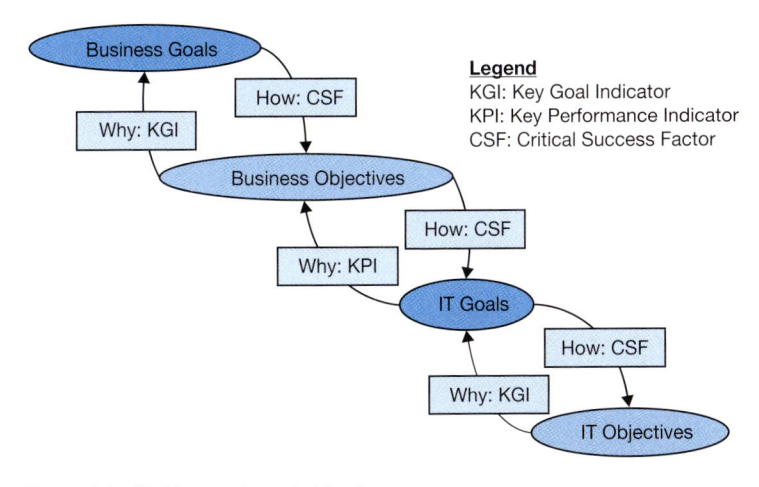

Figure 4.4 Linking goals and objectives

General definitions and criteria are as follows:
- **Goal** - a goal is an aspiration of the company that provides the direction in which the company will focus its resources and efforts in support of its mission. Some typical goals for a company could be:
  - Increase market share
  - Increase profits
  - Reduce time to market
  - Improve customer service

Some typical IT goals could be:
- Create IT agility
- Account for and protect all IT assets
- Optimize the use of information
- Improve IT cost efficiency and its contribution of business profitability

- **Objectives** - objectives are the short-term targets (typically 12-24 months or less) of defined measurable achievement. Goals and objectives together identify what the organization intends to support, as well as how it will be measured. Some typical IT objectives could be:
  - Decrease costs, errors or reworks by a specific percentage
  - Decrease processing or turnaround times by a specific percentage
  - Increase productivity or capacity by a specific percentage
  - Eliminate backlogs by a specific percentage
  - Reduce risk by a specific percentage
  - Improve service levels by a specific percentage
  - Comply with regulatory requirements (avoid fines or penalties)
  - Provide better access to data needed for decision making within a specific time limit

4.5 Defining goals, objectives & metrics

In selecting goals, objectives and metrics, the ITIL® V3 SD "Service Design" book[9] suggests that it is important that they are well defined. They must be specific, measurable, actionable, relevant and timely (SMART) to answer the questions "how will we get?" and "were we successful?"

A model was developed in the mid 1980s by Victor Basili at the University of Maryland called the GQM (Goals Questions Metrics) paradigm[10]. Well designed goals and objectives help to focus on the end-results and tell if they are being achieved through verification with metrics. Victor Basili described his six-step GQM process as follows:
1. Develop a set of corporate, division and project business goals and associated measurement goals for productivity and quality.
2. Generate questions (based on models) that define those goals as completely as possible in a quantifiable way.
3. Specify the measures that need to be collected to answer those questions and track process and product conformance to the goals.
4. Develop mechanisms for data collection.
5. Collect, validate and analyze the data in real time to provide feedback to projects for corrective action.
6. Analyze the data in a post-mortem fashion to assess conformance to the goals and to make recommendations for future improvements.

For example, the following goals/objectives are ambiguous:
- implement change management (why?)
- more effective & efficient IT service management (what does effective & efficient mean?)
- higher quality of IT service support (quality in terms of what?)
- increased customer satisfaction (satisfaction with what?)
- reduced incidents (with what aim?)

Basic concepts

The following questions are useful to better define SMART goals and objectives:
- What are the specific outcomes?
- Can the desired outcomes be measured?
- What do we need to ask ourselves to determine if we have achieved these goals?
- What constitutes a realistic success?
- What are the time boundaries?

The following questions are useful to define the metrics required to support the goals and objectives:
- What are the metrics that will support the determination if the goals and objectives have been achieved?
- What are the metric that will help diagnose where the issues are?
- What are the metrics required to produce performance or goal indicators?
- Decide if and how to report on KPI and metrics

4.6 Core elements of a metric

Metrics have a number of elements, the core elements of basic metrics include the following terms:

Actual
The actual or current value of the metric for the most recent period and expressed in numerical fashion that is number, percent, currency, time, et cetera.

Previous
The previous value of the metric for the last period and expressed in numerical fashion, that is number percent, currency, time, et cetera.

Trend
The trend is the change direction of the actual value when compared to the previous value. For example, trending can be up – increasing; the same – no change; or down – decreasing.

Unit of measure
The unit of measure refers to what is being measured in numerical terms. For example, # incidents, satisfaction levels, # calls, minutes, hours, days, cost, changes, et cetera.

Polarity
The polarity of a metric is the desired directional change. For example, increasing is better (More successful changes) or decreasing is better (Less unsuccessful changes).

- **up** – actual metric value is higher than last period
- **same** – actual metric value is same as last period
- **down** – actual metric value is lower than last period

Progress

The progress indicates the movement of the current metric value compared to the last period and takes polarity into consideration, that is, did an improvement occur? For example:
- **better** – actual metric value is better than last period
- **same** – actual metric value is the same as last period
- **worse** – actual metric value is worse than last period

Thresholds

Thresholds provide the expected ranges for the metric to use as a reference and comparison. This is to determine if the actual value is above or below its target and danger values; and between the upper and lower limits. This approach is often used to set the status of metric, that is green = OK, yellow = caution, and red = alert.

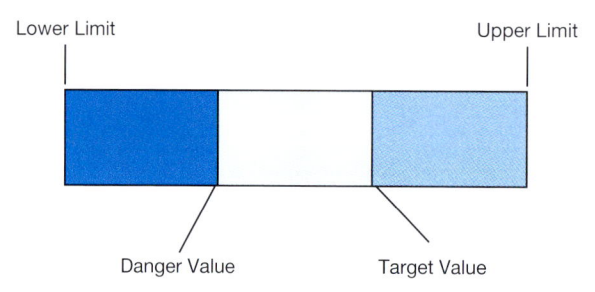

Figure 4.5   Metric thresholds

Reporting period

The reporting period refers to the point-in-time in which the metric was measured. For example, Financial Year 2007, 1st Calendar Quarter 2007, March 2007, March 31st 2007.

Reporting frequency

The reporting frequency refers the intervals in which the metric is measured. For example, hourly, daily, weekly, monthly, quarterly, semi-annual, yearly, et cetera.

Target value

The target value is used to set the metric's target threshold or green status condition which is also dependent on the polarity of the metric, that is lower is better versus higher is better.

Danger value

The danger value is used to set the metric's danger threshold or red status condition which is also dependent on the polarity of the metric, that is lower is better versus higher is better.

Low limit

The low limit value is used to indicate the lowest possible value for the metric. Note that when the metric's actual value falls below the low limit, a potential data entry error or a wrong threshold value exists.

High limit
The high limit value is used to indicate the highest possible value for the metric. Note that when the metrics actual value falls above the high limit, a potential data entry error or a wrong threshold value exists.

Baseline
A baseline is the normal operating value for a specific metric. The baseline could be an average of a number of actual measures or a point-in-time snapshot of an actual measure. Baselining is used to compare current performance against a historical or accepted standard. For example, if you measured the performance of a process over a period of time, you could use that performance figure as a comparative baseline if you made a change to the process. Baselines are also used to set threshold ranges like the target-value and danger-value.

Benchmark
A benchmark is similar to a baseline but uses external comparison data for example industry or similar peer group's high/low/average data value for the metric.

Status indicators
Status indicators are used to display the current condition of a metric relative to its thresholds. Status indicators are often color coded like a stop-light or sometimes represented through a graphic symbol or gauge display. For example, a stop-light color code would normally indicate:
- **green** – OK
- **yellow** – caution
- **red** – attention

Alerts
When a metric exceeds its danger value, an alert condition exists and is usually displayed through a color coded status indicator in red. An alert is generally used to initiate some form of, or a set of prescribed actions.

Metric weight
Sometimes one or more metrics may have more significance than the others when aggregating them into a theme or a group. For example, one metric could have more weight and therefore more influence than the other metrics included in the aggregation method. See 'Metric Themes' and 'Aggregation of Measures' for more examples.

Metric owner
The metric owner or measurement process owner is the person in the organization who is accountable and/or responsible for managing the metrics. The metric owner is often the owner of the measurement process.

Data source
The data source provides the details on where the data was obtained to produce the metric, that is database, surveys, source transactional systems or files. It also provides an overview of how the data is captured; the location or department it represents; any manipulation or calculations

required; and the expected data quality specifications. For example, for a change management metric "% Successful - changes on time":
- **data sources** – change management sub-system
- **how captured** – extract the count of closed on time and the count of total closed
- **location** – division A of company XYZ
- **calculations** - count of [Successful - closed on time] / [Successful - closed] for period
- **data quality** – potential 2% error rate

Figure 4.6 provides examples of various data sources:

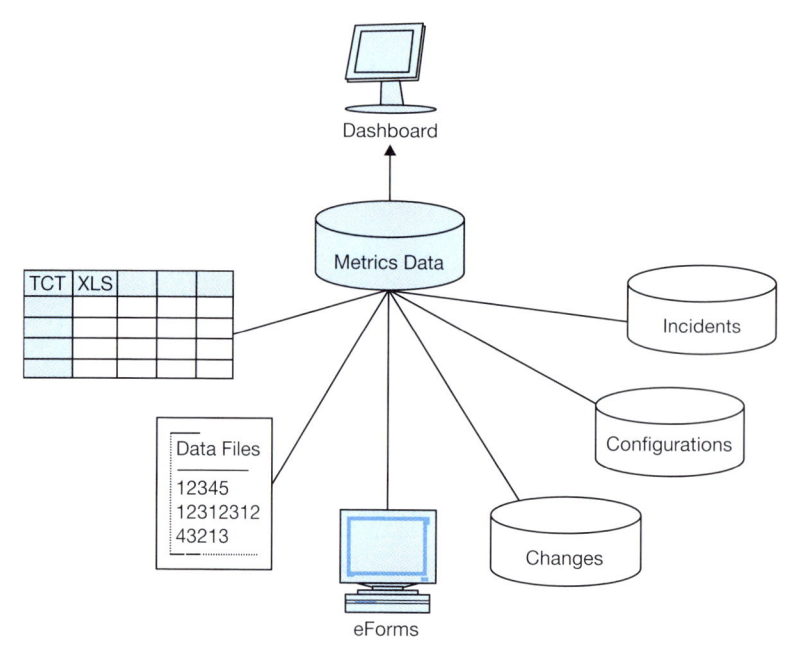

Figure 4.6   Sample data sources

Metric dimension

A metric dimension is a data element that helps to characterize the data to provide filtering, grouping and labelling. Dimensions provide structured labelling information to otherwise unordered numeric measures providing a means for "slice and dice" reporting. For example, metric dimensions could include date, organization, customer, service, process, technology, priority, et cetera.

Metadata

The simplest definition of metadata; "metadata is data about data - more specifically information (data) about a particular content (data)". The metadata for a metric describes the purpose of the metric in terms of analyzing the data, tracking performance, detecting patterns and trends, and helping make better decisions. For example:
- **goal** – the goal the metric supports
- **mission** – the mission the metric supports

- **objective** – the objective the metric supports
- **description** – a short description of what the metric is all about
- **specification** – a description of how the metric is measured or calculated
- **justification** – a description of what the metric is used for and why it is useful
- **audience** – a list of whom the metric is to be provided
- **constraints** – any issues that limit the application or interpretation of the metric
- **owner** – person accountable or responsible for managing the metric
- **source** – where the data was obtained from
- **calculations** – the formulas used for calculations

Measure dictionary

Each metric should have its associated elements registered in a master measure dictionary for quick reference. Figure 4.7 provides an example of a measurement dictionary.

Example KPI Measure Dictionary

Perspective/Theme: Internal Process	Measure #/Name: *IM001% incidents resolved by 1st line support*	Process Owner: *D. Smith, Incident Manager*	
Goal: *To minimize the impact of service disruptions to the business by restoring that service through effective management of incidents.*		Objective: *To prevent a breach in agreed service levels by ensuring the timely resolution of incidents.*	
Description: *How many incidents require no escalation to second line support?*			
Lag/Lead: *Lag*	Frequency: *Monthly*	Unit Type: *Percentage*	Polarity: *High values are good*
Danger Value: *<65%*	Target Value: *>85%*	Low: *0%*	High: *100%*
Threshold Actions: *Owner to present new initiatives to correct deviation*		Accountability: *ITSM Manager*	
Formula: *A count of incidents that require no escalation.*			
Data Source: *Data is extracted from incident management system monthly.*			
Data Quality: *> 95% Confidence Level*			Data Collector: I. Jones, IT Analyst
Baseline: *Our most recent data from incident management system indicates 75% of incidents are resolved by 1st line support.*		Target: *Q1:75% Q2:75% Q3:80% Q4:80%*	
Target Rationale: *This is a measure of a few things. If the Service Desk has a good Known Error DB supplied by Problem Management the number of incidents resolved by the first line support will increase.*			
Initiatives:	1.*Training all 1st line support staff by Q2 on new applications*		
	2. *Increased use of knowledge base system by 25% by Q3*		
	3. *Customer service training pass level > 60% for all 1st line support staff*		
Comments/Notes:			

Figure 4.7   Sample measurement dictionary

Examples of metric core elements

The following list provides an example of the core elements of a metric for 'Temperature' (see figure 4.8):

- **actual** – today's temperature
- **previous** – yesterday's temperature
- **trend** – up or down
- **polarity** – increase/decrease is better
- **progress** – warmer is better
- **unit type** – Celsius/Fahrenheit
- **thresholds/banding** – seasonal range
- **alerts** – public warnings
- **period** – day
- **frequency** – daily, hourly
- **target** – optimal setting
- **baseline** – last year's temperature
- **benchmark** – high/low/average
- **status Indicators** – thermometer
- **weighting** – relative importance, i.e. temperature versus precipitation
- **data quality** – accuracy
- **data source** – weather network system
- **data owner** – environment Canada
- **time stamp** - date and time the measure was taken

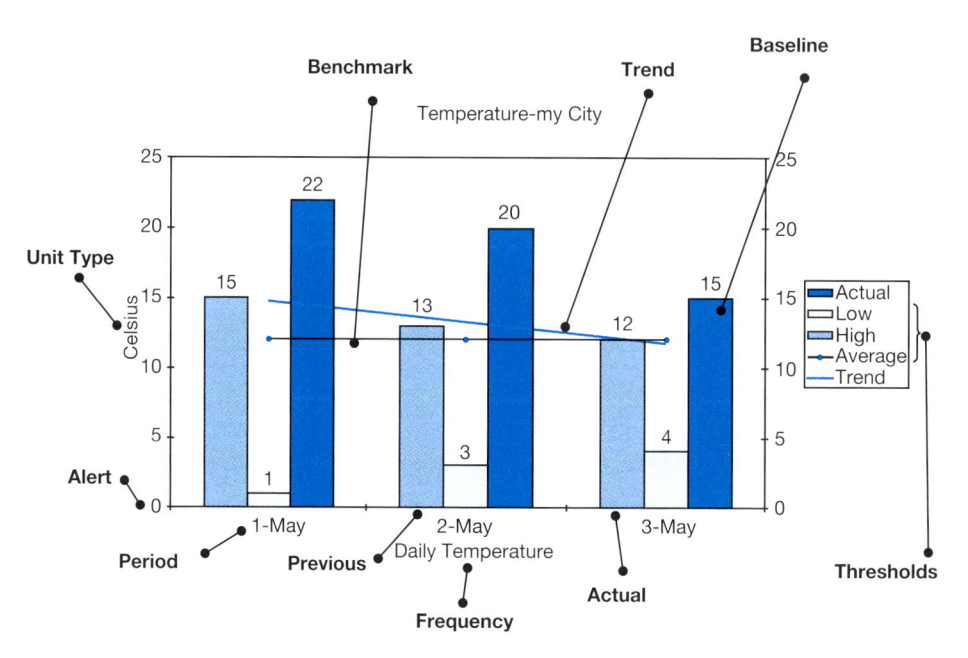

Figure 4.8 Sample metric elements – Temperature

Metric themes

Metrics can be grouped or classified by themes to create key performance indicators. Themes enable metrics to be viewed from different perspectives and context. This method is called 'aggregating' which is a means of looking at a group of metrics together as a whole. For example, an Effectiveness KPI may consist of two or three metrics viewed as a group. The following list provides other examples of metric themes to produce key performance indicators:

- **effectiveness** – goals and objectives are being met
- **efficiency** – cycle time and/or costs are improving
- **cost effective** – optimal performance for lowest cost
- **quality** – defects are down and/or satisfaction is up
- **workload** – volumes are manageable within resource constraints
- **utilization** – processes/services are operating at optimal capacity levels
- **performance** – performance is acceptable or improving
- **compliance** – compliance requirements are being met
- **improvements** – initiatives are working and making improvements
- **benefits** – value is being realized
- **utility** – the functionally and features of a service
- **progress** – desired change over time

Chapter 5
Reporting techniques

There are many techniques for reporting metrics. At the lowest level, trending of individual metrics provides detailed information to operational management about the state of the process or service activities. Using aggregation methods, metrics are classified and grouped together by themes for process owners and senior management to determine the health of a process or service. At the highest level, using dashboards and scorecards reporting techniques helps to visualize the end-to-end process or service to quickly drill-down into the details and determine opportunities for improvement.

5.1 Trending

Monitoring and reporting trends of individual metrics helps identify potential problem areas within a process or service. Trending helps pinpoint the hot-spots or weak links throughout the process or service. Trending typically includes monitoring the inputs, activities and outputs of the process over time. Trending indicates variations over time and whether variations are moving in a positive or negative direction, if improvements are required and if corrective actions are making a difference. Trending can be used to trigger alerts to the metric owner who in-turn would initiate a set of prescribed corrective actions or remedies. Figure 5.1 provides an example trending report for an incident management metric:

5.2 Aggregation of measures

Metrics can be aggregated together using indexing techniques and viewed as a group-theme to create key performance indicators. For example, a key performance indicator for quality may require looking at defects rates throughout the process and include customer satisfaction. Figure 5.2 provides an example of quality for the Configuration Management process:

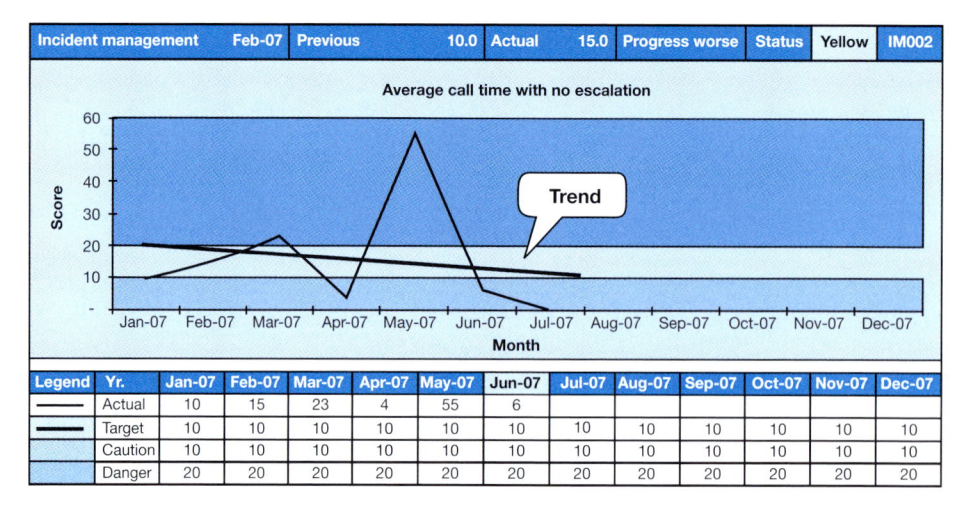

Implementing Metrics for IT Service Management

| Incident management | Feb-07 | Previous | 10.0 | Actual | 15.0 | Progress worse | Status | Yellow | IM002 |

Average call time with no escalation

(Trend chart: Score vs Month, Jan-07 to Dec-07)

Legend	Yr.	Jan-07	Feb-07	Mar-07	Apr-07	May-07	Jun-07	Jul-07	Aug-07	Sep-07	Oct-07	Nov-07	Dec-07
	Actual	10	15	23	4	55	6						
	Target	10	10	10	10	10	10	10	10	10	10	10	10
	Caution	10	10	10	10	10	10	10	10	10	10	10	10
	Danger	20	20	20	20	20	20	20	20	20	20	20	20

Figure 5.1 Sample trending report

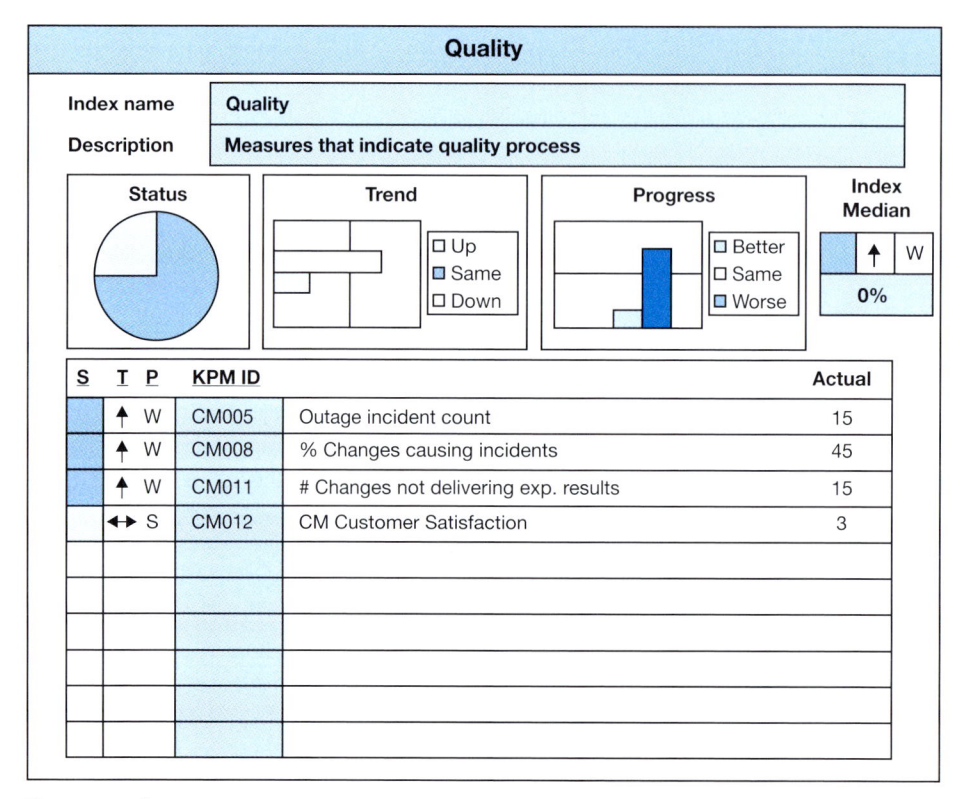

Quality

Index name: Quality
Description: Measures that indicate quality process

Status | Trend (Up / Same / Down) | Progress (Better / Same / Worse) | Index Median ↑ W 0%

S	T	P	KPM ID		Actual
	↑	W	CM005	Outage incident count	15
	↑	W	CM008	% Changes causing incidents	45
	↑	W	CM011	# Changes not delivering exp. results	15
	↔	S	CM012	CM Customer Satisfaction	3

Figure 5.2 Sample aggregation of measures

5.3 Classification of measures

Measures can be grouped by types and classified to produce strategic and tactical types of key indicators and metrics. Classification is a method of categorizing measures into groups that help steer, control, direct, justify, verify, correct and optimize value. Some examples of classification are as follows:

- **Key Goal Indicator (KGI)** - A key goal indicator (KGI) is used to confirm (after the fact) that a business or IT goal has been achieved. KGIs are the measure of success and verification of accomplishment. KGIs can be thought of as 'lagging' indicators that tell us if the goal has been achieved. For example, a KGI for a fully optimized Information Technology (IT) service could be that all objective targets for efficiency, effectiveness and quality measures were met.
- **Critical Success Factor (CSF)** - A critical success factor (CSF) is a business term for an element which is necessary for an organization to achieve its objectives. CSFs are used to steer, control and monitor the actions required to reach the desired outcomes. For example, a CSF for a successful change management process could be "protect services when making changes". For another example, an objective of achieving a high level of customer satisfaction might have a critical success factor of hiring the right calibre of staff. The latter is not a business objective in its own right, but may be a critical prerequisite to achieving the objective.
- **Key Performance Indicator (KPI)** - Key performance indicators (KPIs) are metrics used to quantify objectives to reflect the performance of a process or service. KPIs are used to assess the present state of the process and to prescribe a course of action. KPIs can be thought of as "leading" indicators that tell us how well a process is performing in its objective to achieve an objective or CSF. The act of monitoring KPIs in real-time is known as activity monitoring. KPIs are frequently used to 'value' difficult to measure activities such as the value based benefits, efficiency, effectiveness, quality and satisfaction.
- **Key Performance Metrics (KPM)** - Key performance metrics are a system of parameters or ways of quantitative and periodic assessment of a process/service that is to be measured. KPMs are used to assess and interpret inputs, outputs and activities of a process in light of previous or comparable assessments. KPMs are frequently used to assess trends and initiate corrective actions when necessary. KPMs are often used together to formulate key performance indicators using aggregation and indexing techniques.
- **Key Fact Metrics (KFM)** – Key fact metrics are the quantitative data which provide fact-based information on the process activities during a period of time. For example, volumes, frequency rates, workload, effort, utilization, throughput, costs, defects, et cetera. KFMs are often used to produce KPIs and KPMs using formulas or calculations.

5.4 Alignment of key measures

Aligning the key measures requires a top-down view of what is important to the organization and its stakeholders. Then, a bottom-up build of the facts, metrics and indicators to support the desired outcomes. Executive management is most interested in executing strategy and vision to meet the goals and objectives; KGIs, CSFs and KPIs that support strategy attainment are most important. Senior management are concerned with justifying, directing and controlling services and processes to meet the strategy and vision requirements; KGIs, CSFs, KPIs and KPMs that support operational excellence are important. Managers and staff are focused on service and process execution and within the guidelines required of senior and executive management; CSFs, KPIs, KPMs and KFMs help them tactically to stay-the-course, see figure 5.4.

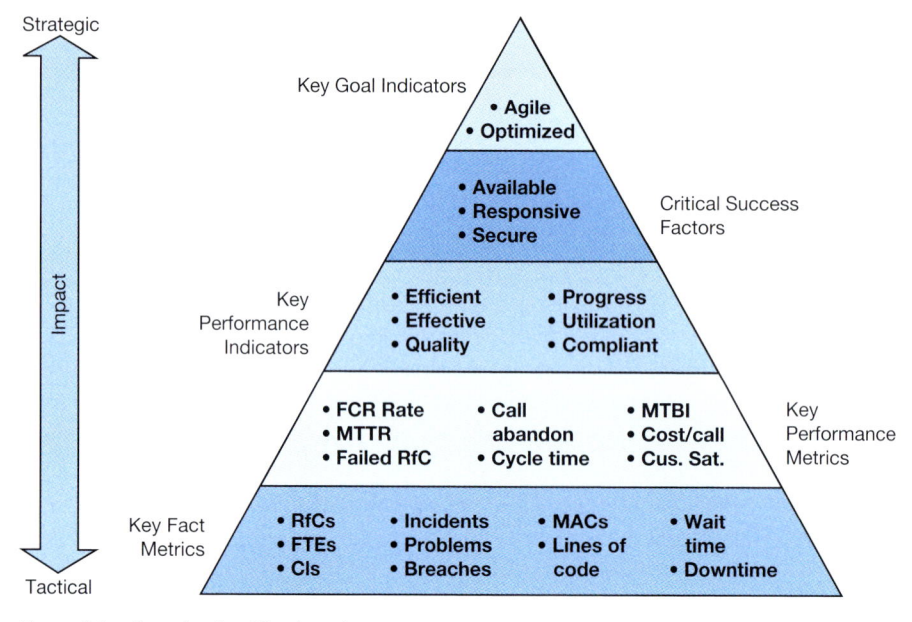

Figure 5.3 Sample classification of measures

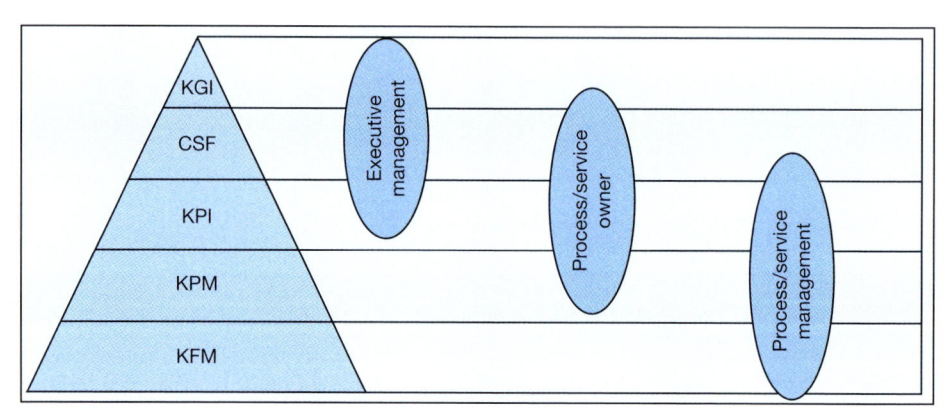

Figure 5.4 Alignment of key Measures

5.5 Dashboards

Dashboard reporting helps provide the instrumentation for management control. Summarised and visual in nature, dashboards make it easier to concentrate on what's important. Dashboards can also identify successes and trouble areas at a glance and usually provide drill-down capability to get to the details. Dashboards can be configured and personalized to provide strategic, operational and tactical views of the organization, processes, services and activities. For example, figure 5.5 provides an example overview of performance, goals, benefits and initiatives for all IT service management processes:

Reporting techniques

5.6 Role based dashboards

Role based dashboards help make it easier to view, map and align relevant information by role. Figure 5.6 provides an example of mapping strategic information for a Chief Information Officer (CIO); summarised IT service management results for senior IT management; and specific process and service based results by process/service owners (Service Level Manger "SLM", Incident Manager "IM" and Change Manager "CM"):

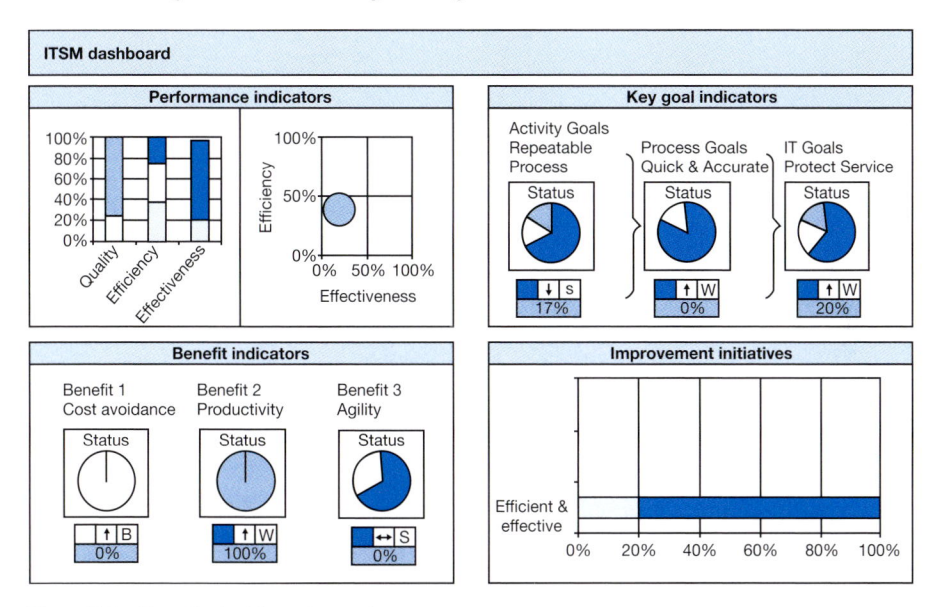

Figure 5.5   Sample dashboard report

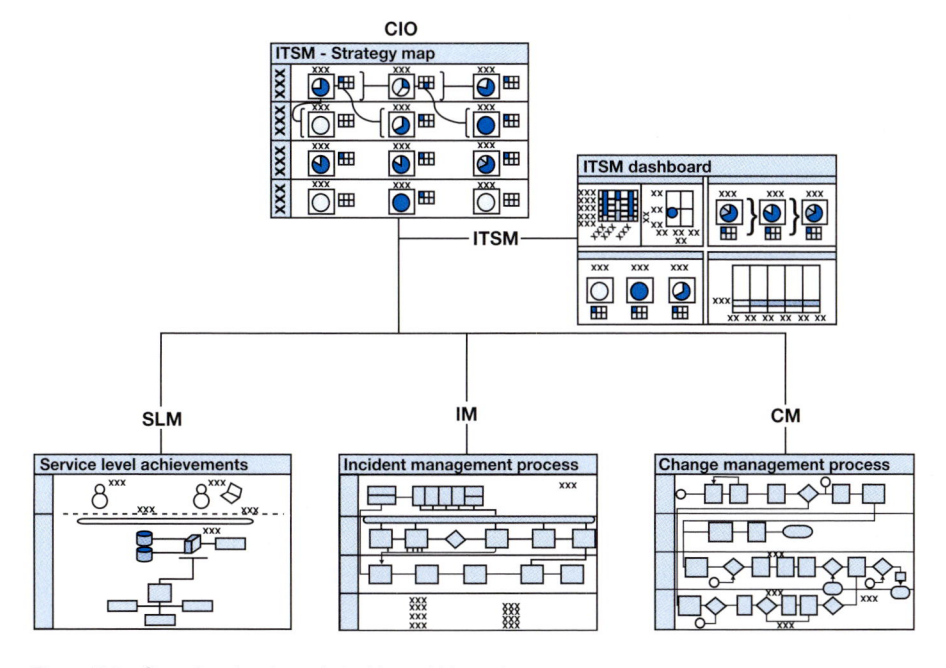

Figure 5.6   Sample roles-based dashboard hierarchy

5.7 Balanced scorecards

The balanced scorecard (BSC) is a methodology developed by Robert Kaplan & David Norton[11]. The balanced scorecard helps translate the organization's strategy into performance objectives, measures, targets and initiatives. This popular methodology prescribes breaking the strategy down into perspectives using cause and effect linkages. Then developing and using objectives, measures and initiatives to support each perspective. Figure 5.7 provides an example of four BSC perspectives:

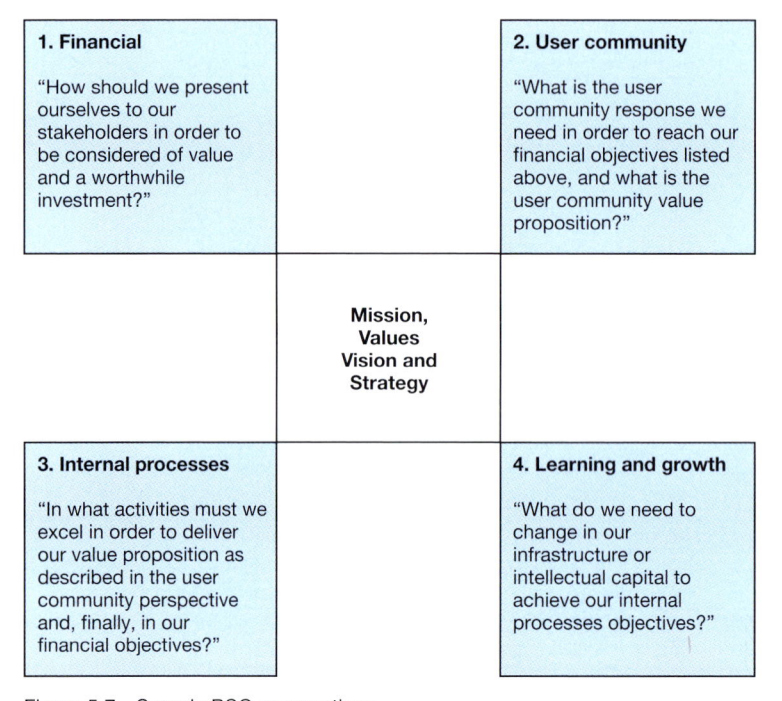

1. Financial	2. User community
"How should we present ourselves to our stakeholders in order to be considered of value and a worthwhile investment?"	"What is the user community response we need in order to reach our financial objectives listed above, and what is the user community value proposition?"
3. Internal processes	4. Learning and growth
"In what activities must we excel in order to deliver our value proposition as described in the user community perspective and, finally, in our financial objectives?"	"What do we need to change in our infrastructure or intellectual capital to achieve our internal processes objectives?"

Centre: Mission, Values, Vision and Strategy

Figure 5.7 Sample BSC perspectives

5.8 General scorecards

General scorecards are used to present specific and summarised information by groups, themes or initiatives. Figure 5.8 provides an example of a series of scorecards related to a Performance theme:

Reporting techniques

Change Management - Performance Scorecards

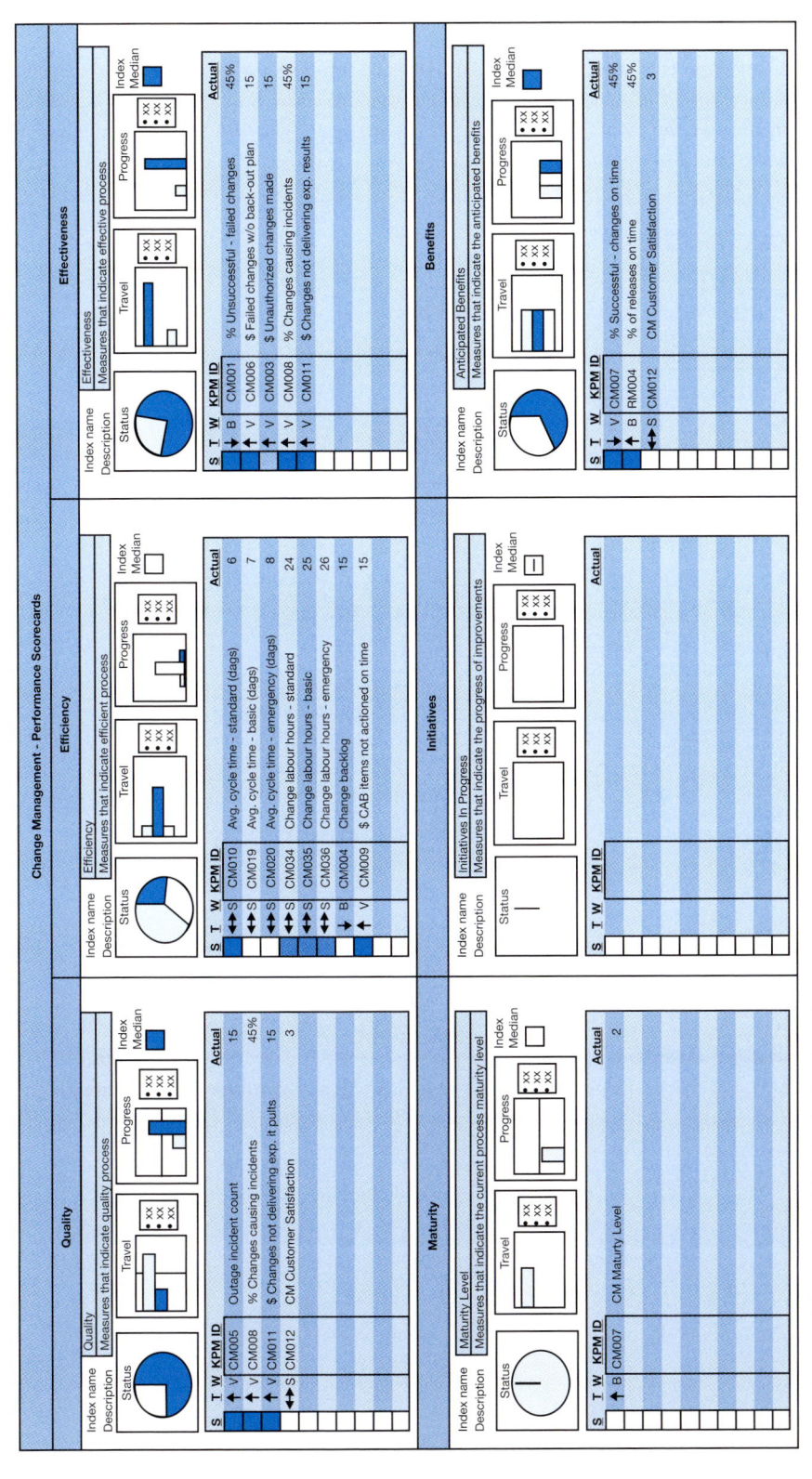

Quality				
Index name	Quality			
Description	Measures that indicate quality process			
Status	Travel	Progress	Index Median	

S	T	W	KPM ID		Actual
	↑	V	CM005	Outage incident count	15
	↑	V	CM008	% Changes causing incidents	45%
	↑	V	CM011	$ Changes not delivering exp. it pults	15
	↑↓	S	CM012	CM Customer Satisfaction	3

Efficiency				
Index name	Efficiency			
Description	Measures that indicate efficient process			
Status	Travel	Progress	Index Median	

S	T	W	KPM ID		Actual
	↑↓	S	CM010	Avg. cycle time - standard (days)	6
	↑↓	S	CM019	Avg. cycle time - basic (days)	7
	↑↓	S	CM020	Avg. cycle time - emergency (days)	8
	↑↓	S	CM034	Change labour hours - standard	24
	↑↓	S	CM035	Change labour hours - basic	25
	↑↓	S	CM036	Change labour hours - emergency	26
	→	B	CM004	Change backlog	15
	←	V	CM009	$ CAB items not actioned on time	15

Effectiveness				
Index name	Effectiveness			
Description	Measures that indicate effective process			
Status	Travel	Progress	Index Median	

S	T	W	KPM ID		Actual
	→	B	CM001	% Unsuccessful - failed changes	45%
	↑	V	CM006	$ Failed changes w/o back-out plan	15
	←	V	CM003	$ Unauthorized changes made	15
	↑	V	CM008	% Changes causing incidents	45%
	↑	V	CM011	$ Changes not delivering exp. results	15

Maturity				
Index name	Maturity Level			
Description	Measures that indicate the current process maturity level			
Status	Travel	Progress	Index Median	

S	T	W	KPM ID		Actual
	↑	B	CM007	CM Maturity Level	2

Initiatives				
Index name	Initiatives In Progress			
Description	Measures that indicate the progress of improvements			
Status	Travel	Progress	Index Median	

Benefits				
Index name	Anticipated Benefits			
Description	Measures that indicate the anticipated benefits			
Status	Travel	Progress	Index Median	

S	T	W	KPM ID		Actual
	→	V	CM007	% Successful - changes on time	45%
	↑	B	RM004	% of releases on time	45%
	↑↓	S	CM012	CM Customer Satisfaction	3

Figure 5.8 Sample general scorecards by themes

5.9 Cascading of scorecards

Using a cascading approach, scorecards should be designed top-down with the business goals and objectives in mind then built bottom-up to create cause-and-effect linkages. When populating the scorecards they are fed from the bottom-up. This approach helps ensure there is alignment and cohesiveness from top to bottom, see figure 5.9.

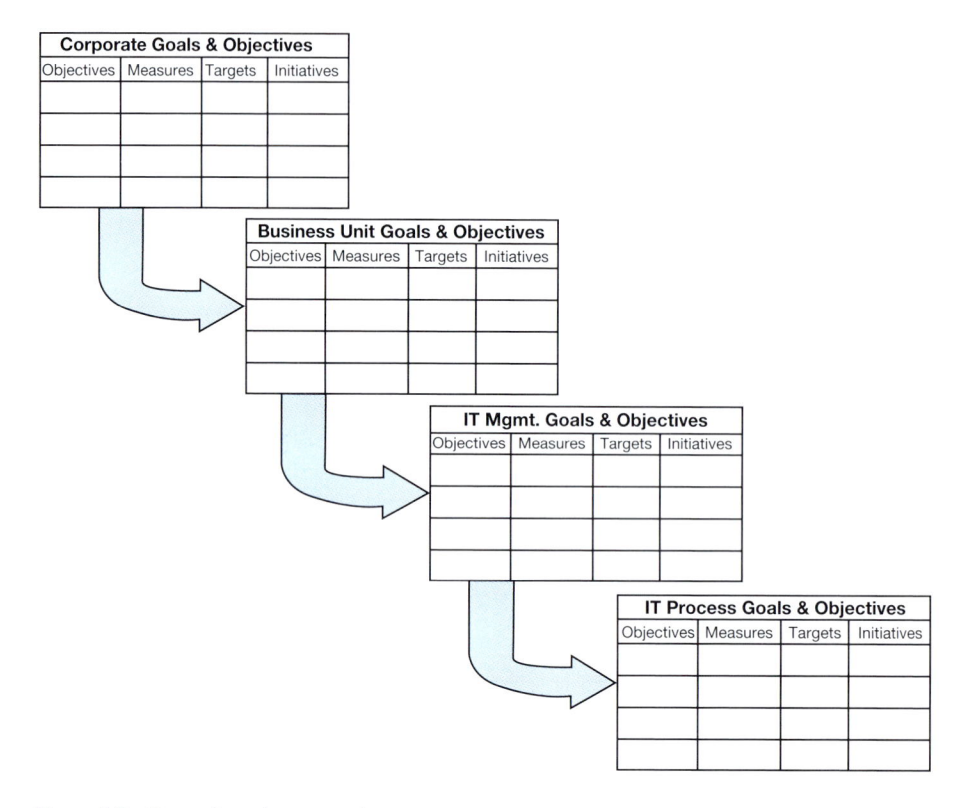

Figure 5.9   Cascading of scorecards

5.10 Strategy maps

Strategy maps are another form of a scorecard which visually displays the cause-and-effect relationships necessary to achieve the organization's vision and mission. Figure 5.10 provides an example of a strategy map with the following characteristics:
- **theme** – increase the value of IT
- **perspectives**:
    - user community – fulfill the value obligation to the user community
    - internal CIO processes – through being able to deliver effective services
    - learning and growth – by having the necessary available tools
    - financial resources – by securing and prioritizing the use of limited resources
- **legend**
    - green – OK
    - yellow – investigate
    - red – attention

- **coloured bubbles** – objectives and their cause and effect relationships
- **ghosted bubbles** – metrics

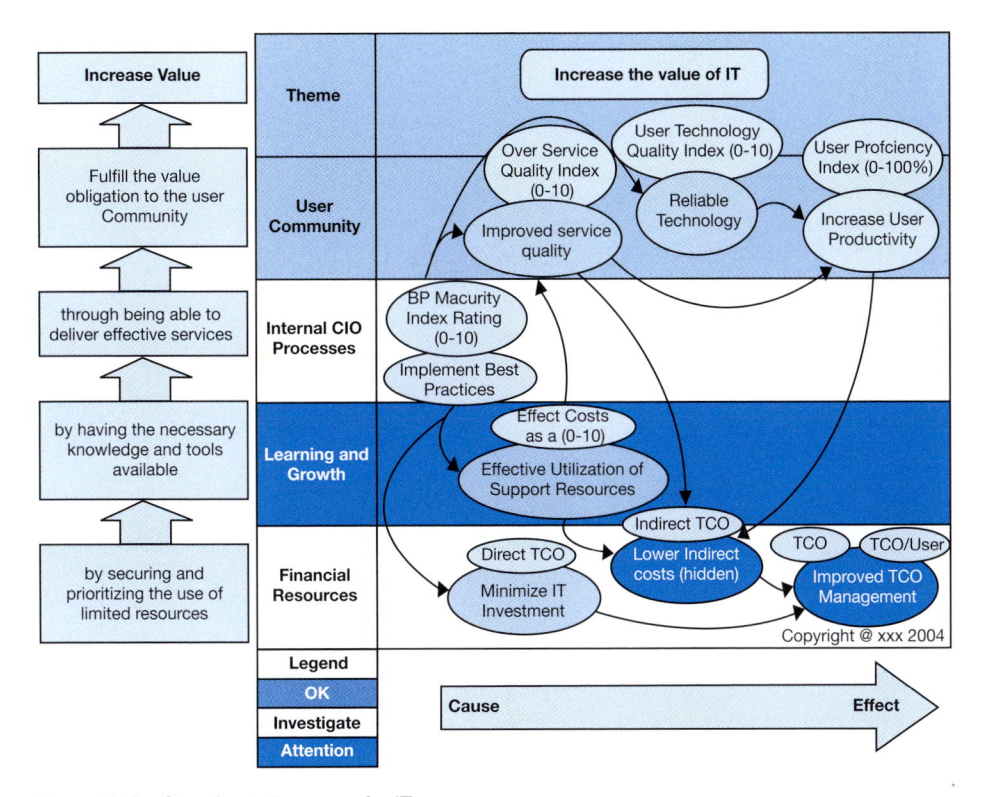

Figure 5.10 Sample strategy map for IT

5.11 Process scorecards

Process scorecards are another type of scorecard which help to summarise the health of a process/service; steer and control the process/service; to pinpoint hot-spots requiring attention; and predict where areas of improvement are required. Process scorecards should contain a mix of outcome measures and causal measures. Process scorecards help view and visualize a process or service end-to-end as a whole. Process scorecards are process/service centric regardless of who is responsible for the individual tasks or activities.

Process scorecards help to determine the health of a process/service by assessing the performance using theme based metric groups to form key performance indicators. Themes enable the process to be viewed from different perspectives. For example, typical performance themes could include:
- **quality** – free from defects and/or meeting high levels of customer satisfaction
- **effectiveness** – goals, objectives, and activities are being met as planned
- **cost effective** – optimal performance for lowest cost
- **efficiency** – cycle time and/or costs are as planned

- **maturity** – process/service is optimized by exploiting known best practices
- **benefits** – expected value of the process/service is being realized
- **initiatives** – improvement initiatives are executing as planned
- **dependencies** – identify other processes that this process/service is dependent on

Process scorecards can be used to steer, control and manage the process with predefined critical success factors using theme based metric groups. For example, critical success factors for the change management process could be:
- **repeatable process** – a repeatable process for making changes consistently
- **quick & accurate** – make changes quickly and accurately (business driven needs)
- **protect service** – protect services when making changes
- **efficient & effective** – deliver expected process efficiency & effectiveness benefits

Process scorecards can also be used to pinpoint problem areas that require attention by using key fact metrics and key performance metrics as 'process sensors' to indicate process states. The sensors are strategically placed throughout the process to take process state readings to monitor specific aspects of the process. Some examples of process sensors could include:
- **inputs** – indication of the volume of work, requests and/or feedback received
- **activities** – indication of the success of various activities, leading indicators of workload and/or backlog of work
- **outputs** – indication of the outcomes and/or results produced

Process scorecards can be used for predictive analysis by anticipating where problems might occur and having some prescriptive remedies on-hand to deal with situations if required. This is possible by placing process sensors close to activities on the process scorecard to indicate potential root causes and to act as leading indicators. It is possible that more than one activity could be a suspected cause; in this case each activity would require investigation to determine the root cause. When placing sensors in this fashion it is highly recommended that 'Diagnostic Reasoning' for the sensor placement is documented to minimize confusion and trouble-shooting effort. Diagnostic reasoning should include 'Suspect Root Causes' and 'Prescriptive Remedies' information for each process sensor. For example, an output metric "# of failed changes w/out back out plan" in the Change Management process could be a result of:
- **suspect root causes**
  - inadequate planning in the Release & deployment management process
  - emergency change decision resulted in by-passing back out plan creation
  - Change Advisory Board (CAB) risk assessments not rigorous enough or overlooked.
- **prescriptive remedies**
  - improve Release & deployment management planning
  - reduce emergency changes, revise approval policy
  - improve CAB risk assessments

Some basic rule-of-thumb guidelines for placing the sensors throughout the process include:
- **keep it simple** – too many sensors will congest the process and make interpretation difficult and confusing
- **inputs** – generally placed at the beginning of the process as leading indicators
- **activities** – generally placed throughout the process as leading indictors

- **outputs** – generally placed at the end of the process as lagging indicators
- **root-cause approach** – place sensors close to activities which may be the source or potential cause of problem areas
- **leading/lagging approach** – use interrelationship and Ishikawa diagrams to determine leading and lagging indicators. See 6.7, section "Reactive analysis techniques"
- **documentation** – good record keeping of the diagnostic reasoning behind sensor placement

Figure 5.11 provides an illustration of a process scorecard from the "Metrics for IT Service Management[12]" book and includes references to quality, efficiency and effectiveness measures:

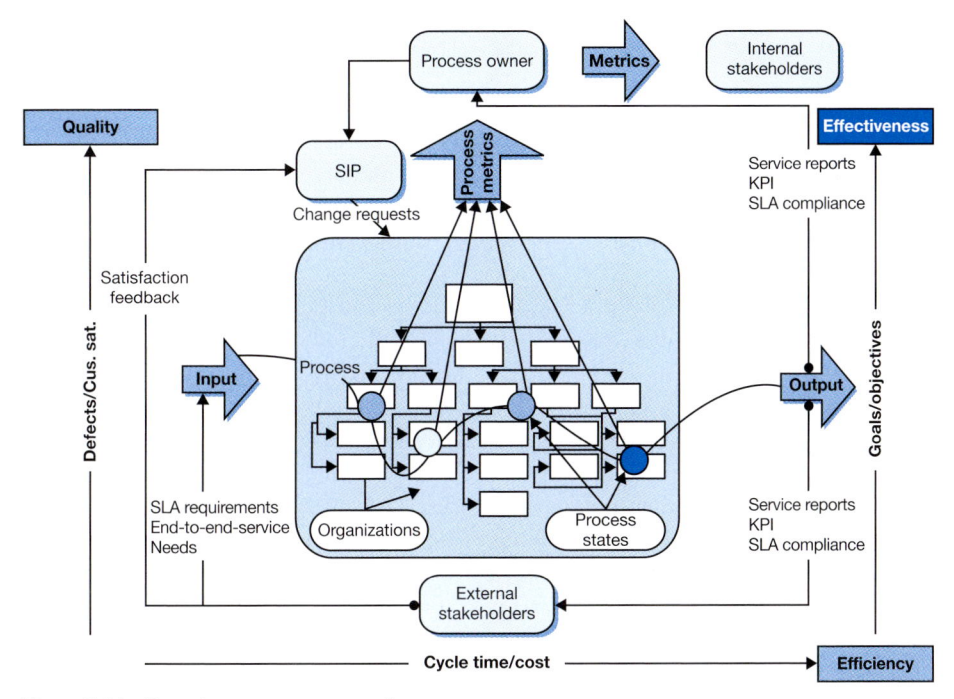

Figure 5.11 Sample process scorecard

5.12 Analysis techniques

There are a number of analytical techniques which are useful in performing investigative analysis. Analysis techniques can be reactive and used only when issues present themselves; or they can be proactive in nature and used to remediate weaknesses before issues occur. For example, a reactive analysis may reveal more staff is required to correct a degrading service level; a proactive analysis may reveal that workload is increasing which will require more staff to prevent service levels to degrade. In the reactive example the service level has already degraded and needs to be remediated. In the proactive example the increase of workload triggers an action which prevents a service level breach. The following sections provide an overview of useful tools and techniques, further information can be found in section 6.7 Analysis of Metrics.

Reactive analysis

The reactive analysis techniques are concerned with handling deficient processes or services (problems) in an efficient and effective way when they occur. Useful reactive analysis techniques include:

- **Compare & contrast analysis** - The compare and contrast analysis observes similarities and differences between various measures allowing the team to observe whether the current measurement value is better than or worse than other points of reference. This helps to set goals and prioritise actions based on the degree of variance between the measures being observed once the similarities and differences are understood.
- **Process flowcharting** - Process flowcharting creates a picture of the process which allows the team to identify the value chain and actual sequence of events in a workflow for any process or service. Flowcharts can also be used to identify who is responsible for key activities, where key measure points should be taken, where decisions are made and what interfaces are required. This is a pre-requisite for developing the Process scorecard.
- **Affinity diagrams** - The affinity diagram is used for gathering and grouping of ideas. This allows a team to creatively generate a number of ideas or issues and organize them into common themes or natural groupings. This analysis method is useful to help understand the nature of a problem and develop creative ideas to solve them. This method is also useful for identifying themes for key indicators.
- **Cause & effect** - The cause-and-effect diagram (also referred to as an Ishikawa, Tree or Fishbone diagram) helps display the factors that affect a particular quality, benefit, outcome, or problem. The diagram is named after its developer, Kaoru Ishikawa[13] (1915-1989), a leader in Japanese quality control.
- **Relations diagrams** - The relations diagram is used to look for drivers and outcomes to allow the team to systematically identify, analyze, and classify the cause and effect relationships that exist among key issues. This enables the team to focus on effective solutions that address critical drivers and outcomes. This method can also support the creation of Ishikawa diagrams.
- **Kepner-Tregoe problem analysis** - The Kepner-Tregoe problem analysis is a useful method to analyze problems and distinguish between symptoms and root cause(s), developed by Charles Kepner and Benjamin Tregoe[14]. They state that "Problem analysis should be a systematic process of problem solving and should take maximum advantage of knowledge and experience". They distinguish five phases for problem analysis.

Proactive analysis

Proactive analysis techniques are concerned with identifying and resolving problems before process or service degradation occurs. This helps minimize the adverse impact on the service deliver processes, service levels and business-related costs. Useful proactive analysis techniques include:

- **Trend analysis** - The objective of trend analysis is to identify 'weak' processes or components of the service management process and investigate the reasons for their weakness and correct them. Trending of key performance metrics or indicators help the team to recognize and identify variances over time. Trend analysis also helps to tell the difference between a trend and an anomaly (an exception to the norm). Trend analysis can be used for reactive analysis as well.
- **Brainstorming** - The objective of brainstorming is to produce more and better ideas. Using an open-forum method free of criticism and judgement, the team can generate a number of

quality ideas on any topic. Brainstorming is useful for planning and defining all aspects of a measurement framework design and program implementation.
- **Predictive analysis** - The objective of predictive analysis is to develop a course to steer to help achieve the desired outcomes. Like the cause-and-effect diagrams that are used to troubleshoot problems to determine the root-cause, the same approach can be used in a reverse order to predict desired outcomes. A predictive analysis is used by the team to map out a cause and effect sequence of disparate but connected measures which provide the desired results for the organization. This method uses a balance of leading and lagging indicators that help to articulate a strategy or hypothesis and to help visualize the cause and effect relationships in a strategy map diagram. A leading indicator is one that predicts that something may or is about to happen whereas a lagging indicator confirms an outcome has already taken place or has happened.

5.13 Tuning

The main objective of tuning is to determine, prioritise and plan the most cost effective implementation of improvements for IT service management. Analysis of the monitored data may identify areas of the process or service that could be tuned to improve performance of the process through improvement initiatives. The main activities of tuning include:
- review of the alternate options to implement improvements
- a review of gaps and actionable items required for implementation
- the anticipated benefits from the implementation of the changes including key performance metrics and timelines
- decision analysis criteria review

Initiatives are used to create continual step-by-step process improvements to increase maturity and operational optimization over time. They can be minor (actionable items) or significant (project based) in nature. There are four main decision analysis criteria for consideration when prioritizing competing initiatives sometimes referred to as 'The Business Case':
- **cost of making the change** – time, money, resources
- **time to recover costs** – break even point
- **risks, impact or potential problems that may be encountered** – from implementation or from status quo
- **anticipated business benefits** – quantitative, qualitative and alignment

Chapter 6
The measurement process

As stated earlier "The goal of the measurement process is to provide a measurement framework that helps align IT with the business objectives and create value through continual improvements". The three main objectives are identified as:
- to help align IT with business objectives and verify results
- to help maintain compliance requirements for business and IT operations
- to drive operational efficiencies, effectiveness and quality

The critical success factors for an effective measurement framework are the ability to validate, direct, justify, and intervene when necessary to achieve the goal and objectives. The following definitions of the four critical success factors are provided from the ITIL® V3 CSI "Continual Service Improvement" book[6]:

- **To validate** – Monitoring and measuring to validate previous decisions.
- **To direct** – Monitoring and measuring to set direction for activities in order to meet set targets. It is the most prevalent reason for monitoring and measuring.
- **To justify** – Monitoring and measuring to justify, with factual evidence or proof, that a course of action is required.
- **To intervene** – Monitoring and measuring to identify a point of intervention including subsequent changes and corrective actions.

The measurement process is a structured set of activities designed to achieve the goals and objectives. The "Administration" sub-process receives inputs from various sources that trigger subjects or objects to be monitored and measured. The core operational sub-processes provide four main activities of monitoring, analysis, tuning, and implementation which forms continual feedback loops. The reporting process provides communication outputs which are fed into the continual service improvement process. The measurement process is critical success factor for any continual service improvement process.

Figure 6.1 shows the inputs to, the activities within and the outputs from the measurement process.

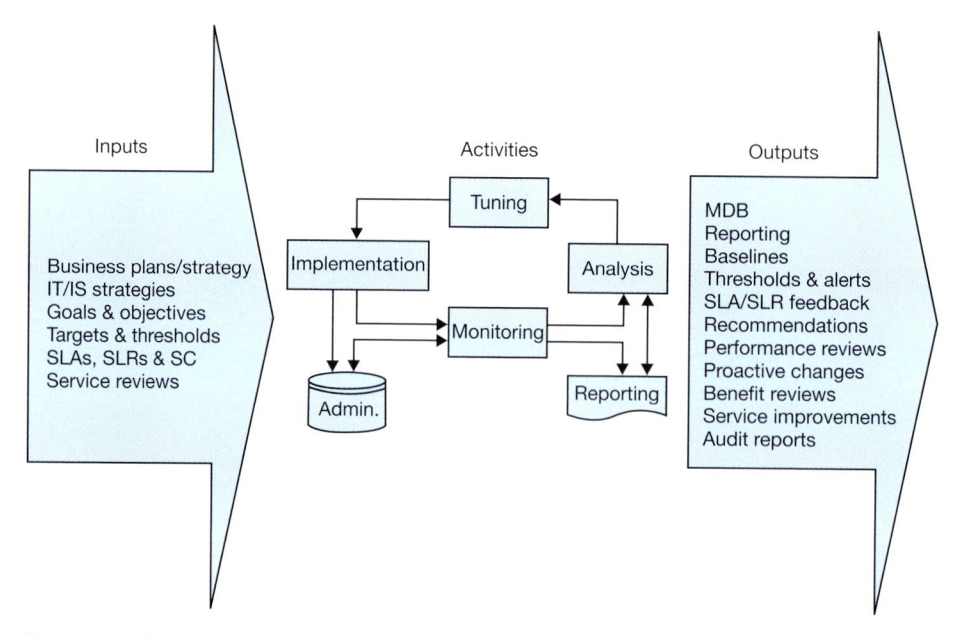

Figure 6.1 Measurement process inputs/activities/outputs

6.1 Inputs

There are a number of sources of information that are relevant to the measurement process. Some of these are as follows:
- the organizations business plans, strategy and financial plan
- the IT/IS strategy, plans and current budget
- any goals & objectives set by business or IT management
- service level agreements, service level requirements and service catalogues
- agreed service level targets and/or thresholds to maintain or achieve service levels
- the rolling business- and IT-program, project calendar or change schedule
- customer satisfaction surveys and/or feedback
- authorized service improvement plans or initiatives to be monitored as a result of service reviews or improvement activities
- external or industry benchmarks

6.2 Activities

The measurement process consists of a number of sub-processes, within which there are various activities structured in a continual improvement cycle. The sub-processes of the measurement process are:
- **Administration** - The sub-process is responsible for the administration of the metrics and measurement database (MDB) maintenance activities. The Administration sub-process can also act as the entry point for planning and implementation of the measurement program, framework and measures.
- **Monitoring** - The monitoring sub-process is responsible for the data gathering, calculations and validation of the required measurements.

- **Analysis** - The analysis sub-process is responsible for comparative, causal and predictive analysis of the measurements.
- **Tuning** - The tuning sub-process is responsible for identifying improvement opportunities and recommendations for the subject process or service which is being measured.
- **Implementation** - The implementation sub-process is responsible for implementing the recommended changes through process/service owners and normal change management processes.
- **Reporting** - The reporting sub-process is responsible for reporting the findings and recommendations to process/service owners, management and various stakeholder groups keeping them informed and aware.

6.3 Outputs

The outputs of the measurement process are used to report the status, findings and recommendations of various service management processes and services to key stakeholder groups within the organization. Some of these are as follows:
- process and service based performance reports
- exception handling reports
- notices and alerts
- root cause analysis and observations
- predictive analysis and observations
- change requests
- status of new and existing service improvement initiatives
- evaluation of benefits/value derived from processes or service improvements
- service improvement initiative recommendations
- audits and reviews

6.4 Measurement activities

The activities described in this section are undertaken when carrying out any of the sub-processes of the measurement process. The sub-processes are carried out on a sequential basis normally on a predefined and agreed schedule (for example monthly). Each sub-process requires inputs; performs activities; and produces outputs which then provide the inputs to the next sub-process in the sequence. The sub-processes are performed on a cyclical basis which forms a feed-back loop providing a basis for continual improvement. The measurement process supports the ITIL Continual Service Improvement – 7-Step Improvement Process[27]. The seven steps are outlined as:
1. Define what should be measured – Administration
2. Defined what can be measured – Administration
3. Gather the data – Monitoring
4. Process the data – Monitoring
5. Analyze the data – Analysis
6. Present and use the information – Reporting & Tuning
7. Implement corrective actions – Implementation

The measurement process is also similar in nature to the ITIL® capacity management[15] process and the Problem Management[21] process. The capacity management process activities are cyclical and proactive in design. Like the Problem management process, some activities in the measurement process are reactive, while others are proactive. A powerful feature of how the sub-processes can be used with the same data is the perspective from which it is analyzed, in terms of reactive (prescriptive) versus proactive (preventive). For example, the decline of a service level or a critical process measure could set off a series of reactive event triggers. The triggers set an alert which automatically start an investigation to determine the root cause and initiate corrective actions (prescriptive). Another example might be where a decline of a service level or a critical process measure could set off a series of reactive event triggers. The triggers set an alert and start an impact analysis to determine which dependent services or processes are at risk and initiate preventive actions (preventive). These event triggers and actions are similar to the ITIL® event management[16] process.

The proactive (preventive) activities of measurement process should:
- provide the information necessary for actions to be taken before the issues occur
- produce trends of the current process or service workload (utilization) and estimate the future resourcing requirements
- provide insight to identify the changes that need to be made to the appropriate processes to maintain service levels
- actively seek to improve the service performance and provision

A number of the activities need to be carried out iteratively and form a natural lifecycle as illustrated in figure 6.2:

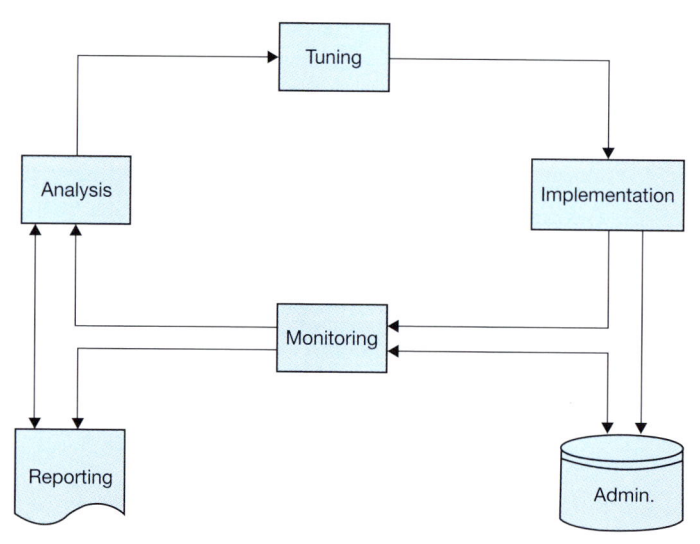

Figure 6.2   Measurement Process Lifecycle

Data collection (extraction) should be established and automated for each of the processes or services being measured. The data should be transformed, loaded and analyzed, using systems to compare actual values against performance thresholds. The results of the analysis should be included in

The measurement process

reports, and recommendations made as appropriate. Decision analysis and management control mechanisms may then be put in place to act on the recommendations. This may take the form of adjusting service targets, modifying policies, making process improvements, implementing tools and/or automation, developing new scorecards/metrics and adding or removing resources. The cycle then begins again, monitoring any changes made to ensure they have had a beneficial effect and collecting the data for the next day, week, or month. The suggested frequency for managing the sub-processes is:

- **on-going** – main sub-process activities and the storage of data in a measurement database (MDB), the production of the service reports, review of benefits realized and improvement initiatives
- **ad hoc** – proactive and reactive activities to initiate improvements to strategic, operational or tactical processes and/or services
- **periodically** – audits and reviews

Figure 6.3 shows the sub-process activities together with the other activities of the measurement process that need to be carried out:

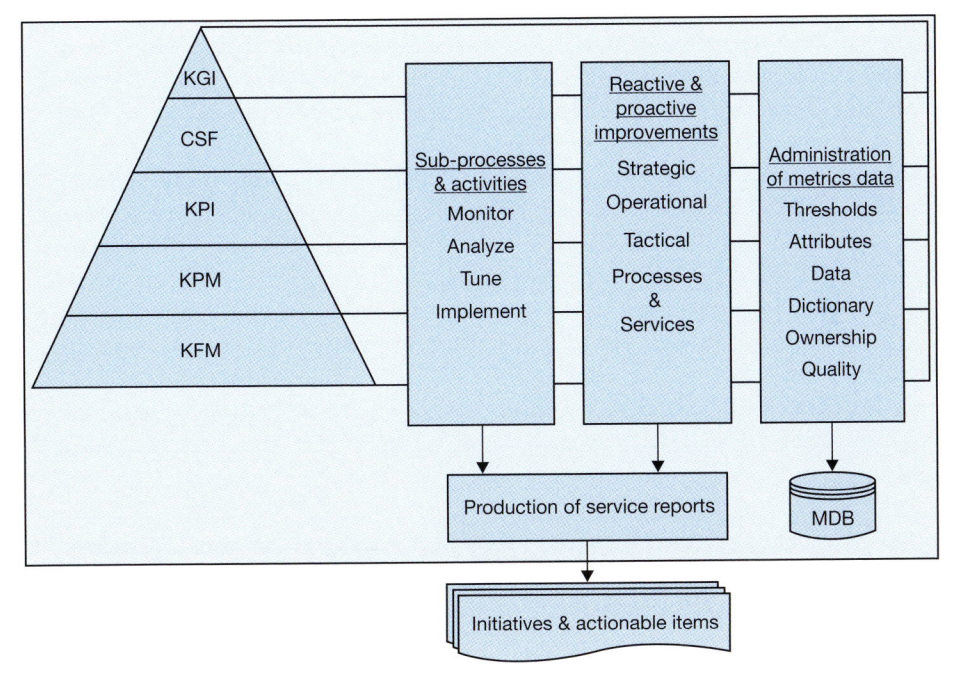

Figure 6.3 Measurement sub-process activities

The following sections describe each of the measurement sub-processes in detail.

6.5 Administration of metrics data

Objective
The objectives for administration sub-process is to plan, design, administer and control the metrics data in a central repository for analysis and provision of performance and management reporting. Administration can act as the entry point for the implementation of the measurement program. See section 8.0 Implementing a Measurement Program.

Description
The administration process provides governance over the measurement framework and process. It helps plan and design what should be measured and how it will be measured. It also provides guidance and support on the scope, policies and procedures for the overall measurement program. Lastly it is responsible for the administration, control and integrity of the metrics data.

The Measurement Database (MDB) is the cornerstone of a successful measurement process. The MDB is like the ITSM Metrics Data Mart of a data warehouse. A data warehouse is the main repository of an organizations' historical data. A data warehouse is used to perform complex queries and analysis on information without compromising the operational systems performance. Most organizations have a Data Warehouse group and these solutions are often referred to as Business Intelligence (BI) systems. While the data warehouse is designed to manage bulk data, the "Data Mart" is selections of data which is extracted for presentation to Decision Support users to meet specific management needs. Two pioneers and influential practitioners in data warehousing techniques are Bill Inmon[17] and Ralph Kimball[18]. Data stored in the MDB is specific to ITSM metrics. Data in the MDB is stored and used by all the sub-processes of the measurement process. The MDB will hold a number of different types of data including business, service, process, financial, workload and utilization. However the MDB will most likely extract source data from several source transactional systems. For example, source data may be located in the financial management, incident management or change management systems. Thus requiring data to be extracted, transformed and loaded on a regular basis into the MDB for analysis. The MDB may also be considered part of the Service Knowledge Management System (SKMS). Managing the MDB has similar characteristics to the ITIL knowledge management[19] process.

The information in the MDB is used to provide performance, measurement and control process information and reports for process/service owners, management and key stakeholders. The information can also be used generate future forecasts enabling management to plan for future resource requirements should service levels or workload characteristics be significantly altered.

Metrics and performance data from the source transactional systems that support the process or service should be identified, extracted, transformed and loaded into the MDB. The performance metrics can then be processed for analysis, provision of performance and management reporting, decision analysis and be acted upon when necessary.

The measurement process

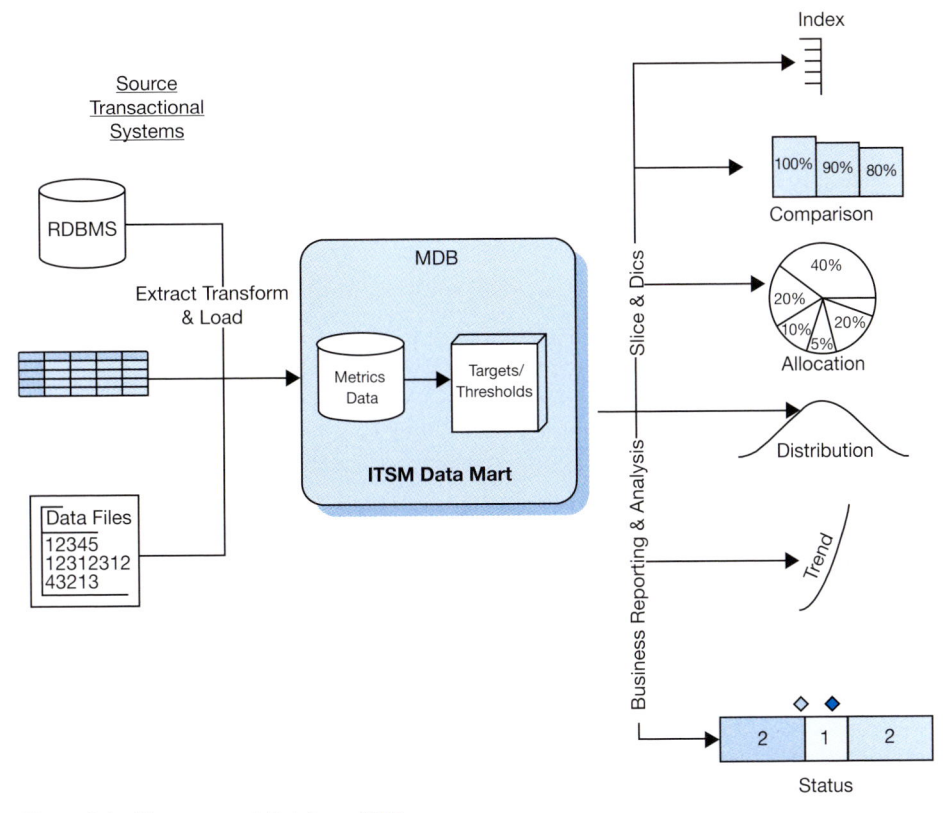

Figure 6.4 Measurement Database MDB

Inputs
Many inputs are required for the planning, design, administration and control of the metrics data and MDB. Each of the measurement sub-processes generates and uses many of the types of data stored in the MDB. For example, the monitoring sub-process sometimes uses baseline data from previous measurements to set targets and thresholds. Analysis scorecards may indicate that the metric in question is influenced by three other causal metrics. Additionally, that the metric in question belongs to a group of aggregated metrics which together represent an indication of efficiency. The metric may also be part of an initiative and used to indicate the status of an improve program that has been initiated.

The types of data that could be hosted in the MDB include:
- **Core Data Elements** - Make up the units of data required for the base measurements and include items such as "Actual", "Previous", "Trend". See section 4.6 on "Core Elements of a Metrics" for more examples.
- **Metadata** - metadata is information (data) about a particular content (data). An item of metadata may describe an individual datum (content item) or a collection of data (content items). Metadata is used to facilitate the understanding, use and management of data. Metadata can be managed in spreadsheets or static web pages, but at scale there are specialized "metadata repositories" to facilitate efficient management of hundreds of metrics. Without the metadata, the metric is meaningless and the entire IT metrics initiative may be at risk because people

can't find or interpret the data correctly. Data warehouses typically have associated metadata repositories for this and related purposes. The main purpose of metadata is to help organize, navigate and locate information in the MDB. For example:
  - What data do we have?
  - How is the data described, organized, classified, dimensioned?
  - Where is it located?
  - What format is it stored in?
  - Who is responsible for the content?
  - When was the source data last updated?
  - Which tools should be used for retrieval?
  - Has someone prepared the scorecard or report I need?
  - How do I access or initiate it?
- **Data Dimension** - is a data element (unit of data) used to categorize information to provide filtering, grouping and labelling. For example, in an ITSM MDB where each process metric is categorized as having a theme of efficiency, effectiveness or quality, a user of the MDB would then be able to filter or categorize themes by process or processes by themes. Dimensions can also be structured into hierarchies. For example the "Date" dimension could have several hierarchies: "Day > Month > Year", "Day > Week > Year", "Day > Month > Quarter > Year". The "Location" dimension could have several hierarchies: "Department>Division>Company", "City>Province>Country". Dimensions provide the means to "slice and dice" data for reporting.

What needs to be measured

Input is required to determine what needs to be measured. The in-scope processes and/or services that are being measured need the appropriate metrics identified, established, configured, tested and released into operational measurement processes. This starts with selecting the in-scope processes and/or services that are to be operationally monitored as part of the measurement process, including populating the core elements, dimensions and metadata information for each of the active metrics to be monitored. Some examples of processes that could be considered in-scope included in table 6.1.

Strategic	Tactical	Operational
• Business Perspective Metrics • Continual Service Improvement Program • Risk Management • Document Management • Competence, Awareness and Training • Program & Project Management	• Service Level Management • Problem Management • Financial Management • Availability Management • Capacity Management • IT Service Continuity Management • Security Management	• Service Desk • Incident Management • Configuration Management • Change Management • Release Management • Application Development • Application Support • Operations Management

Table 6.1   Sample IT service management processes

Data sources – what can be measured

Input is needed on the availability of data from existing data sources to answer the question "What can be measured?" Data sources are the source transactional systems that contain much of the factual information about the business, service, process, financial and technical data.

Data sources within the organization and source transactional systems they reside in need to be identified and documented to help automate the collection of measurement data. This will need to include details about:
- **data sources** – where existing information resides
- **how captured** – method of extracting the data from its host
- **frequency** – how often the data needs to be collected
- **calculations** – what calculations are required to transform the data
- **data quality** – what validation techniques are required to verify data quality and accuracy
- **import method** – what steps are required to map and load the data

Finding clean sources of this data is non-trivial. This is where the IT measurement team needs to recruit the enterprise data architects, analysts and administrators, who should understand the best sources for such data. The team should be prepared for poor data quality, multiple competing sources, or no available source at all. Overall goals and objectives for the measurement effort may need to be re-considered based on data quality and availability. More information can be found at the Data Management Association[20] web site.

Data Perspectives
There can be many types of data perspectives. Data about the business, services, process, financial aspect and technical infrastructure are useful in planning the measurement process.

Business data
Business data is required to understand the patterns of business activity. To understand exactly what drives the workload and performance of an IT organization, it is essential to have quality business data. The business plans of the organization need to be considered, and the effects on the IT Services understood. The business data is used to forecast and validate how changes in business drivers affect the workload and performance of the processes and services. Typically business data includes:
- number of accounts and products supported
- number of calls into call centres
- number and location of branches
- number of registered users of a system
- number of PCs
- anticipated workloads
- seasonal variations of anticipated workloads
- number of web site business transactions, et cetera
- external and legislative requirements

Service data
It is essential that the measurement process considers at all times the effect that the IT organization has on the productivity of the user. To achieve this service-orientated approach, service data should be stored within the measurement database for trending and analysis. Typical service data are end-to-end service transaction response and turn-around times that are consistent with the perceived level of service delivered to the user. Service transactions can be service or process centric and span the interval from request through fulfillment. For example, a process transaction could be a Request for Change to add a new user to the sales network, a service transaction could

be the time to process a new sales order. This could involve logging at the service desk, filtering and coordination by the change management group, execution by the network management group and request closure by the service desk. Many functions and roles may be required to work together in a chain to provide a simple service to the customer. The strength of the chain is its weakest link.

Monitoring Service Level Targets (SLTs) can avoid service level breaches. Service Level Agreements (SLAs) and Service Level Requirements (SLRs) provide the SLT objectives that the measurement process needs to record and monitor to help ensure that the service levels are achieved. Targets and thresholds should be configured, so that the monitoring activity can measure and detect looming SLA breaches and trigger alerts or exception reports. By setting the thresholds below or above the actual targets (based on polarity), service data can be analyzed and acted upon to avoid SLA breaches.

Process data
Process data is required to manage efficiency, effectiveness and quality. In many internal IT organizations, processes are often designed to accommodate an expected range of activity (volume and throughput) with less design consideration for quickly scaling up to meet unexpected growth or workload fluctuations. Therefore, many of the processes in the IT organization have limitations on the level to which they can be utilized. Beyond this level of utilization the process will be over-utilized and the performance of the services using the process will be impaired causing a backlog to build and/or quality and effectiveness to be compromised. The capacity management process can act on this data to optimize resource utilization.

Process metrics help manage resource utilization. Resources have various physical limitations beyond which greater productivity or use is not possible. For example there are only 24 hours in a day, 5 working days in a week; there may only be a limited number of trained or skilled personnel; limited physical space from which to work; limited number of technology tools, assets, phone lines, software licenses, et cetera. Metrics can identify when over-utilization situations are approaching or exist.

Process metrics help plan for workload fluctuations. The technical limits and constraints on the individual processes can be used by the monitoring activities as the thresholds at which alerts are raised and exception reports are produced. For example if the average Incident volume increases by 25% then the existing process will be at risk and require additional resources to scale the process and maintain quality and service levels. Metrics can identify potential bottlenecks.

Financial data
The measurement process requires financial data to help measure cost effectiveness. Financial data is useful in determining cost efficiency metrics. For example, cost per call, cost per transaction, cost per user and total cost per ownership are important key performance metrics that measure cost effectiveness and efficiency. Financial data is also useful for planning improvement initiatives. For example, when proposing various scenarios for service improvements, the investment cost together with information about the current IT budget is required for decision analysis.

Financial data can be obtained from a number of sources, including:
- financial plans, which may indicate long-term plans to reduce the costs of IT Service provision
- IT budgets, which may include specific budgets for capital and/or operational expenditure in the next year
- external suppliers, for the cost of new assets, tools, services and/or service levels improvements
- the configuration management systems, for the purchase or rental costs of current configuration items
- the human resources department for costs relating to people resources and/or skills development
- the project management system, because it is a primary source for effort accounting in most large shops for incremental spend and sometimes base spend

Technical data
Technical data is required to measure the performance of infrastructure components.

Potentially there are vast amounts of performance data available in existing infrastructure and source transactional systems. Summary technical performance information is useful and sometimes required to determine end-to-end service levels. There are many hardware and software systems that monitor component performance across many infrastructure platforms. Some are utilities within a management system, while others form part of a larger system or management sub-system. Data from these systems needs to be extracted, filtered, aggregated and transformed into meaningful metrics.

Stakeholder requirements
Inputs are required from key stakeholders to determine their reporting requirements. This includes identifying the stakeholders. Determining the categorization types which will appeal to different stakeholder groups and provide answers to varying degrees of questions they may ask. Identify the level of detail required by stakeholders. Some of these for consideration include:

Key stakeholder groups
- Customers/Users
- Executive Management
- Process/Service Owners
- Process/Service Managers

Classification of metrics (Themes)
- key goal indicators (KGI)
- critical success factors (CSF)
- key performance indicators (KPI)
- key performance metrics (KPM)
- key fact metrics (KFM)

Level of detail
- metrics
- scorecards
- dashboards

Surveys

Some inputs to the measurement process can be obtained from periodic surveys conducted with customers, users, IT personnel and external vendors. Surveys can be either formal or informal in nature and can be conducted through many mediums including email, forms, telephone surveys, focus groups, interviews, et cetera. Surveys are useful for collecting more subtle and sometimes subjective information. Some examples include:

- satisfaction
- perception of service levels
- hidden costs
- best practices maturity
- process and capability maturity
- suggestions for improvements
- allocation of effort to activities
- determining gaps in service provision
- changing business needs and priorities
- customer user demographics

Surveys can be performed on an ad-hoc basis to help answer a specific question or periodically to help determine patterns and observe trends over time.

Initiatives in progress

Input is required on any service improvement initiatives that are in progress. Initiatives are used to make improvements to processes, services and the IT organization. Initiatives by nature will have goals, objectives, critical success factors and therefore key performance indicators and metrics to track the success of implementing the initiatives to drive the desired outcome. The relevant measurements identified in the initiative details need to be included in the measurement process to determine if the desired results or outcomes are being achieved.

R.A.C.I. authority matrix

Input is required to determine who is playing what roles. An R.A.C.I. authority matrix[21] identifies who are accountable, responsible, consulted and/or informed within in a standard organizational framework. Understanding the roles and responsibilities for each process is critical for effective governance. Documenting an R.A.C.I. matrix for each process helps to map the key stakeholders more effectively for the measurement sub-processes. Accountable means the person who provides direction and authorizes an initiative or activity. Responsibility means the person who gets the task done. The other two roles (consulted and informed) ensure that everyone who needs to be is involved and supports the process. The following table 6.2 summarizes the R.A.C.I. authority matrix roles:

R	Responsible	Correct execution of process and activities. The person or people responsible for getting the job done.
A	Accountable	Ownership of quality, and end result of process. The one person who has the authority for the decision, activity or process results.
C	Consulted	Involvement through input of knowledge and information.
I	Informed	Receiving information about process execution and quality.

Table 6.2   R.A.C.I authority matrix

Extracting, transforming, and loading (ETL)

Input is required from the technical departments on how to collect the data. A data loading process can help automate the collection of data by mapping the source data to the measurement systems. Extract, transform, and load (ETL) as is a process that loads any data warehouse or database and involves:
- extracting data from outside sources
- transforming it to fit business needs, and ultimately
- loading it into the database

The ETL process can be documented and automated to build a data loading process which can help automate the data collection process. Data quality assurance and load exception reporting are also critical aspects of ETL. The following sections provide an overview of each ETL activity:

Extract
The first part of an ETL process is to extract the data from the source systems. Most data warehousing projects consolidate data from different source systems. Each separate system may also use a different data organization/format. Common data source formats are relational databases and flat files, but may include non-relational database structures. Extraction converts the data into a format for transformation processing.

Transform
The transform stage applies a series of rules or functions to the extracted data to derive the data to be loaded. Some data sources will require very little manipulation of data. In other cases, one or more transformations types may be required. For example, deriving a new calculated value (e.g., sale_amount = qty * unit_price).

Load
The load phase loads the data into the data warehouse. Depending on the requirements of the organization, this process ranges widely. Some data warehouses merely overwrite old information with new data. More complex systems can maintain a history and audit trail of all changes to the data.

Activities

Planning & design
The planning and design of the measurement process should reference existing procedures and plans wherever possible, in order to keep things simple and to avoid duplication. A measurement process plan should define:
- the purpose, scope and objectives of measurement process (and how it fits in with the organization's overall IT service management plan)
- related policies, standards and processes that are specific to the support group
- governance application generic controls – for example, CobiT®[2]
- measurement process roles and responsibilities
- measurement scope and context – what should be measured and from what context
- measurement naming conventions

- the schedule and procedures for performing measurement activities: monitoring, analysis, tuning, implementation, administration and reporting
- interface control with data sources, for example incident management, change management, service level management, et cetera.
- measurement process systems design, including scope and key interfaces, covering:
  - MDB
  - locations of measurement data and libraries
  - controlled environments within which metrics are manipulated
  - links and interfaces to other service management systems
  - support tools (for example analytical, modeling, reporting)
- housekeeping, including management, archiving and the retention period for metrics
- planned metric baselines, releases, milestones, workload and resource plan for each subsequent period.
- stakeholders and reporting package definition

Plan the first two to three months in significant detail and the following twelve months in outline. Performance relative to the plan should be reviewed regularly – at least every six months – and should include the measurement process workload for the period and the resources needed to service it. Checks should be made to ensure that the staff, IT resources, and support tools – including the size of the MDB to be made available to the measurement process – are likely to be adequate.

Where deficiencies are identified, steps should be taken to obtain further resources or procure enhanced sub-system support tools.

The measurement process activity and data volume will grow with the passage of time. The number of metrics under control and the frequency of changes affecting them will vary. Information on growth should be available from the organization's business plans, IT service plans, workload and capacity plans. IT service management may also decide to implement changes in the light of management reports, efficiency/effectiveness reviews, and audits of the measurement process function.

At each review point, measurement process plans for the preceding period should be compared with actual events. Any deficiencies in the planning process should be rectified to improve future planning.

In considering the future work of the measurement process group and IT service management should ensure that only required metrics data is handled; redundant or non useful data should be purged and/or archived. Failing to do so will burden the system and process. The cost of keeping and capturing metric details should be compared with current and potential benefits; if the current level of detail is costing too much, do not store it; if the overhead attached to capturing the current level of detail is excessive, the fiscally responsible organization must revisit the value of the information and determine if its value exceeds the cost of collection and storage.

Measurement scope & context

Measurement scope & perspective answers the questions "What should be measured and in what context?" For example, an organization could mandate all support processes (incident & problem management) be measured for efficiency, effectiveness, and quality. In this case the scope is the incident and problem management processes which have been selected for measurement; efficiency, effectiveness and quality represent the context theme in which they will be viewed. An organization may not know where to start or what to measure. This may require assistance from external consultancy organizations to perform independent benchmarks or maturity assessments to determine which processes or services present the best opportunity. More examples are included in 8.3, section "Plan the approach".

As a first step, the IT organizational processes and services should be broken down and uniquely identified and catalogued. Next, prioritize the list processes or services that should be measured (subjects) to enable effective control, recording and reporting of performance to the level that the business requires. As a rough guide, this could be to the level of planned or adopted 'IT service management processes' for example incident, problem, change, release, configuration, et cetera. Another approach could be to align the measurement process with the existing Service Catalogue in support of Service Level Agreements (SLAs) and/or Operational Level Agreements (OLAs). Lastly, determine the context themes in which the subjects will be viewed.

The scope should include a blend of strategic, tactical and operational metrics which satisfy the business requirements to improve overall management of the subject processes or services, see figure 6.5. Examples of the metrics that should be identified:

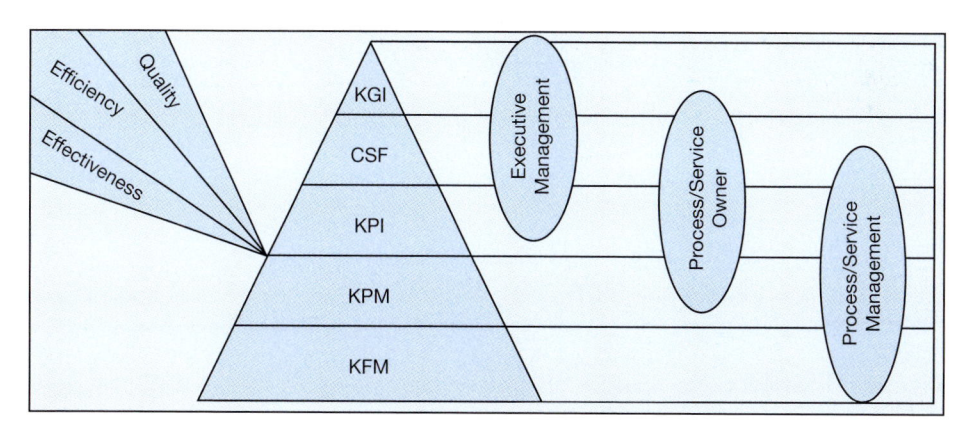

Figure 6.5   Classification of measurements

To determine context themes, consider who is interested in what kind of information and the degree of granularity they will require. Is it sufficient, for example, to just measure efficiency, effectiveness and/or quality of a process/service or to go deeper and measure the inputs, workload and outputs? The same question can be applied to what is required by the key stakeholder groups in terms of the level, depth, complexity and types of question they will ask.

Scope and context themes drive complexity and database size. Consider the size of database to be created and the problems of maintenance and audit. Before deciding on these issues, consider how to plan maintenance of the database and what to do with the information being maintained. What is the value to the business of holding low level data?

Measurement structure & selection of metrics

Measurement structures should describe the relationship and dimensions of various types of metrics for each in-scope process or service as shown in figure 6.6. This should include the subject processes or services, time frames, metric classes and perspective themes. For example, the structure could be the in-scope processes for all ITIL tactical processes measured monthly by metrics classes that support the IT goals and objectives.

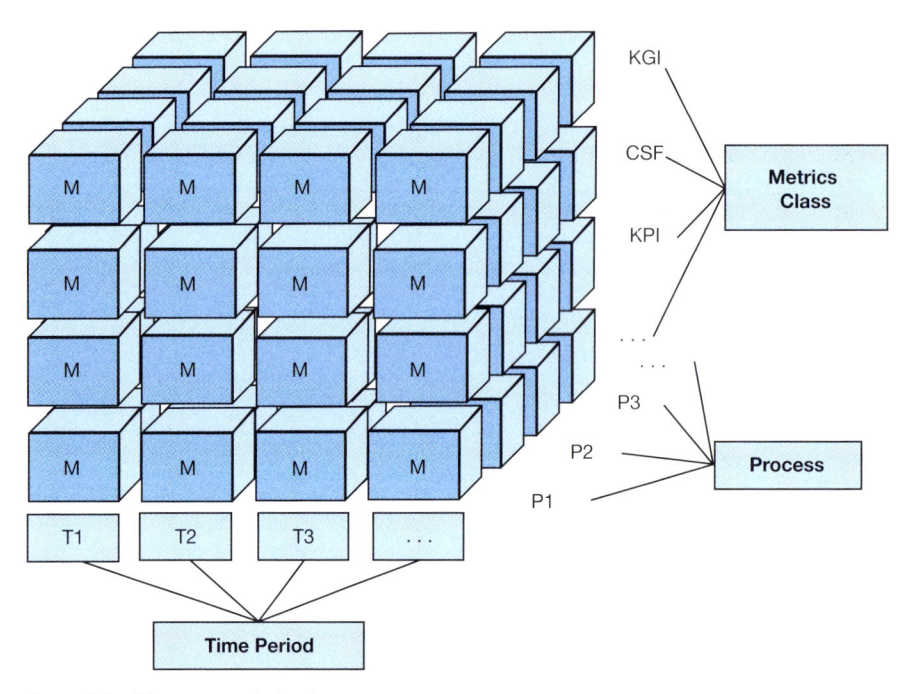

Figure 6.6   Measurement structures

Metrics should be selected by applying a decomposition process to the top-level item using guidance criteria for the selection of metrics. For example, goal alignment could be the guidance criteria, see 8.3, section "Select the measurements" for examples of this approach. Next determine the dimensions required to view the metrics. This is the perspective themes that the stakeholders are interested in viewing. For example, dimension that are by "monthly time periods", "service", "process", or "metrics class".

A metric can be viewed as a single entity (KFM) or can form part of many sets of metrics that are viewed together to produce different classes of metrics (KGIs, KPIs, KPMs) using aggregation. For example, the number of incidents in a given period (KFM: '# of Incidents/month') could be

The measurement process

used by many metrics or groups (KPI: Quality index for successful change management process, KPM: Incident Workload).

The measurement structure should be designed to reuse common metrics. For example, a measurement structure for an email service could use process metrics such as "effective incident resolution", "effective access requests" as well as technology metrics such as "availability", "performance" and "reliability". Reusing common metrics improve repeatability.

The ability to have multiple views through different measurement structures and dimensions improves root-cause analysis, impact analysis and service reporting, measurement administration, change and release & deployment management, see figure 6.7.

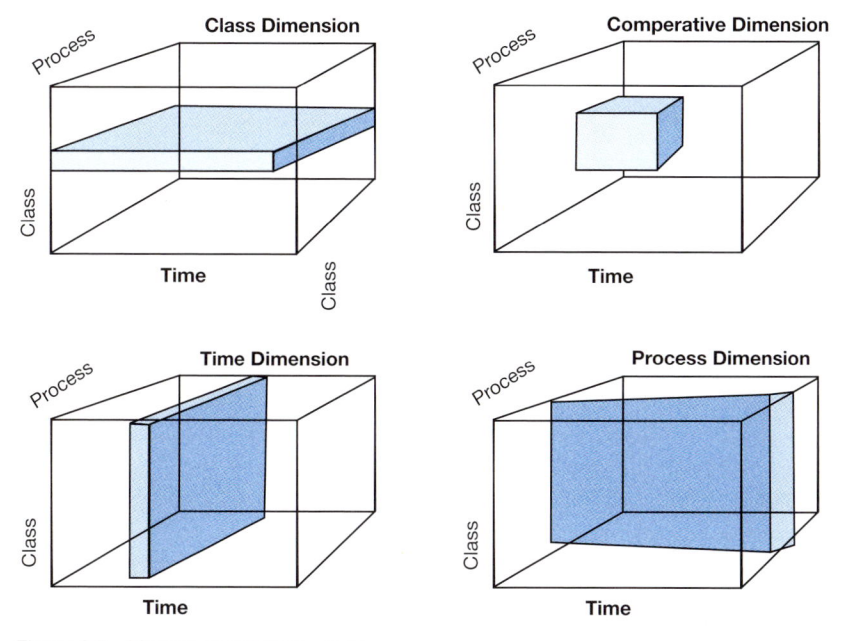

Figure 6.7   Measurement dimensions

The metric level chosen depends on the business, process and service requirements. Try to decide in advance the breadth of processes/services to be measured and to the lowest metric level that will be required, even if you do not immediately populate the MDB down to that level. It is worthwhile spending time on this activity and being as forward-looking as possible. It may save costly reorganizations of the MDB in the future. However, deciding the right level of metrics in advance is not always easy. If possible, obtain a measurement design and support tool that does not unduly constrain further breakdown of measurements to lower level ones. If this is not possible select a tool that allows the recording of properties of individual metrics. Examples of a measurement structure and dimensional breakdown are shown in figure 6.8.

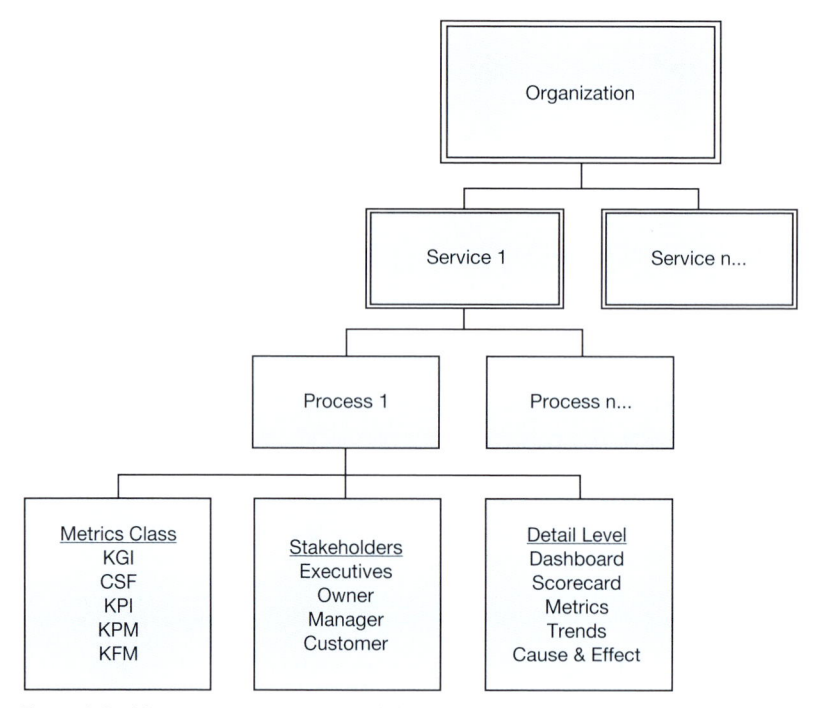

Figure 6.8 Measurement structure and dimensional breakdown

Metric classification, themes and lifecycle

Measurements should be classified by types then by themes aligned by stakeholder groups. Organizing the metrics in this manner provides the right detail level by stakeholder group for better interpretation and analysis. Typical metric classification types are KGIs, KPIs, KPMs and KFMs. Example themes are efficiency, effectiveness, quality, workload, utilization, performance, conformance, improvements, benefits, utility, progress, et cetera.

The lifecycle states for each metric theme should also be defined and reviewed on a periodic basis; for example a key goal indicator may be registered, accepted, active, or withdrawn. The role that can promote the metric should be defined, for example service asset & configuration management, release & deployment management. An example of a lifecycle for a key goal indicator is shown in figure 6.9.

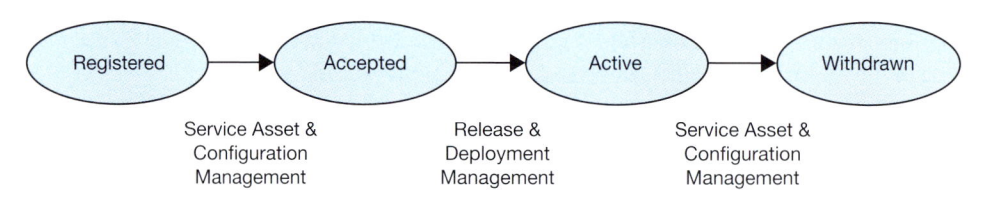

Figure 6.9 Measurement lifecycle states

The measurement process should plan which elements are to be recorded for metric themes; as the required elements may vary for different classifications of metric themes. Note that some support tools may dictate the necessary elements to be recorded. The section 4.6 "Core Elements of a Metric" in this book gives a suggested list of elements that should be recorded. It is useful to have an element to identify when a metric theme should be reviewed, that is, review date.

Metric relationships
The relationships between metrics should be stored so as to provide dependency information. For example:
- A metric is a part of another metric theme group (for example a key performance metric is part of a key performance indicator group) – this is a 'parent/child' relationship.
- A metric influences or is influenced by another metric as part of a cause & effect chain (for example service level performance influences customer satisfaction; service level performance is influenced by number of trained and qualified staff).
- A metric is used to calculate and create another metric (for example total number of transactions per period divided by number of staff equals average transactions per staff).

IT is useful to define a so-called metric-tree that defined the hierarchy and the relationships between metrics if there are any (e.g. input, output, sequential, causal relationship). There may be many more types of relationships, but all of these relationships are held in the MDB.

Identification of metric targets and thresholds
The organizations IT service management top-level goals need to be made concrete during the implementation phase in order to answer the question "How do we know that we have achieved our goals?" It is important that a dialogue occurs between the key stakeholders and the IT organization in order to ensure that top-level goals are made concrete. Questions to ask might include:
- "What do we need to ask ourselves to determine if we have achieved these goals?"
- "What constitutes a success?"
- "What are the metrics that will support us in determining if the goal has been achieved?"
- "What are the metric that need to be monitored to maintain goal achievement?"

It is this information that should be used to drive the continual service improvement initiatives, procedures, activities, inputs and outputs of the processes to ensure they realize the goals and deliver the necessary metrics.

By using this type of method for establishing goals and metrics an IT organization can:
- identify which processes would be most beneficial in demonstrating goal achievement
- ask probing questions that demand an answer if the goal is to be realized
- provide clearer guidelines and focus for implementing specific activity sets within the processes
- give all involved something concrete to aim at
- help determine quick wins and longer term results

For each of the goals and metrics, targets and thresholds need to be assigned to determine the current level of achievement. It is recommended that initial targets and thresholds are set to be

easily attainable to help maintain interest and motivation. There are generally three types of targets:
- **short term** – up to six months
- **mid-term** – six to 24 months
- **long term** – next two to three years

There are four common sources for obtaining ideas on where to set targets and thresholds:
- **internal baseline** - for example, internal previous measures
- **industry norms** – for example, generally known industry best practices
- **external benchmark** - for example, external comparison of similar peer organizations
- **internal benchmark** - for example, other departments within the same organization

The most common and best place to start is the 'internal baseline' which in most cases is the quickest and easiest to obtain.

Naming conventions

Naming conventions should be established and applied to the identification of metrics and versions. The names should be unique and take into account any existing corporate or standard naming/numbering structures. The naming conventions or information management system should permit the management of:
- hierarchical relationships between metrics within a measurement structure
- hierarchical or subordinate relationships in each metric theme
- relationships between metrics and their associated cause & effect peers

The measurement process should arrange for a naming convention to be established for all metrics and classification groups, for example KPIs. Individual instances of a metric should be uniquely identifiable by means of the metric identification name/number and version. The details of identification name/number and version need to be in the MDB, but need not be part of the unique identifier. The version identifies a changed version of what can be regarded as the same metric. More than one version of the same metric can coexist at the same time, for example two departments in the same company tracking the same metric but with different threshold target settings, owners, reporting periods, et cetera. They must be uniquely identified and be easily distinguishable to avoid confusion and or mistakes.

When the naming convention is being planned, it is very important that sufficient account is taken of possible future growth. Identifiers should be relatively short, but meaningful, and should re-use any existing conventions wherever possible.

Administration and control

The administration and control activity, within the measurement process, primarily includes planning, development, maintenance, administration and control of the metrics and measurement database. Control of the MDB and metrics should come under change management. Administrative and controlling activities can include:

Control of measurements

The objective of measurement control is to ensure that only authorized and agreed metrics are recorded and managed in the MDB. The procedures should protect the integrity of the enterprise's measurement data, systems and processes. When a change is processed, the components being changed move through a number of planned/agreed states. Examples of states are: 'registered', 'accepted', 'active', and 'withdrawn'.

The on-going measurement control processes are:
- Register all new metrics and versions
- Update metric records with regard to
  - Value changes that occur to metrics current measurement sample (for example This months incident count)
  - Updating elements
  - Changes in ownership or roles
  - Relating new versions of metrics arising from element variations (for example New definition of metric)
  - Linking metrics to related scorecard or dashboard reporting, aggregation indexes, metrics theme groups, cause & effect linkages
- Update and archive of metrics and their associated details when metrics are deleted or retired

Sources for metrics information

There are multiple sources for metrics information including off-the-shelf industry metrics (for example the five ITIL® V3 core books[1], itSMF Metrics for IT Service Management book[4], Control Objectives for IT V4 CobiT®[2]) and internally developed custom metrics.

New metrics and versions

Good planning and measurement controls ensure that updated metric versions are configured correctly and put into production to improve management control of processes and services. The measurement process along with Change and Release & deployment management should plan, design, build, test, deploy, manage and review the desired metrics. This includes:
- details of the target processes/services in which the metrics are designed for in terms of mission, goals, objectives and R.A.C.I. details
- expected benefits and/or outcomes anticipated from putting the processes/services under measurement control
- details of the thresholds and targets from which the metrics will trigger alerts and/or actions
- specifications on data accuracy and quality control parameters and processes
- cross-references to other metrics that may be influenced or dependent on the new metrics and/or processes/services
- sources for obtaining fact data from source transactional systems through the ETL process

When measurement planning quality-control checks are successful, the metrics are authorized for acceptance and are released into the production measurement environment.

Updating metrics

The current values of metrics change as they progress from reporting-period to reporting-period. Ideally, the MDB update should be automated as much as possible and where appropriate to

gather the current value of metrics as they change each period. This could be possible through any of the following update methods:
- manual data entry update
- batch process update
- manual import
- automated data connections, for example ETL

Changes to the elements of the metrics in the MDB should be updated with a related Request for Change (RFC) that authorizes the change to the element. If corrections need to be made to the elements – for example, after an audit – a change record should be raised to track the element updates.

In many organizations it is difficult to keep up with changes in ownership and roles, particularly where there is high staff turnover or a high use of contract staff. Procedures to update the MDB with changes in ownership are essential in order to ensure that Requests for Change, alerts, reports, initiatives and action requests are notified to the right parties.

To ensure all measurement metrics are as authorized by change management, a record of all authorized changes and enhancements is made on the MDB. Once a change is implemented, the MDB should be amended to show the change in status of metrics affected by the change.

Archiving of retired or withdrawn metrics
Scheduling and controlling the removal and disposal of retired metrics is often important for good maintenance reasons. However, if a metric is retired too early then it is not possible to measure year on year improvement. Metrics need to have an 'inactive' state where they are not on the scorecard, but can be referred back to for like-for-like comparisons. This is particularly true of there is a high rate of change. There should be procedures in place for retiring metrics so as to ensure they are not used erroneously to make management decisions. The MDB should be updated and the status of the metrics promoted to the final state, for example 'withdrawn' or 'archived'.

MDB back-ups, archives and housekeeping
Back-up copies of the MDB should be taken regularly and securely stored. It is advisable for one copy to be stored at a remote location for use in the event of a disaster. The frequency of copying and the retention policy will be dependent on the size and volatility of the measurement metrics and the MDB. Certain tools may allow selective copying of metric records and data that are new or have been changed.

Consider the size of database to be created and the problems of maintenance and audit. Before deciding on these issues, consider how to plan maintenance of the database and what to do with the information being maintained. What is the value to the business of holding low level data?

The amount of historical information to be retained depends on its usefulness to the organization. The retention policy on historical metrics records should be periodically reviewed, and changed if necessary. If the cost to the organization of retaining metric information is greater than the current or potential value, archive it.

Typically, the MDB should contain records only for items that are actively monitored or needed for historical baselines, and under the control of the measurement process. When measurement process has been operating for a period of time, regular housekeeping should be carried out to ensure that redundant metric records are systematically deleted.

Outputs

The output from the administration process is to provide a measurement service to assist in driving continual improvements. The aim of a MDB is to provide the relevant performance and management information to the appropriate sub-processes to aid in defining and executing strategy, management decision making, benefits realization, and management control.

A measurement program or service should add value to the IT service management organization. Recommended service functions comprise:
- implementing the measurement framework and processes
- policy, procedures, roles and responsibilities for the measurement process
- sample measurement programs and plans
- advice on setting up measurement for new processes or services
- reports that help to identify how to reduce the number of variant metrics and the complexity of the data reported
- regular information and an ad hoc reporting service
- efficient capture, maintenance and deletion of records
- a library service to manage measurement templates
- measurement process audit and review

6.6 Monitoring the metrics

Objective

The main objective of the monitoring sub-process is to monitor, measure and review the metrics in order to determine if the service management objectives and plan are being achieved.

It is important that the metrics of each process and service are monitored and updated on an on-going basis to ensure the optimum performance from the process; that all agreed performance targets and service levels can be achieved; and that business volumes are as expected.

Description

Data that support the metrics need to be gathered on a predefined frequency and used to update the current value of the active metrics stored in a MDB.

The monitoring should be specific to required key fact metrics, key performance metrics, indicators and critical success factors for the in-scope processes and services. Some of the monitoring may be automated through standard reporting tools using existing source transactional systems like management tool sets, service desk software, change management and service asset & configuration management systems ITIL® V3 ST "Service Transition" book[22]. Other information may be more labor intensive and require manual reporting, custom data loading process, independent surveys, spreadsheet calculations, et cetera. It is important that the monitoring collect all the data required by the measurement process for the specific processes and/or services and include a data validation process to determine the quality of the data received.

Typical data collected includes:
- **current** - most recent measure value
- **time stamp** - date and time the measure was taken
- **source** - where the data was obtained from

Part of the monitoring activity should be comparison of the current metric value to its thresholds and baselines or profiles of the normal operating levels. If these are exceeded, alerts should be raised and exception reports produced. These thresholds and baselines should have been determined during implementation based on the analysis of previously recorded baseline data or from external benchmarks, and can be set on:
- **individual metrics** – for example, monitor that "% Unsuccessful - failed changes" does not exceed 10% for a sustained period of one month
- **specific services** - for example, monitor that the "Avg. time waiting for call to be answered" by a service desk does not exceed 20 seconds

Many SLAs have user response times as one of the targets to be measured, but many organizations have great difficulty in supporting this requirement. Availability management ought to have end-to-end metric measurement (and other metric measurement) as part of its set of design criteria. User response times of IT and network services can be monitored and measured in several ways:
- incorporate specific code within client and server applications software to report performance
- use 'Robotic scripted systems' with terminal emulation software
- use distributed agent monitoring software
- use specific passive monitoring systems tracking a representative sample number of client systems

In some cases a combination of a number of systems may be used. The monitoring of response times is a complex process even if the service is an in-house service running on a private network. However if this is an external Internet service, the process is much more complex because of the sheer number of different organizations and technologies involved.

Inputs

The inputs to the monitoring sub-process are primarily concerned with obtaining current values for the active metrics from the source data source transactional systems within the required time-frames and desired accuracy levels.

Active metrics
The MDB will have a list of active metrics which need to be reported on.

Data collection frequency
Based on the active metrics list, each metric will have a designated frequency of data collection referred to as the Period. For example, hourly, daily, monthly, quarterly, semi-annual, annual, et cetera.

Required elements
Each metric should have a list of mandatory and optional elements which need to be collected each period. For example, current value, time-stamp, data source, et cetera.

Source data
Each metric should indicate the source of where the data comes from, any related procedures or work instructions. For example, sub-system management tool sets, service desk software, change management, service asset and configuration management systems, manual reporting, custom data connections, independent surveys, spreadsheet calculations, et cetera.

Data calculations/processing
Each metric should indicate how any metric data is calculated, transformed or processed to produce the current value. For example, 'Percentage of rejected RFCs' calculated by Count of all [Rejected - unauthorized] / [Logged] Request for Changes.

Data validation parameters
Data must be accurate and reliable. Each metric should indicate data tolerance requirements and how the data should be validated for accuracy. One example could be a range of values the data is expected to be within. Anything outside the expected range would flag a potential accuracy issue. For another example, if using a survey sample approach to collect random survey data, the population size would dictate the number of random survey responses required to provide a representative sample with an accuracy level of 95% with a (+/-) 2% confidence level. Data should be validated to determine the level of accuracy.

Activities

Data collections
Once the measurement framework planning has been defined and implemented, the data collection process begins. Data collection is the sampling and update of the metric's current value based on the specified periods, schedules and frequency outlined in the measurement plan. Ideally, source data is imported from existing systems using the ETL process with predefined and tested data loading process. If not automated, the data collection process can be labour intensive and prone to errors. Care should be given using the data validation process activity.

Data validation
Once the source data has been extracted, the data needs to be verified or validated to assure the data is within the quality guidelines defined by the data validation parameters in the measurement dictionary. If the data does not meet the quality criteria, steps should be taken to correct or cleanse any errors before performing any calculation and processing the data.

Perform data calculations/processing
Once the data has passed the data validation process activity, any additional calculations or processing can be performed. For example, counting, summing, averaging, division, et cetera. Careful design is necessary so that the metrics are available in a timely way; they may have their own SLA!

Outputs

The aim of the monitoring process is to provide reliable data to produce the metrics which in turn can be reported, analyzed and acted upon.

KGIs/CSFs/KPIs/KPMs/KFMs

The monitoring process is responsible for the production of the current facts, metrics, indicators and critical success factors for the reporting and analysis activities. For example, the monitoring activity would publish and communicate the new measurements once all data validation processes compliance requirements have been met.

Data validation reports

The monitoring process may produce data validation reports to indicate data validation issues and resolutions; accuracy ratings of specific measurements; documenting data sources, methods, or calculations for audit purposes.

Alert notifications

The monitoring process may generate alert notifications for specific key performance metrics or indicators based on business rules tied to monitoring thresholds. For example, a key performance indicator for monitoring workload may trigger a process to initiate temporary staffing requirements through the human resources department.

Dashboards/scorecards

The monitoring process is responsible for the production of any business friendly dashboards and/or scorecards and for publishing or delivering this information to the business, process or service management and users as required.

Metrics trending reports

The monitoring process is responsible for the production of metrics trending reports for key metrics or indicators including the publishing and delivery of trending information to individuals identified by the R.A.C.I. matrix model.

6.7 Analysis of metrics

Objective

The main objective of the analysis sub-process is to identify areas to improve the efficiency, effectiveness and quality for IT service management.

The metrics data collected from the monitoring should be analyzed to identify trends from which the normal workload, utilization, service level, or *baseline*, can be established. By regular monitoring and comparison with this baseline, exception conditions in the workload and utilization of individual processes or service thresholds can be defined, and breaches or near misses in the process targets or SLAs can be reported and acted upon. Also the data can be used to verify or confirm that targets have been met; predict events which may follow; predict future resource usage; or to monitor actual business growth against predicted growth.

Description
Comparison and analysis of the metrics data to the baseline, target thresholds and benchmarks can identify issues and concerns which require corrective or preventive actions. Data can also be used to predict and prescribe answers to business problems.

Analysis of the data may identify issues or concerns that need to be addressed to improve IT service management such as:
- performance is not improving, for example efficiency, effectiveness, quality
- goals and objectives are not being met, for example IT goals, process, activity
- benefits are not being realized, for example cost avoidance, productivity, agility
- initiatives are not making an impact, for example benefits, performance, satisfaction
- service levels are not being achieved, for example response, availability, performance

Analysis of the data may predict or determine events which will require corrective or preventive action such as:
- customer satisfaction may be at risk because:
  - performance is declining, for example efficiency, effectiveness, quality
  - service levels are not being achieved, for example response, availability, performance
- expected benefits may not be realized because:
  - goals and objectives are not being met, for example IT goals, process,
  - activity initiatives are not making an impact, for example benefits, performance, satisfaction

The analysis process may identify improvement areas on a micro or macro level. This would include:
- improvements to an individual process or service that can be implemented by the process owner or service manager with the usual staff resources, for example performing individual corrective and preventive actions
- improvements across the organization or across more than one process or service

Inputs
The inputs to the analysis sub-process are primarily concerned with interpretation of the outputs obtained from the monitoring sub-process. The inputs include:
- KGIs/CSFs/KPIs/KPMs/KFMs for subject processes and services to be analyzed
- reports to indicate any validation issues anomalies
- alert notifications to consult with parties to see if any corrective/preventive actions are underway
- dashboards/scorecards by business, process, service, owner or responsible manager
- trending of metrics and indicators
- initiatives which may already be in-progress

Activities
There are three questions one must answer when analysing the current values of the active metrics:
1. What has happened?

2. What will happen next?
3. What actions to take?

The main activities of the analysis sub-process include:
- collect and analyze data to baseline, targets and benchmarks
- determine any exceptions which may be explained
- determine areas of interest, risk or concern which require further investigative analysis
- use analytical tools and techniques to determine cause and effect relationships
- identify, assess and prioritise corrective or preventive actions
- consult with all parties involved
- document findings, conclusions, opportunities and recommendations

The activities of the analysis sub-process are similar in nature to the ITIL problem management process[23]. There are a number of analytical techniques which are useful in performing investigative analysis, some of which are summarised in the following sections:

Reactive analysis techniques

The reactive analysis techniques are concerned with handling deficient processes or services (problems) in an efficient and effective way. The aim of the reactive analysis techniques is to identify the root cause(s), such as the components that are at fault and solve the problem. They provide the process owners and service managers with information and advice on improvement initiatives or corrective actions when available.

The main reactive analysis techniques are compare & contrast analysis, process flowcharting, affinity diagrams, cause & effect, relations diagrams and Kepner-Tregoe problem analysis.

Compare & contrast analysis

The compare and contrast analysis observes similarities and differences between various measures allowing the team to observe whether the current measurement value is better than or worse than other points of reference. This helps to set goals and prioritise actions based on the degree of variance between the measures being observed once the similarities and differences are understood.

Some common measure comparison reference points for compare and contrast analysis against the current actual measures include:
- **worst** - related industry peer group with the worst in class results
- **baseline** – internal previous measures over time or averaged
- **target** – desired state or goal
- **benchmark** – best external peer group based on similarities
- **best** – related industry peer group with the best in class results

Figure 6.10 depicts a number of common reference points for comparison:

The measurement process

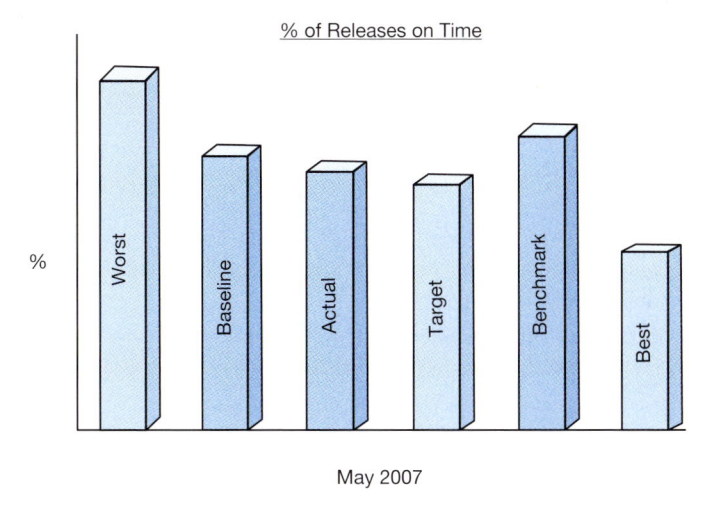

Figure 6.10 Compare and contrast references

When selecting a peer group to be compared to, it is important that they are of similar by size of organization, by technologies they manage and by the complexity of their user, software and hardware environments. When comparing and contrasting, it is useful to identify what is similar and different about the people, process, technologies, best practice maturity, user satisfaction and total costs of ownership. For example, you may compare certain measures to external benchmark reference points to notice significant variances between costs. The real value is to understand what is driving the contrasting (different) areas. In many cases the degree of maturity and successful implementation of best practices is what sets the best in class organizations apart from the rest of the pack.

Use the following steps to develop a compare and contrast analysis:
1. Determine what the frame of reference is, that is, measures to be compared or contrasted.
2. Determine the grounds for comparison, that is, common technologies, size, complexity.
3. Compare and determine what is similar and what is different, that is, same, higher-than, lower-than.
4. Determine which items are of importance and need to be understood, that is, look at what is contrasting, determine if it matters, determine the underlying reasons or causes.
5. Present the arguments of your compare and contrast, that is, what is the significance or outcome of your findings.

Process flowcharting

Process flowcharting creates a picture of the process which allows the team to identify the value chain and actual sequence of events in a workflow for any process or service. Flowcharts can also be used to identify who is responsible for key activities, where key measure points should be taken, which activities are adding value, where decisions are made and what interfaces are required. This method is also useful for developing Process Map scorecards.

Use the following steps to develop a flowchart of your process or service:
1. Determine the scope, detail level and boundaries of the process.
2. Brainstorm the major activities of the process including inputs, activities, decisions and outputs.
3. Order and sequence the activities from the beginning to the end of the process.
4. Identify which activities are value-adding.
5. Draw the process diagram using appropriate symbols.
6. Test the flowchart for completeness by performing a walk-through for each scenario with the team.
7. Finalize with the team by determining critical measure points throughout the process.

Processes can not only be drawn in visual flowcharts, they can also be automatically simulated using discrete event simulation tools, which can be another useful technique for predicting or analyzing.

Figure 6.11 provides an example of a change management process flowchart depicted in a process scorecard with critical measures (process sensors) numbered throughout the process:

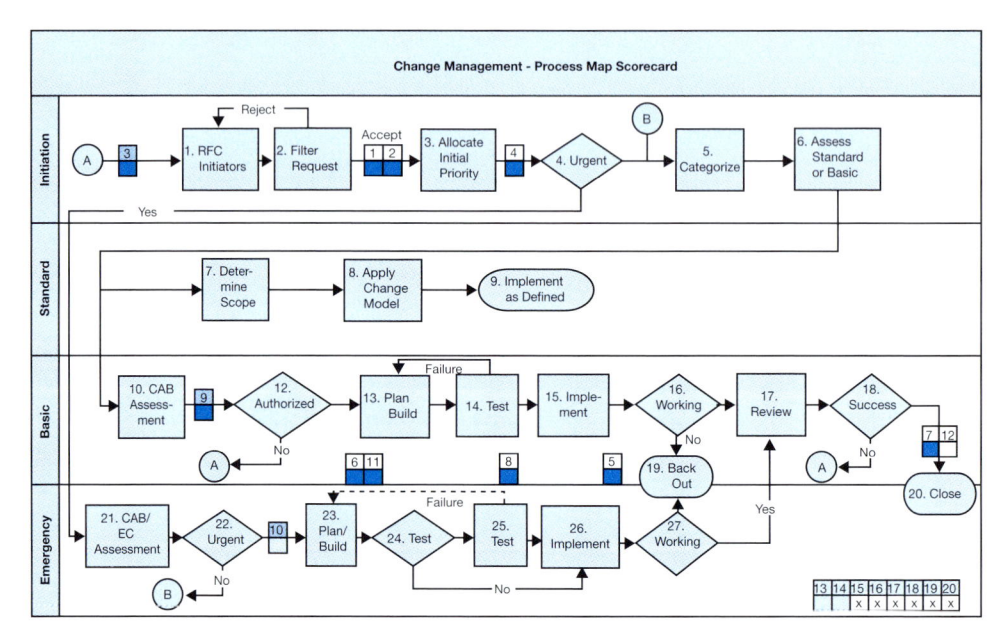

Figure 6.11 Sample Change Management process flowchart

Affinity diagram
The affinity diagram is used for gathering and grouping of ideas which may contributor to the root cause. This allows a team to creatively generate a number of ideas or issues and organize them into common themes or natural groupings. This analysis method is useful to help understand the nature of a problem and develop creative ideas to solve them. This method is also useful for identifying themes for key indicators.

The measurement process

Use the following steps to develop an affinity diagram:
1. List the issue or problem under discussion in a full sentence
2. Brainstorm a number of ideas on the issue or problem
3. Sort the ideas into related groupings
4. Create a summary or header description for each grouping

The following example, see figure 6.12, is trying to determine the likely contributors to high operational costs. After brainstorming a number of ideas and issues, there are three main groupings of people, process and technology related issues. This can be further analyzed to determine the relationships amongst them using the Relationship Diagram.

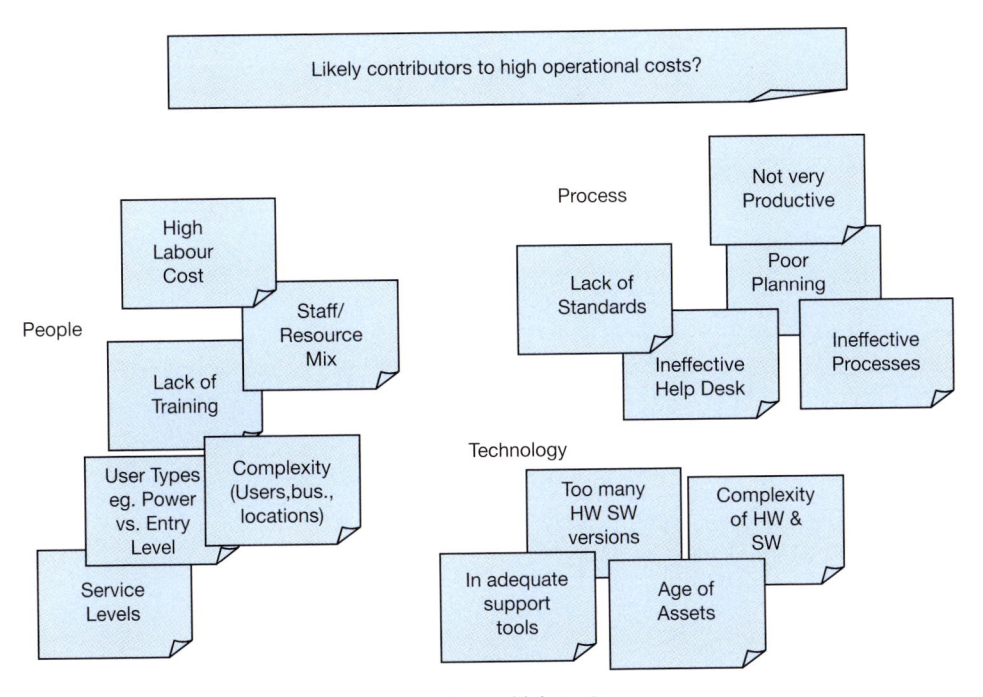

Figure 6.12 Affinity Diagram – likely contributors to high costs

Cause-and-effect diagram (Ishikawa)

A cause-and-effect diagram is typically the result of a brainstorming session in which members of a group offer ideas on how to improve a product, process or service. The main goal is represented by the trunk of the diagram, and primary factors are represented as branches. Secondary factors are then added as stems, and so on. Creating the diagram stimulates discussion and often leads to increased understanding of a complex problem.

The cause-and-effect diagram helps to find and cure causes not symptoms by allowing the team to identify, explore and graphically display, in varying levels of detail, all possible causes related to a problem or outcome to discover its root cause(s).

Use the following steps to develop the cause-and-effect diagram:
1. Select the most appropriate format to categorize the primary branches of the cause and effect format, there are two main formats:
   - **Theme Classification Type** – categorize the primary causal branches by major themes, then attach secondary or individual stem causes to the primary. Continue to detail the causes by repeatedly asking the question "Why does this cause (theme) happen?" until the team exhausts all possibilities.

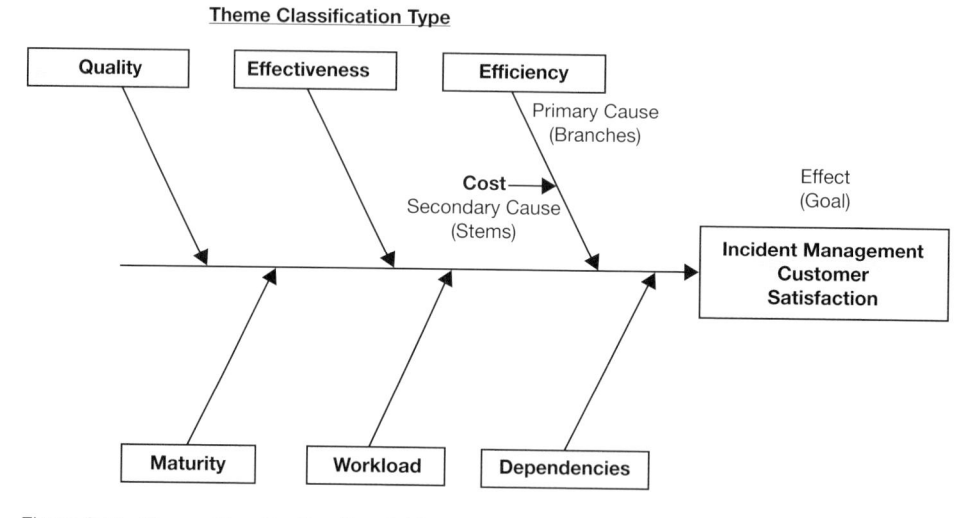

Figure 6.13 Theme Classification Type Ishikawa

   - **Process Classification Type** – Uses the major steps of the process for the primary causal branches, attach individual causes to the primary. Continue to detail the causes by repeatedly asking the question "Why does this cause (process) happen?" until the team exhausts all possibilities.

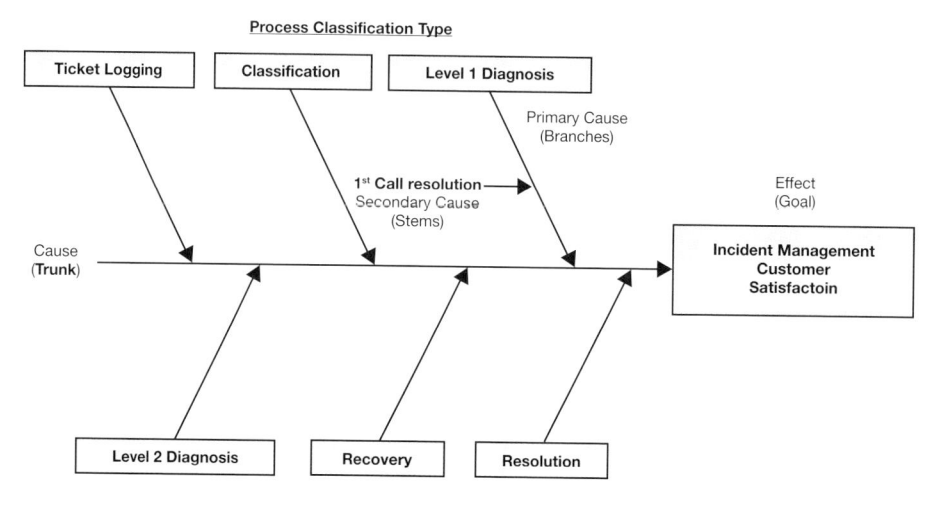

Figure 6.14 Process Classification Type Ishikawa

The measurement process

2. Generate the causes needed to build the cause and effect diagram using predetermined check lists or through a Brainstorming process.
3. Construct the cause and effect/fishbone diagram and assess the status of each cause, that is there any evidence that suggests Suspects and potentially an underlying Cause?
4. Determine the root cause versus symptoms by asking the questions "Why does this happen?" or "What could happen?"

Figure 6.15, provides an example of the Theme Classification Type for the change management process using metrics displayed on a Root Cause Analysis scorecard. The current status of metrics are visually displayed (■ (green) = OK, □ (yellow) = caution, and ■ (red) = alert) to identify potential causes. In this example the anticipated benefits are not consistently being achieved (red status); the suspect themes (major cause bones) are maturity, effectiveness and quality (red status). Further analysis will be required for each of the secondary cause bones to determine any underlying causes.

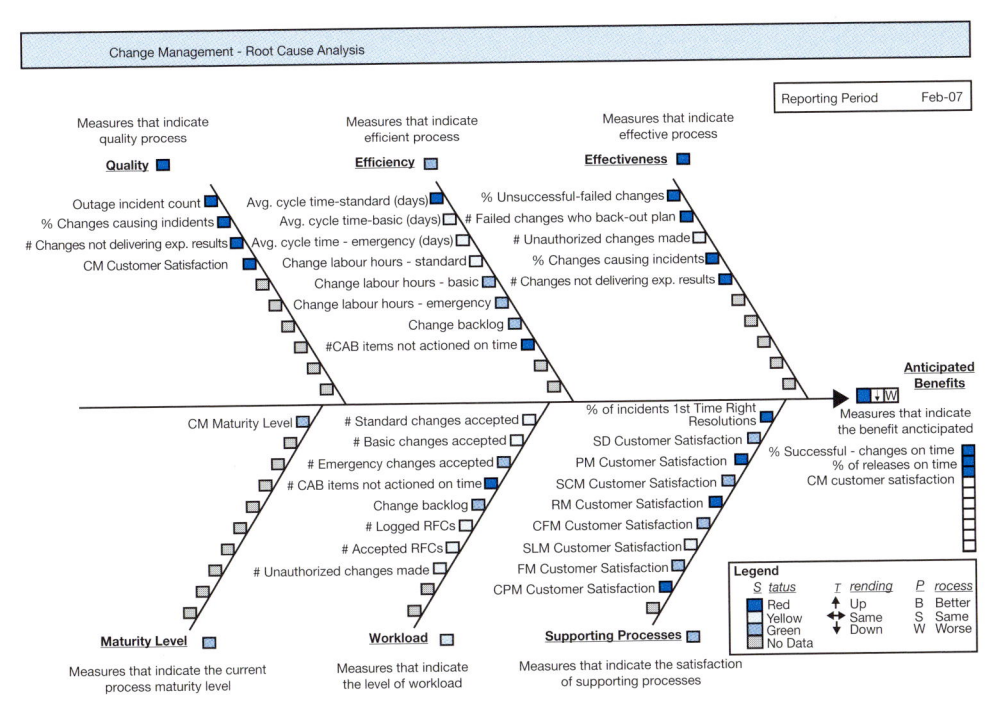

Figure 6.15 Sample Theme Classification Type Ishikawa

Relations diagram (interrelationship diagram)
The relations diagram is used to look for drivers and outcomes to allow the team to systematically identify, analyze, and classify the cause and effect relationships that exist among key issues. A relations diagram helps answer the question "What are the likely contributors to symptom/problem X". The relations diagram is most useful when paired with the Ishikawa to enable drill down of the secondary cause bones to determine underlying drivers of the effects produced. This enables the team to focus on effective solutions that address critical drivers and outcomes.

Use the following steps to develop an interrelationship diagram:
1. Agree on the issue or question – what are the likely contributors to symptom/problem "X"?
2. Lay out all ideas/issues in circular fashion that have been brought from other tools or brainstorming activities
3. Compare elements to each other looking for cause/influence relationships between all of the ideas and draw relationship arrows
4. Tally the number of outgoing and incoming arrows and select key items for further investigation
5. Items with the most number of outgoing arrows (labelled: Out) will be root causes or drivers
6. The items with most number of incoming arrows (labelled: In) will be the key outcomes or results

Figure 6.16, has identified one of the likely contributors to high asset costs is under-utilised assets, of which there are five potential causes.

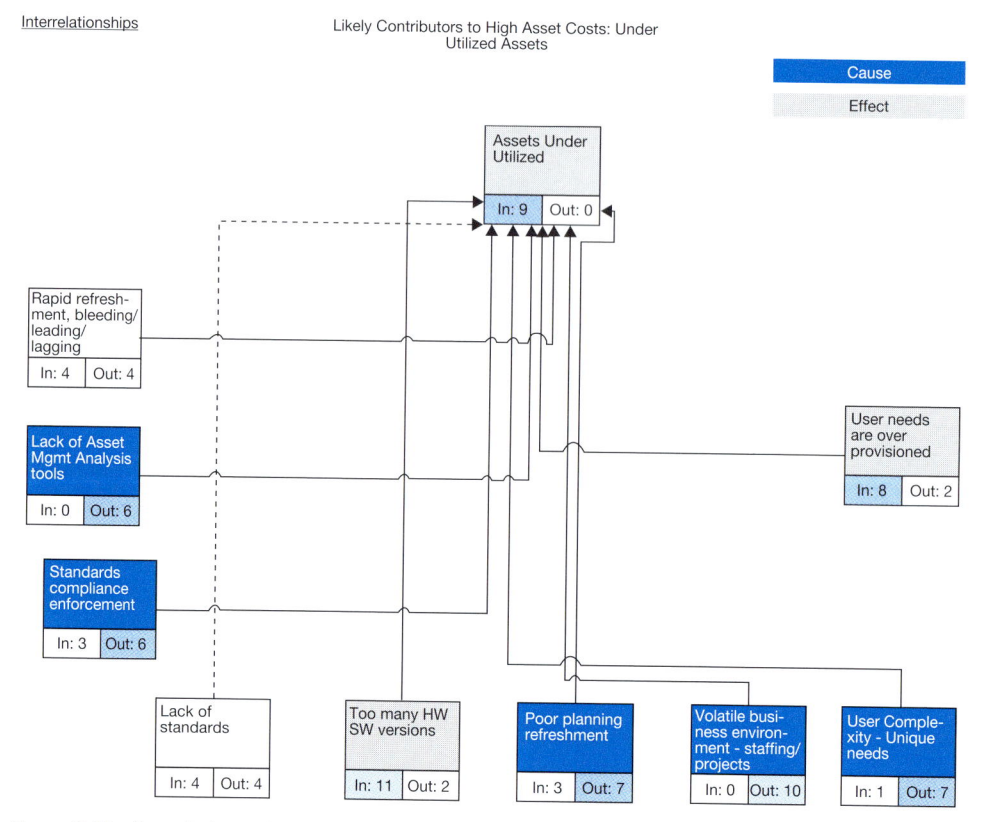

Figure 6.16 Sample Interrelationship Diagram

Kepner-Tregoe problem analysis

The Kepner-Tregoe problem analysis is a useful method to analyze problems and distinguish between symptoms and root cause(s), developed by Charles Kepner and Benjamin Tregoe.[15]

Kepner and Tregoe state that "problem analysis should be a systematic process of Problem solving and should take maximum advantage of knowledge and experience". They distinguish the following five phases for problem analysis (described further below):
1. Defining the problem
2. Describing the problem with regard to identity, location, time and size
3. Establishing possible causes
4. Testing the most probable cause
5. Verifying the true cause.

Depending on time and available information, these phases can be realized to a greater or lesser extent. Even in situations where only a limited amount of information is available, or time pressure is high, it is worthwhile adopting a structured approach to problem analysis to improve the chances of success.

1. **Defining the problem** - Because the investigation is based on the definition of the problem, this definition has to state precisely which deviation(s) from the agreed service levels have occurred.

   Often, during the definition of a problem, the most probable problem cause is already indicated. Take care not to jump to conclusions, which can guide the investigation in the wrong direction from the beginning.

   In practice, problem definition is often a difficult task because of a complicated IT infrastructure and non-transparent agreements on service levels.

2. **Describing the problem** - The following aspects are used to describe the problem:
   – Identity - Which part does not function well? What is the problem?
   – Location - Where does the Problem occur?
   – Time - When did the Problem start to occur? How frequently has the problem occurred?
   – Size -What is the size of the problem? How many parts are affected?
   – Who - For whom does it affect?

   The 'is' situation is determined by the answers to these questions. The next step is to investigate which similar parts in a similar environment are functioning properly. With this, an answer is formulated to the question 'What could be but is not?' (Which parts could be showing the same Problem but do not?). This is similar to the Compare and Contrast analysis technique.

   It is then possible to search effectively for relevant differences in both situations. Furthermore, past changes, which could be the cause of these differences, can be identified.

3. **Establishing possible causes** - The list of differences and changes mentioned above most likely hold the cause of the problem so possible causes can be extracted from this list.

4. **Testing the most probable cause** - Each possible cause needs to be assessed to determine whether it could be the cause of all the symptoms of the problem.

5. **Verifying the true cause** - The remaining possible causes have to be verified as being the source of the problem. This can only be done by proving this in one way or another – for example by implementing a change or an improvement initiative. Address the possible causes that can be verified quickly and simply first.

Proactive analysis techniques

Proactive analysis techniques are concerned with identifying and resolving problems before process or service degradation occurs, thus minimizing the adverse impact on the IT service management processes, service levels and business-related costs.

Problem prevention ranges from prevention of individual problems, such as repeated difficulties with a particular process flow or service feature, through to strategic decisions. The latter may require major expenditure to implement, such as investment in better tools, process, training, systems. Analysis focuses on providing recommendations on improvements for the process owners or service managers, for example provision of online technical tools may reduce the time taken to resolve incident, thereby reducing the total number of calls reducing the overall support workload.

The main proactive analysis techniques are trend analysis, brainstorming and the predictive analysis.

Trend analysis

Trending indicates variations over time and whether variations are moving in an undesirable direction. The objective of trend analysis is to identify 'weak' processes or components of the IT service management process; mapping out potential problem; investigate the reasons for their weakness; and correct them. Trending of key performance metrics or indicators, help the team to recognize and identify variances over time and to be able to tell the difference between a trend and an exception to the norm (anomaly or one-time occurrence). A negative trend may indicate a process is degrading and requires improvement. An exception may indicate an unusual event which may also require changes to prevent if from affecting performance in the future.

Use the following steps to develop a trending diagram:
1. Select the process to be observed
2. Select the key performance metrics or indicators to be analyzed
3. Determine the frequency and time span for obtaining measurements and initiate data collection
4. Plot the measurements and then use a trending function using a software plotting tool to display a trend line
5. Assess whether the trend is positive (better) or negative (worse) by observing the polarity of the metric

The following elements should be considered:
1. Trends can be: up, same or down from last period
2. Polarity can be: up is better, down is better, no change is better
3. Progress can be: better, same or worse than previous
4. Status can be: Red = warning, Yellow = caution, Green = normal.

The measurement process

Figure 6.17 provides an example of a measure that is trending down in Jun/07 which in terms of progress is worse, because the polarity for the measure is "More is better" however the entire trend is showing a significant improvement since Jan/07.

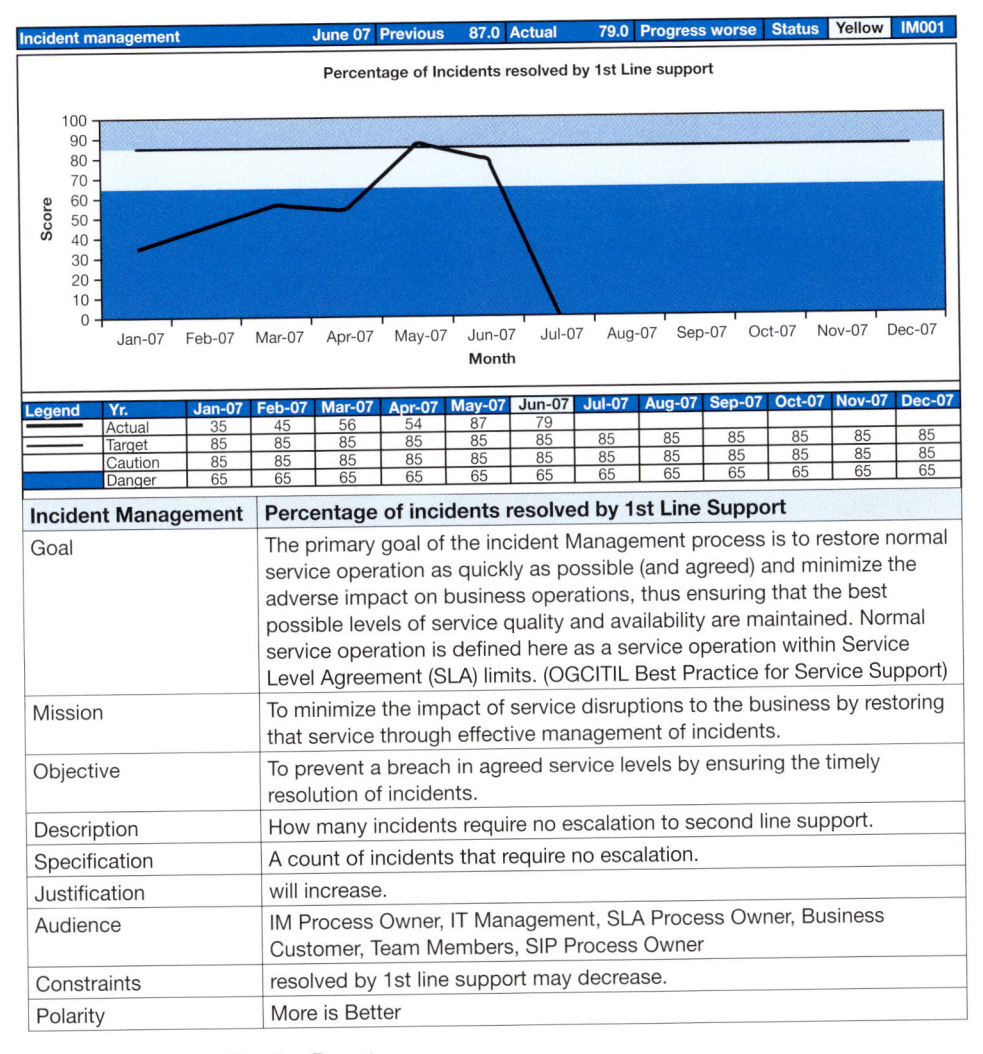

| Incident management | | | June 07 | Previous | 87.0 | Actual | 79.0 | Progress worse | Status | Yellow | IM001 |

Percentage of Incidents resolved by 1st Line support

Legend	Yr.	Jan-07	Feb-07	Mar-07	Apr-07	May-07	Jun-07	Jul-07	Aug-07	Sep-07	Oct-07	Nov-07	Dec-07
	Actual	35	45	56	54	87	79						
	Target	85	85	85	85	85	85	85	85	85	85	85	85
	Caution	85	85	85	85	85	85	85	85	85	85	85	85
	Danger	65	65	65	65	65	65	65	65	65	65	65	65

Incident Management	Percentage of incidents resolved by 1st Line Support
Goal	The primary goal of the incident Management process is to restore normal service operation as quickly as possible (and agreed) and minimize the adverse impact on business operations, thus ensuring that the best possible levels of service quality and availability are maintained. Normal service operation is defined here as a service operation within Service Level Agreement (SLA) limits. (OGCITIL Best Practice for Service Support)
Mission	To minimize the impact of service disruptions to the business by restoring that service through effective management of incidents.
Objective	To prevent a breach in agreed service levels by ensuring the timely resolution of incidents.
Description	How many incidents require no escalation to second line support.
Specification	A count of incidents that require no escalation.
Justification	will increase.
Audience	IM Process Owner, IT Management, SLA Process Owner, Business Customer, Team Members, SIP Process Owner
Constraints	resolved by 1st line support may decrease.
Polarity	More is Better

Figure 6.17 Sample Trending Report

To determine the difference between a trend and an exception, ask the following questions when significant deviations from the norm are present, a 'yes' answer may trigger a root cause investigation to see if the exception has occurred and can be explained.
- Are there differences in the process or methods used by different personnel?
- Were any untrained personnel involved in the process at any time?
- Are employees afraid to report bad news?
- Are there any significant differences in the measure accuracy?
- Is the process affected by the environment? That is, temperature, humidity

- Has there been a significant change in the environment?
- Is the process affected by predictable conditions? That is, increased workload
- Has there been any change to the source inputs? That is, information
- Is the process affected by employee fatigue?
- Has there been a change in policies, procedures, tools? That is, new software tools, patch releases
- Is the process adjusted frequently?
- Did the measurements come from different shifts or individuals?

Trend analysis can lead to the identification of bottlenecks through root cause analysis of the subject IT service management process. Negative trends should be analyzed, investigated for root cause and corrected as described in the Tuning and Initiatives sections. Trend analysis can help identify both general problem areas and exceptions requiring attention.

Brainstorming
The objective of brainstorming is to produce more and better ideas. Using an open-forum method free of criticism and judgement, the team can generate a number of quality ideas on any topic.

There are two main methods of brainstorming: formal where everyone takes turns providing an idea; and informal where ideas are presented in random order at anytime.

Use the following steps to conduct a brainstorming session:
1. The main problem or question is written down for everyone to see and agree upon.
2. Each team member provides an idea in turn (formal) or at anytime (informal). No idea is ever criticised.
3. Record ideas on post-it notes, flipcharts or whiteboards until exhausted.
4. Review for clarity and discard duplicates.

Predictive analysis
The objective of predictive analysis is to develop a course to steer to help achieve the desired outcomes. Like the cause-and-effect diagrams that are used to troubleshoot problems to determine the root-cause, the same approach can be used in a reverse order to predict desired outcomes. A predictive analysis is used by the team to map out a cause and effect sequence of disparate but connected measures which provide the desired results for the organization. This method uses a balance of leading and lagging indicators that help to articulate a strategy or hypothesis and to help visualize the cause and effect relationships in a strategy map diagram. A leading indicator is one that predicts that something may or is about to happen whereas a lagging indicator confirms an outcome has already taken place or has happened.

Figure 6.18 provides an example of predictive analysis whereby the goal or desired outcome is customer satisfaction. By repeatedly asking the question "What causes this to happen?" or "What prevents this from happening?" other influencing factors will surface which when measured, become successive leading and lagging indicators.

The measurement process

For example, what causes high Customer Satisfaction?
1. Good Change Management success rate.
   What prevents this from happening?
   a. High level of incidents.
      What causes this to happen?
      i. Untested changes causing more incidents.
2. Support being available when needed.
   What prevents this from happening?
   a. Unplanned work causing a backlog to develop.
   What causes this to happen?
      i. Unexpectedly high incident volumes.
         What causes this to happen?
         1. Untested changes causing more incidents.
      ii. Takes longer than usual to fix incidents.
         What causes this to happen?
         1. Unknown problems taking longer to resolve.

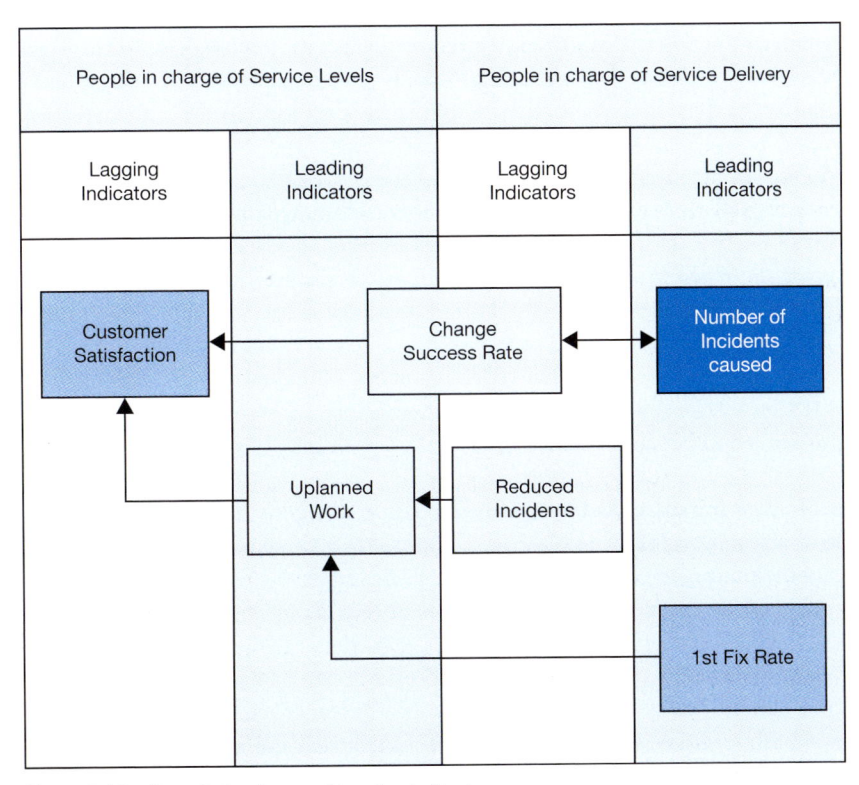

Figure 6.18   Sample leading and lagging indicators

Use the following steps to conduct predictive analysis:
1. Agree on the primary desired outcome and what it's lagging measure indicator might be.
2. Brainstorm what secondary leading/lagging measure indicators would influence the primary by asking the question "What causes this to happen?" or "What prevents this from happening?"
3. Brainstorm what tertiary leading/lagging measure indicators would influence the secondary by asking the question "What causes this to happen?" or "What prevents this from happening?"
4. Repeat until list is exhausted.
5. Map all cause and effect linkages and gain consensus.

Predictive analysis can be brainstormed in advance and mapped using strategy maps which can be automatically populated by the measurement system to produce color coded key indicators highlight potential risks or issues that need to be addressed.

A hand book called "The Memory Jogger™"[24] is another useful book covering many of these analytical techniques and more.

Outputs

The aim of the analysis process is to identify areas to improve the efficiency, effectiveness and quality by providing analytical techniques to interpret the changes in the metrics data. This helps process owners and service managers to make informed business decisions in the Tuning process. Some of the common outputs from the analysis would include observations from the following perspectives:

- **Improvements, degradations and exceptions assessment** - Assess and highlight any significant changes to any of the processes or services. Significant changes may be a top ten list approach or anything that improves/degrades by a predetermined percentage, that is all processes or services whose metrics improve/degrade by 10% in a given analysis period.

  In both cases of improvements or degradations, the analyst(s) should determine any reasonable explanations for the change and whether this was an exception due to some external influence or if it is a problem requiring corrective action.

- **Service improvement initiatives status assessment** - Assess all service improvement initiatives to determine if they are progressing as planned or require any assistance. The approach would be to compare the process improvement initiatives to the targets or plans to determine the deviation and if there are any problems requiring corrective action.

- **Benefits realized assessment** - Assess all anticipated or expected benefits from the processes or services to determine if they are producing results as planned or require any investigation. Again, the approach would be to compare the anticipated benefits to the targets or plans to determine the deviation and if there are any problems requiring corrective action.

- **Findings, observations, problems & predictions review** - Use the lessons learned to gain knowledge and wisdom for further improving IT service management. From the various assessments, develop the findings, observations, problems and/or predictions review. The review should be documented and discussed with the appropriate processes owner(s) and service manager(s) and include opinions on:

- what was done right
- what went wrong
- what could be done better next time
- how to prevent any problems from happening again
- what eminent risks if a status-quo course is maintained
- what are the service innovation initiatives

6.8 Tuning the process

Objective
The main objective of the tuning sub-process is to assess, prioritise, align and evaluate the most cost effective implementation of improvements for IT service management. Analysis of the monitored data may identify areas of the process or service that could be tuned to improve performance of the process through improvement initiatives.

Description
Tuning techniques can provide recommendations and invoke initiatives or changes to: refine processes, redistribute workload, revise targets, remove bottlenecks, introduce tools & automation, update policies, define better procedures, improve work instructions, increase skill-sets, et cetera. The scope of the initiatives can be minor adjustments through to major or significant projects.

Before implementing any of the recommendations arising from the tuning techniques, it is appropriate to test the validity of the recommendation. For example, "Can workload be redistributed or a policy revised to avoid the need to carry out any tuning?" or "Can other approaches be used to solve a particular problem?" or "Can the proposed change be modelled to show its effectiveness and return on investment (ROI) before it is implemented?"

One of the main challenges is deciding which initiatives to implement given limited time, fixed budgets and scarce resources. This can be compounded further if the processes or services are not that mature resulting in a constant reactive fire-fighting mode of operation; or if there is already perceived to be too much change taking place in the organization. There are four main decision analysis criteria for consideration when prioritizing competing initiatives sometimes referred to as 'The business case':

1. cost of making the change – time, money, resources
2. time to recover costs – break even point
3. risks, impact or potential problems that may be encountered – status quo or from implementation
4. anticipated business benefits – quantitative, qualitative and alignment

Inputs
The inputs to the tuning sub-process are primarily concerned with understanding the outputs from the analysis and reviewing options available that provide the most feasible solutions for implementation. The inputs include:
- business, service, process, financial, workload and utilization data
- improvements, degradations or exceptions to the processes or services
- current initiative and process improvements underway

- maturity and readiness of the organization involved
- benefits realized, their alignment and priority to the business
- findings, observations, problems and predictions from the analysis

Activities

There are four questions one must answer when determining which improvement initiatives to recommend and implement:

1. What alternative approaches or options were considered for this improvement? that is, workload balance, policy change, tool automation
2. What is required to implement the change? that is, effort, cost, timelines
3. What are the anticipated benefits? that is customer satisfaction, cost reduction, productivity gain
4. What is the business case for making the change? that is, ROI, break-even, risk reduction

The main activities of the tuning sub-process include:
- gap assessment – a review of gaps and actionable items required from implementation
- initiative options – a review of the alternate options to implement changes
- a review of gaps and actionable items required from implementation
- the anticipated benefits from the implementation of the changes including key performance metrics and timelines
- setting and aligning goals – a review of goals for alignment
- anticipated benefits – a review of the anticipated benefits from the implementation of the changes including key performance metrics and timelines
- decision analysis – a review of the decision analysis criteria review.

Gap assessment

The results of the analysis lead to identification of gaps in terms of people, process and technology issues. A documented gap assessment is the catalyst to prioritizing where to begin formal process improvement. The gap report is used when there is a need to compare data, contrasting one set of numbers or opinions against another, such as current state versus future state, 'Initiative A' versus 'Initiative B', and so on. Gap reports are primarily used when there is a need to present quantitative data for decision.

Categorizing of the data facilitates analysis, assists in identifying trends, and divides data results and reporting into more manageable pieces. Assessment reports can often produce vast amounts of data, but the value of that data depends on how it is organized and interpreted; the data can be transformed into information that will help an organization successfully achieve change and process improvement. The results must clearly display the gaps, identify the risks of not closing the gaps, facilitate prioritization of development activities, and facilitate communication of this information.

The success of every IT project relies on a combination of people, process, and technology; the mix of these elements needed for success in a specific project has to be identified by the organization itself. Therefore understanding the importance of the organizational capabilities or competencies is critical to properly prioritizing gaps and identifying areas for development.

A gap analysis will provide insight to risks and development opportunities
Gap analyzes identify the risks and development opportunities an organization has in front of it in preparing itself for successful IT improvements. If all processes cannot be implemented simultaneously, the organization has to decide which process(es) will give the greatest business benefit in the least amount of time with the lowest risk.

Once credibility for the assessment process and gap document data has been established, the results must be articulated in an understandable and actionable manner. The problems with suspected causes should be described and next steps clearly articulated. A gap analysis summary of results and key priorities should be presented to a cross-functional group of key stakeholders who will be pivotal in furthering the change. Understanding and buy-in from this group is needed before any action planning can occur. If an organization does not buy into the diagnosis, then they surely will not buy into the cure. Establishing credibility for the assessment or benchmark and its results are important for fostering buy-in.

Initiative options
Initiatives options are the alternative approaches an organization could take to improve a process or service. Each alternative must be explored to select the best approach. The tuning sub-process assesses the alternative options using decision criteria and recommends the best approach.

Most organizations have limited resources (time, priorities, people, and money) and must make decisions wisely on how to use them. For that reason implementing new initiatives should be reviewed to determine the best method of making 'fit for purpose' changes with the least amount of disruption, yet provide maximum business benefit. This means looking at more than one option, approach or solution to implement an initiative and determining the best approach given the organizational circumstances "time", "priorities", "people", "risk" and "money". It is useful to weight and grade your initiatives and alternative approaches to determine which ones are the highest priority, with least amount of effort and maximum benefit. For example, the following bubble chart tool (figure 6.19) ranks initiatives by "priority" versus "benefit" versus "cost" into opportunity quadrants, making it easier to make a selection.

Initiatives that generate quick wins are sometimes highly desirable. This would require another dimension of time to be compared to benefits. Quick wins help to keep improvement initiatives on track and help to keep the energy and commitment levels high. Quick wins can be used to:
- help convince change sceptics of the benefits
- prove early successes, and enable success to build on success
- help retain support of influential stakeholders
- help expand the guiding coalition and get more people on board and committed to the program
- help build credibility and confidence to tackle even more complex implementation issues and process integration

Setting and aligning goals
One of the key areas where improvement initiatives often go wrong – not setting clear goals and success criteria as they relate to the stakeholder needs. Although this is a difficult and sometimes time-consuming exercise it is one that helps:

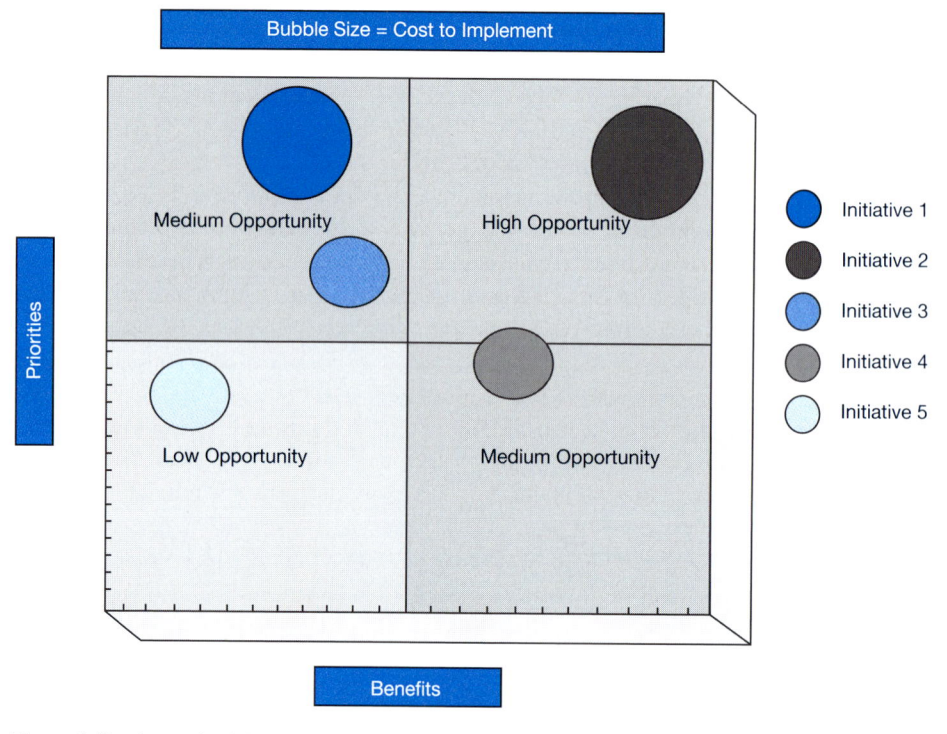

Figure 6.19 Assessing initiative options

- focus on real results that are measurable and understood by the business and the sponsors for the initiative
- get buy-in from all management levels and stakeholders
- set priorities to steer initiatives
- define procedures, working instructions and reports that underpin the goals
- help identify if desired outcomes of the initiatives have been realized

It is important that goals are measured to determine if the IT strategy is successfully meeting the customer's needs. There are various methods for setting and measuring goals.

The ITIL® V3 CSI "Continual Service Improvement" book[25] states that the primary purpose of continual service improvements is to continually align and re-align the IT services to the changing business needs by identifying and implementing improvements. The first stage in setting and aligning goals is to establish some top-level goals that support the business objectives. The top-level goals need to be supported with objectives and anticipated benefits that can be measured to verify goal achievement. These top-level goals, objectives and benefits help provide guidance and focus on results:
- Reduced time to realize infrastructure changes
- Increased reliability of the infrastructure in support of key business operations
- Increased availability of IT functionality to the key business operations
- Increased throughput and performance of business processing through the optimal use of IT
- Reduced volume of complaints related to IT functionality support and problem resolution

- Reduced business impact of IT outages and User experienced problems
- Increased skills and competency levels of IT staff in order to better support business needs and offer a career growth to IT staff

Reassess objectives and anticipated benefits – expected outcomes

Things change. The economy, competitors, company strategies, technologies and customer needs are constantly shifting. An important step in key objectives and benefits identification is to periodically reassess what the priorities are from your leadership. Key objectives and benefit identification can be somewhat of a moving target, what was a burning platform last year may not be the same issues today and certainly will be different next year.

In the tuning process it is important to verify that the objectives and anticipated benefits are relevant to the current business conditions. However, it is also important that the metrics are as consistent as possible over time so they can be compared historically. A balance must be maintained and where appropriate, modifying the metrics only if necessary to reflect the changing times.

For each of the initiatives, identify and quantify the anticipated or expected benefits. This is useful for deciding which initiatives to implement and provides a means to track their success. For example, if the goal was "reduced time to realize infrastructure changes" a metric like "Percentage of changes on time" could be used to track benefits attained. Like key goal indicators, the benefits should be measured with metrics to indicate their realization.

Decision analysis

The final stage is to choose the initiative(s) that best meet the business and IT organization key goals and objectives. The goal of a decision analysis is to quickly identify the initiatives that provide the best cost/benefits while considering risks and other qualitative and quantitative aspects.

An important step in key objectives and benefits identification is to periodically determine what the priorities are from your leadership. Key objectives and benefit identification can be somewhat of a moving target, what was a burning platform last year may not be the same issues today and certainly will be different next year.

A decision analysis tool is useful in identifying the key objectives/benefits, weighting them according to management's priorities, scoring each of the initiatives on a 'fit for purpose' scale and providing a total weighted score to help select the best candidates.

The following decision analysis, figure 6.20, compares three initiatives to one another. Initiative 1 is the winner even though it did not have the highest score because the other two initiatives did not meet the mandatory requirements.

Decision Analysis Tool

Key Objectives/Benefits	Weight	Initiative 1 Score (0 to 5)	Initiative 1 Total Score (B x C)	Initiative 2 Score (0 to 5)	Initiative 2 Total Score (B x E)	Initiative 3 Score (0 to 5)	Initiative 3 Total Score (B x G)
Low effort	3	3	9	2	6	2	6
Low Cost	3	4	12	3	9	3	9
Quick payback	2	3	6	1	2	4	8
Low risk	2	2	4	3	6	3	6
High ROI	2	2	4	3	6	3	6
Staff buy-in	2	1	2	3	6	3	6
Total Weighted Score			37		35		41

Scoring Legend	
Exceeds requirements	5
Somewhat exceeds requirements	4
Meets requirements	3
Moderately meets requirements	2
Barely meets requirements	1
Does not meet requirements	0

Weighting Legend	
Mandatory	3
Required	2
Nice to have	1

Scoring Legend	
Pass	Green
Fail	Red

Figure 6.20 Sample Decision Analysis Tool

6.8.5 Outputs

The aim of the tuning process is to make decisions on which initiatives and actions to take for the purpose of making continuous continual service improvements to the organizational processes and services. Additionally, to develop an adequately detailed plan to ensure that changes will be delivered at the agreed cost, time and service quality.

Initiative scope can range from minor adjustments to major projects; plans need to be scaled accordingly; approvals may vary accordingly. The plans may include information like:
- overview description of the initiative recommendation in common business terms
- roles and responsibilities for implementing, operating and maintaining new process or service changes including activities to be performed by customer or suppliers
- changes to the existing service management processes or services
- new or changed underpinning contracts and service level agreements to align with the changes
- manpower or recruitment requirements
- skills and training requirements
- processes, measures, methods and tools to be used in connection with the new or changed service, e.g. capacity management, financial management
- budgets and time-scales
- service acceptance criteria
- the anticipated benefits and expected outcomes from implementing the new changes expressed in measurable terms

Initiative recommendations

The initiative recommendations should include a brief synopsis written for executive management. The recommendations should be quantified and qualified in terms of:
- scope of initiative
- business benefits to be expected
- potential impact of carrying out the recommendations
- risks involved

- resources required
- timing required
- cost, both set up and on-going

Initiative implementation plans

Sufficient details should be provided to describe the proposed roles and responsibilities for implementing, operating and maintaining process or service changes including activities to be performed by customer or suppliers. This may take the form of a project charter describing for example the key goal, objectives, methods, time-scales and business outcomes, etc. The following example list provides an outline of topics which may be included:
- project plan/project charter name
- project number
- project overview
- goals & objectives
- delivery methodology
- background
- scope
- assumptions
- concept and definitions
- areas of impact
- risks
- constraints
- contingency plans
- implementation approach
- timing
- budgets
- functional requirements
- key performance indicators
- approval and reviews
- project/executive ownership
- business case

Initiative activity plans

The activity plans are the details required for the project management and quality management approaches. Some examples of what a project management approach may include:
- work breakdown structure (WBS) Gantt chart
- basis of estimates
- project effort estimation
- project standards
- project roles and responsibilities
- change and issue management approach
- communications and control approach

Some examples of what a quality management approach may include:
- activity reviews/walk-through
- tools and techniques

- test approach
- performance/quality standards
- quality management roles
- training

Project resourcing request

If the initiative change is significant or major in nature it may require a project resourcing request and approvals. In this case it is suggested that the organizations normal project resourcing request be used to initiate changes of this type.

The following items should be included in a project resourcing form, whether paper or electronic:
- project description and executive overview
- project charter and details
- project management approach
- quality management approach
- approval process

6.9 Implement process initiatives

Objective

The main objective of the implement sub-process is to introduce to the live operational processes or services any changes that have been identified by the monitoring, analysis and tuning activities in order to assist in meeting the service management objectives and plan.

Description

Implementation of any initiatives should be undertaken through the formal change and release & deployment management processes to gain optimal results. The change management process ensures that standardised methods and procedures are used for efficient and prompt handling of all changes while the release & deployment management process focuses on the protection of the operational environment and its services through the use of formal procedures and checks.

Again, initiative scope can range from minor adjustments to major projects; release plans, testing and coordination details need to be scaled accordingly. Release & deployment management undertakes the planning, design, build, configuration and testing of processes, services, hardware and software to create a set of Release components for a live environment. Activities also cover the planning, preparation and scheduling of a release to many customers and locations. Release & deployment management activities may include:
- design, build and configuration
- acceptance
- rollout planning
- extensive testing to predefined acceptance criteria
- sign-off of the release for implementation
- documentation, communication, preparation and training

- audits prior to and following the implementation of changes
- installation of new or upgraded hardware or software tools

It is important that further monitoring takes place, so that the effects of the change can be assessed. It may be necessary to make further changes or to regress some of the original changes.

Inputs
The inputs to the implementation sub-process are primarily the instructions on what initiative changes are to take place for the improvement of processes or services as a result of the monitoring, analysis and tuning activities. The inputs include:
- approvals
- documentation on project charters, activities, project plans, KPIs, quality plans
- Request for change(s)
- request for project resources

Activities
The implementation of any changes arising from these activities should be undertaken through a formal change and release & deployment management process. The impact of tuning initiatives can have major implications on the customers of the service. Implementing the tuning changes under formal change and release & deployment management procedures results in:
- less adverse impact on the users of the processes and services
- increased user productivity
- increased productivity of IT personnel
- A reduction in the number of changes that need to be backed-out, and the ability to do so more easily
- greater management and control of processes and services
- stable IT environment

Depending on the scope, some of the main activities may include:
- allocation of funds and budgets
- allocation of roles and responsibilities
- developing and coordinating a communications plan
- documenting and maintaining the policies, plans, procedures and definitions for the processes or services
- identification and management of risks to the processes or services
- managing project teams and resources
- managing facilities and budgets
- managing operational teams and resources
- reporting progress against plans

Request for Change
Most initiatives will be implemented through the organization's normal change management process and are initiated by issuing a Request for Change (RFC). The goal of the ITIL change management process is to ensure that standardized methods and procedures are used for efficient and prompt handling of all changes, in order to minimize the impact of change-related

incidents upon service quality, and consequently to improve the day-to-day operations of the organization.

Communications

An effective communication strategy, well executed, is a critical success factor for change initiatives. The value of effective change communication goes well beyond the moment, require ongoing updates, affecting how employees receive and adopt future changes. The most effective communication plan considers the perspective of each stakeholder group, keeping them informed and up to date.

Outputs

The aim of the implementation process is to ensure that changes are implemented at the agreed cost and service quality with minimal disruption to the operational environment; with a method for tracking and reviewing expected outcomes and anticipated benefits; update of the MDB with new key performance measures.

Initiative execution and deliverables

Improvement initiatives are implemented using the details provided by the implementation and activity plans created by the tuning process. The execution of the plans is best performed by the change and release control processes to ensure for efficient and prompt handling of changes and protection of the operational environment.

Initiative benefits evaluation criteria

Initiative goals, objectives, anticipated benefits and expected outcomes need to be made explicit and measurable so they can be evaluated. A series of new key performance metrics or indicators may be required to verify deliverables and outcomes have achieved the anticipated benefits planned.

Initiative key performance metrics

The measurement database (MDB) should be updated to reflect:
- new key performance metrics or verifying attainment of anticipated benefits
- modification to existing measures, that is targets, thresholds
- new scorecards or dashboards to monitor the health and success of new or revised processes or services

Acceptance & review

The service provider should report on the outcomes achieved by the new or changed processes or services against those planned following its implementation. A post implementation review comparing actual outcomes against those planned should be performed through the change management process and/or measurement process.

6.10 Measurement reporting

Objective
The main goal of the measurement reporting sub-process is to keep all stakeholder groups informed and up-to-date on the monitoring, measurement and review of how service management objectives and plan are being achieved. The specific objective of the measurement reporting sub-process is to create and produce agreed, timely, reliable, and accurate reports for informed decision making and effective communications.

Description
Sharing knowledge about the service management objectives and plan achievements is essential to the IT service provider's success. Key stakeholders are identified in the R.A.C.I authority matrix. They want to know what the status is of the service management objectives and plan achievements and how they are affected. The more people are educated about the progress of the measurement program implementation and how it will help them in the future, the more they participate and benefit.

Measurement reports should be created, distributed and communicated to the relevant parties or stakeholders to be acted upon. The measurement reporting process should provide a framework for informing, involving, and obtaining buy-in from all stakeholder groups when and as required.

Inputs
The inputs to the measurement reporting sub-process are primarily the gathering of outputs from all measurement sub-processes. The inputs to the measurement reporting process can include:
- active measurements, for example KGIs, CSFs, KPIs, KPMs and facts
- data validation reports, for example accuracy, sources, calculations
- alert notifications, for example early warning indicators, pre-rehearsed actions
- dashboards/scorecards, for example summarized information by roles
- metrics trending reports, for example fact, KPM trends
- performance improvements, degradations and exceptions assessments
- process improvement initiatives status assessments
- benefit reported assessments
- findings, observations, problems & predictions reviews
- initiative recommendations
- initiative implementation plans
- initiative activity plans
- Request for Change information
- project resourcing requests
- initiative execution and deliverables
- benefits evaluation criteria
- initiative key performance metrics
- acceptance & reviews
- business case

Activities

The reporting process participates in the implementation and operational aspect of the measurement process. There are four questions one must answer when determining best framework for informing, involving, and obtaining buy-in from all stakeholder groups when and as required:
- Who are the stakeholder groups and what are their respective roles?
- Who needs what level of information and at what frequency?
- What is the best communications methodology for your environment?
- What are the best mediums to communicate the information and in what format?

During the implementation the main activities of the measurement reporting process include:
- identifying stakeholder groups and their roles
- mapping reporting information to the roles
- developing a communications methodology and plan
- choosing the mediums and formats to exchange ideas and information

The operational activities of the measurement reporting process include:
- report creation and distribution electronic, hard-copy, announcements, notifications, scorecards
- Ad hoc reporting
- archiving

Stakeholders

The first step is to determine who the stakeholders are: They are people who are either directly involved in the IT service management (providers); people who use the services or processes (consumers); people who can influence the IT service management effectiveness and efficiency (improvers). The need to involve these people is very important because without the key people, the IT service management plan can have incomplete requirements, political issues, implementation problems, and so on. It is recommended to identify stakeholders as early as possible.

Stakeholder could include any of the following:
- IT executive, IT service management
- business executive, business customer, super users, users
- service owners/managers
- process owners/managers
- team members
- external service providers
- Continual Service Improvement (CSI) manager
- business case owner
- anyone else involved

Depending on the size and complexity of the organization, there may be a need to create multiple levels of stakeholder involvement for different levels of communications, reporting and involvement. For example, you could create the following three levels of involvement:
- **Core members** - Consists of the stakeholders actively involved in decision making and strategy development.

The measurement process 93

- **Primary members** - Consists of stakeholders who must be engaged during the operational change of services.
- **Secondary members** - Consists of the stakeholders actively involved in the day-to-day provision, consumption and monitoring of service efficiency, effectiveness and quality.

For example, figure 6.21, illustrates this concept using core, primary and secondary stakeholder groups:

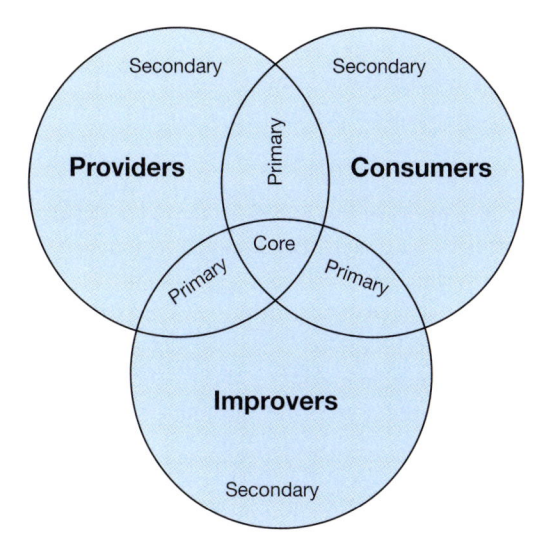

Figure 6.21 Stakeholder types

For example, figure 6.22, further illustrates this concept using mapping to identify the key stakeholders:

		Stakeholder Groups		
Member	Mode	Provider	Consumer	Improver
Core	Strategic	CIO	Customer	IT Owner
Primary	Tactical	Process Owners	Super User	IT Manager
Secondary	Operational	IT Manager	User	IT Staff

Figure 6-22 Stakeholder mapping

R.A.C.I. reporting

The ITIL® V3 CSI "Continual Service Improvement" book states that a characteristic of a process is that all related activities need not necessarily be limited to one specific organizational unit. Service asset & configuration management activities, for example, can be conducted in departments such as computer operations, system programming, application management, network management, systems development and even non-IT departments like procurement, storehouse or accounting. Since processes and their activities run through a whole organization, the activities should be mapped to the existing IT departments or sections and coordinated by process managers. Once detailed procedures and work instructions have been developed, an organization has to map its staff to the activities of the process. Clear definitions of accountability and responsibility are critical success factors for any SIP (Service Improvement Program). Without this, roles and responsibilities within the new process can be confusing, and individuals might revert to how the activities were handled before the new procedures were put in place.

To assist with this task the R.A.C.I. model is often used within organizations indicating roles and responsibilities in relation to processes and activities:
- R - responsibility - correct execution of process and activities
- A - accountability - ownership of quality, and end result of process
- C - consulted - involvement through input of knowledge and information
- I - informed - receiving information about process execution and quality

For Example:
An organization planned to implement change management. It was decided to start with a workshop with the key stakeholders within the IT department: the various IT managers. They drew up a map of all the change management activities and mapped them to the IT sections. They came to an agreement on which IT section was accountable, who should be responsible, who should be consulted and who should be informed. After that a blueprint was set up to clarify the goal, scope, activities (with allocation of roles) and the necessary inputs and outputs were defined. This blueprint was authorized by the stakeholders and communicated across the whole organization.

It is important to understand the distinction between a formal function within an organization and the process roles that the function is expected to carry out. A formal function may fulfil more than one specific service management role and carry out activities relating to more than one process.

This is a difficult and time-consuming exercise but one that helps clarify, to all involved, which activities they are expected to fulfil, as well as identifying any gaps in process delivery and responsibilities. An example of how this could be done for the measurement reporting is provided in figure 6.23.

As can be seen, there is only one person accountable for an activity, although several people may be responsible for carrying out parts of the activity. In this example, the Continual Service Improvement Program (CSI) Manager is fully accountable for the whole Measurement Monitoring process, although informed and helped by other functions. Accountable means to have the end-responsibility for the process. So, in this example, the CSI Manager must understand where the monitoring process is now and where it is going, with specific detailed key performance indicators set up to monitor the health and progress of this process. Note here that, in Tune and Implement, the Process Owner Authority has been identified as the Authority; the SLA owner could easily have been the Authority if the measurement focus was more service oriented.

Possible problems to watch for with the R.A.C.I. model:
- More than one person accountable for a process which means in practice no-one is accountable

The measurement process

	A	B	C	D	E	F	G	H
1	Process	Measurement Reporting Outputs	Client	IT Manager	Process Owner	SLA Owner	Team Members	SIP
2								
3	Monitor	Active measurements, e.g. elements, metrics, KPIs			C	C	I	A/R
4	Monitor	Data validation reports, e.g. accuracy, sources, calculations			C	C	I	A/R
5	Monitor	Alert notifications, e.g. early warning indicators pre-rehearsed actions			C	C	I	A/R
6	Monitor	Dashboards/scorecards, e.g. summarized information by roles			C	C	I	A/R
7	Monitor	Metrics trending reports, e.g. KPM, KPI trends			C	C	I	A/R
8								
9	Analyse	Performance improvements, degradations and exceptions assessments		I	R	A	C	C
10	Analyse	Process improvement initiatives status assessments		I	R	A	C	C
11	Analyse	Benefits realized assessments		I	R	A	C	C
12	Analyse	Findings, observations, problems & predictions reviews		I	R	A	C	C
13								
14	Tune	Initiative recommendations	C	C	A	C	R	I
15	Tune	Initiative implementation plans	C	C	A	C	R	I
16	Tune	Initiative activity plans	C	C	A	C	R	I
17	Tune	Request for change information	C	C	A	C	R	I
18	Tune	Project resourcing requests	C	C	A	C	R	I
19								
20	Implement	Initiative execution and deliverables	I	I	A	C	R	I
21	Implement	Benefits evaluation criteria	I	I	A	C	R	I
22	Implement	Initiative key performance metrics	I	I	A	C	R	I
23	Implement	Acceptance & reviews	I	I	A	C	R	I

Figure 6-23   Mapping measurement reporting

- Delegation of responsibility without necessary authority
- Focus on matching processes and activities with departments
- Wrong division/combination of functions

- Combination of accountability for closely related processes, such as incident management, problem management, configuration management, change management and release & deployment management

Communications methodology & plan

A communications methodology utilizes three directions for effective communication:
- top-down
- bottom-up
- middle-out

Top-Down

It is absolutely crucial that all participants sense the executive support and guidance for any improvement effort, often referred to as 'the tone at the top'. The executive leadership of the organization (business and IT) needs to speak with a unified, enthusiastic voice about the measurement program and what it holds for everyone involved. Not only will the executives need to speak directly to all levels of the organization, they will also need to listen directly to all levels of the organization.

The transition from the improvement management practices of today to the practices envisioned for tomorrow will be driven by a sure and convinced leadership focused on a vision and guided by clearly defined, strategic, measurable goals.

Bottom-Up

To ensure the buy-in and confidence of the personnel involved in bringing the proposed changes to reality, it will be important to communicate the way in which the solutions were created. If the perception in the organization is that solely the improver members created the proposed changes with no input from providers or consumers, resistance is likely to occur. However, if it is understood that all participants were consulted, acceptance will be more promising.

Middle-Out

Full support at all levels, where the changes will have to be implemented, is important to sustainable improvement. At this level (as with all levels), there must be an effort to find and communicate the specific benefits of the changes. People need a personal stake in the success of the project management practices.

A communications plan is also useful to map out who gets what information (target audience), in what medium and when. Figure 6.24, provides an example of how the measurement communications plan could be constructed.

Report creation and distribution

Reports, scorecards and announcements need to be created and distributed on a timely basis to the stakeholders. A schedule of reports should be maintained and followed. The frequency will vary based on the type of information being communicated. For example, alert notifications should be as close to real-time as possible; dashboards and scorecards should be monthly.

The measurement process

Message or Report	Target Stakeholder Group	Vehicle of Communication	Frequency	Medium
Active measurements, e.g. elements, metrics, KPIs	Team members Process Owners	MDB	Monthly	MDB
Data validation reports, e.g. accuracy, sources, calculations	CSI	Issue log	Monthly	MDB
Alert notifications, e.g. early warning indicators, pre-rehearsed actions	Team members	email notifications	Monthly	MDB, email
Dashboards/scorecards, e.g. summarized information by roles	Team members, Process Owners	Status Reports, Monthly	Monthly	MDB, document portal
Metrics trending reports, e.g. KPM, KPI trends	Team members, Process Owners	Status Reports: Monthly	Monthly	MDB, document portal
Performance improvements, degradations and exceptions assessments	IT Mgmt	Executive Staff Presentations	Quarterly	email, document portal
Process improvement initiatives status assessments	IT Mgmt	Executive Staff Presentations	Quarterly	email, document portal
Benefits realized assessments	IT Mgmt	Executive Staff Presentations	Quarterly	email, document portal
Findings, observations, problems & predictions reviews	IT Mgmt, CIO	Executive Staff Presentations	Quarterly	presentation, meetings
Initiative recommendations	IT Mgmt, CIO	Executive Staff Presentations	Quarterly	presentation, meetings
Initiative implementation plans	Team members, Process Owners	Informal meeting- Project Plan	Ad-hoc	document portal
Initiative activity plans	Team members, Process Owners	Informal meeting- Project Plan	Ad-hoc	document portal
Request for change information	Change Mgmt	Change request form	Ad-hoc	email
Project resourcing requests	Project Office	Project request form	Ad-hoc	email
Initiative execution and deliverables	Project Team	Status Reports: Weekly	Friday's by noon	meetings, document portal
Benefits evaluation criteria	Process Owner	Change Management procedures	Per change schedule	meetings, document portal
Initiative key performance metrics	Process Owner	Informal meeting	Ad-hoc	MDB
Acceptance & reviews	Process Owner	Informal meeting	Ad-hoc	email, document portal

Figure 6.24   Measurement communications plan

Ad hoc reporting

There will always be a need for ad hoc reporting to support the analysis and tuning sub-process.

Archiving

A good practice is to archive the reporting information overtime in some type of document management and retrieval systems for future reference.

Outputs

The aim of the measurement reporting process is to produce agreed, timely, reliable, accurate reports for informed decision making and effective communications. Some of the common outputs from the measurement reporting would include:

Production of Measurement Reporting

Regular production of measurement reports from the MDB on the progress and status of metrics. Some examples would include:
- active measurements, for example KGIs, CSFs, KPIs, KPMs and facts
- data validation reports, for example accuracy, sources, calculations
- alert notifications, for example early warning indicators, pre-rehearsed actions
- dashboards/scorecards, for example summarized information by roles
- metrics trending reports, for example fact, KPM trends

Reporting Policy

The measurement reporting process would be responsible for developing the reporting policy on who gets access to what information and to what level of information. Reporting policy outputs would include:
- stakeholder maps, for example producing and maintaining stakeholder groups and their roles
- R.A.C.I. matrix models, for example producing and updating R.A.C.I. models to help map reporting information to roles.
- communications strategy and plan, for example developing an effective communications methodology and plan
- reporting standards, for example determine the content specifications and standards for reports like:
  – performance improvements, degradations and exceptions assessments
  – process improvement initiatives status assessments
  – benefits realized assessments
  – findings, observations, problems & predictions reviews
  – initiative recommendations
  – initiative implementation plans
  – initiative activity plans
  – Request for Change information
  – project resourcing requests
  – initiative execution and deliverables
  – benefits evaluation criteria
  – initiative key performance metrics
  – acceptance & reviews
  – archival policy, for example determining when and how information will be archived

Performance based reports
For each process or service there should be a team of operational staff responsible for its control and management, and management staff who are accountable for the overall process or service. Reports must be produced to illustrate how the process or service and its constituent components are performing in terms of efficiency, effectiveness and quality.

Trend analysis
Trend analysis can be done on the individual performance and management information that has been collected by the measurement sub-processes. The data can be extracted to a spreadsheet for graphical trending; forecasting to show the trend and progress of a particular metric over a previous period of time; and how it may be expected to change in the future.

Exception reporting
Reports that show management and operations staff when the performance of a particular process or service becomes unacceptable are also a required output from a MDB. Exceptions can be set for any process, service or measurement that is stored within a MDB. An example exception may be that the change management success rate percentage has breached 70% for three consecutive months, or that the incident volumes from users exceeded expectations.

In particular, exception reports are of interest to the SLM process in determining whether the targets in SLAs have been breached. Also the IT service management processes may be able to use the exception reports in the balancing of workload and optimizing the cost effectiveness of IT service management.

Process initiative status
The improvement initiatives require status reporting. Initiatives need to be tracked and monitored under the reporting process to report progress status and evidence of success, such as:
- initiative implementation progress
- improved maturity of process
- increased performance in terms of efficiency, effectiveness or quality
- quicker benefits realized
- reduced costs or improving service levels

In all cases, management needs to have a clear view of the Service Improvement Initiatives (SII) in progress and their status as well as have a so-called 'helicopter view' of their contribution to IT service management process improvement.

Benefits reporting
It is important for the IT organization to have a clear definition of what customers can expect from the processes and services provided in terms of features, functions and service levels. This helps to set and manage expectation which in turn enhances relationships, customer satisfaction and the perceived credibility of the IT organization.

It is equally and sometimes more important to consider the business benefits being derived for the beneficiary of the processes and/or services described in terms of outcomes, achievements and/or anticipated benefits realized using the customer's business vernacular.

Business benefits have multiple dimensions of which some may be more important to one customer than another. Further, their priority may change over time due to constantly evolving and changing business drivers. Examples of benefit dimensions include:
- quantitative versus qualitative; for some quantity is more important than quality and vice versa
- tangible versus intangible; example return on investment versus value on investment;
- real versus perceived; example of hard measures versus subjective perceptions
- sense of gain versus avoidance of loss; example to save something versus avoid loosing something

Focusing on expected outcomes, achievements and anticipated benefits helps to align more effectively with meeting objectives, reaching targets or goals, achieving planned results and delivering business value. Also, measuring the benefits realized from the processes and services through metrics helps to maintain alignment of the deliverables to the customer requirements through a continuous feedback loop.

Some examples of the benefits that could be measured include:
- processes/services are in compliance or in conformance with regulatory requirements, that is ISO/IEC 20000[3], SOX, maturity levels are met, service levels are met
- improved quality of service – more reliable business support
- service management objective are being achieved
- demonstrate efficiency and effective improvements of IT service management
- clearer view of current IT capability – maturity of processes or services
- better IT service management effectiveness (and possibly on where changes would bring most benefits)
- cost avoidance or reduction – optimization of processes and services
- increased user productivity – reduction in hidden costs
- enhanced customer satisfaction as service providers know and deliver what is expected of them
- improved cycle time for changes and greater success rate

The importance and level of these will vary between organizations. Collaboration with the key stakeholders is important to defining these benefits for any organization in a way that will be measurable later on. Following ITIL guidance can help to quantify some of these benefits.

Production of the measurement reports

The objective of measurement report production is to produce agreed, timely, reliable, accurate reports for informed decision making and effective communications. There should be clear descriptions of each measurement report including its identity, purpose, audience and details of the data source.

The measurement reports should be produced to meet identified needs and customer requirements. Measurement reports may include:
- **performance improvement assessment** – "against service level targets", "operational level targets", "efficiency", "effectiveness", "quality"
- **exception based reports** – "unexpected workload", "new service start-ups"

- **non-compliance and issues** – "against SLA", "security breach"
- **workload characteristics** – "volume", "resource utilization"
- **performance reporting following major events** – "major incidents and changes"
- **trend information** – "improvements", "degradations", "exceptions"
- **improvement initiative assessment** – "progress to date", "benefits attained"
- **benefits realized assessments** – "cost avoidance", "productivity", "quality"
- **satisfaction analysis** – "internal", "external"
- **findings and observations review** – "problems", "predictions"
- **initiatives** - "recommendations"", plans", "activities", "RFC status", "project status", "reviews"
- **communications** – "plans", "messages", "schedules"
- **risk and management reports**

Measurement reports should be disseminated and communicated to the relevant parties or stakeholders to be acted upon.

Chapter 7
ITSM metrics – case study example

To help further illustrate some of the basic concepts and processes presented thus far, a case study example is provided based on a fictional company called XYZ Corporation.

7.1 Background

XYZ Corporation is a small publicly traded Insurance company based in the United States. XYZ had done well over the recent years but was finding it difficult to keep pace with the competitive marketplace. New product development was critical to differentiating XYZ from the others. Products were sold through a large network of independent Brokers who were able to shop the industry for the best or most creative insurance programs for their clientele. Insurance products are heavily dependent on IT applications, services and support processes. Getting new products developed, tested, deployed and successfully launched and supported by the broker network were critical success factors for the company. There was contention between the Business Units and the IT Department because this process was deemed inefficient, ineffective and of poor quality. It seemed every new product launch was plagued by many problems. The IT Department always came through but took brute-force measures to get things back on track often causing budgets to be exceeded. The credibility of new business products was in question by the broker network. Many stopped promoting new products until they were stabilised; causing competitive advantage to erode.

Compounding the already strained situation, new financial reporting regulations in the United States called the Sarbanes-Oxley Act (SOX), caused additional and significant changes for the IT department's release and control processes. It was determined by external auditors that the existing processes were deficient and required many process risk exposures to be remediated. Seizing the opportunity for improvement, the CIO of XYZ proposed significant changes and a complete over-haul of the release and control processes using industry best practices from the IT Infrastructure Library (ITIL®). A sizable investment was required to transform the processes. The Business Executives realized that this was a make or break situation for the company since the release and control processes were at the heart of their challenge to be competitively agile. The Board of Directors approved the investment but on the condition that XYZ would demonstrate a return on investment and that the improvement benefits were realized through measurements and reporting.

The IT department embraced the ITIL guidance for the release, change and service asset & configuration management processes. New process owners were assigned, trained and delegated the task of revamping the processes to improve efficiency, effectiveness and quality.

Most importantly, to meet the Board of Directors reporting requirement, a measurement framework and metrics were required. The goal of the measurements and reporting was to better align IT with the business and demonstrate benefits realized through continual improvements. This resulted in achieving four main objectives:
1. meet regulatory compliance requirements
2. provide the instrumentation for management control
3. drive cost efficiencies and operational effectiveness
4. increase customer satisfaction levels

7.2 Planning for implementation

The first step in developing the measurement system was a series of planning meetings to determine what measurements already existing, develop a planned approach, and determine how the measurement process would be implemented and reviewed.

Assessments determined that the senior management commitment to the program was strong and included an adequate budget to get the basics in place. A Continual Service Improvement (CSI)) manager role was created and assigned internally with the mandate of managing the continual service improvement process and implementing the measurement program. The CSI manager worked with the release and control process owners to develop and plan a multi-process implementation approach for measuring the change, release and service asset & configuration management processes. Additional processes would be added later based on needs. Figure 7.1 show the Sample console used to navigate to specific process scorecards.

The next step for the implementation team was to develop some policies on how to structure the measurements to support the project charter goals, objectives, critical success factors, indicators and metrics. It was determined that a series of dashboards and scorecards would be the best method for monitoring, analyzing and reporting the metric results. Additional procedures were established for remediation of deficiencies in the process using tuning and implementation guidelines. A series of metrics were identified to help assess the efficiency, effectiveness and quality of the processes. Figure 7.2 show a list of sample change management metrics that were being monitored.

7.3 Implementation

The delivery of these processes involved many sub-groups within the IT department. An R.A.C.I. authority matrix was used to establish roles and responsibilities over the processes. Documenting an R.A.C.I. matrix[26] (who is Responsible, Accountable, Consulted and Informed) for each process helped to map the key stakeholders more effectively for the measurement sub-processes. Figure 7.3 shows a sample R.A.C.I. matrix with some of the role assignments.

ITSM metrics – case study example

itSMF KPI Scorecard© - ITSM Metrics MDB Sample		Home
Strategic	**Tactical**	**Operational**
Business Perspective	Service Level Management	Service Desk
Service Improvement Program	Problem Management	Incident Management
Risk Management	Financial Management	Configuration Management
Document Management	Availability Management	Change Management
Competence, Awareness & Training	Capacity Management	Release Management
Programme and Project Management	Service Continuity Management	Application Development
	Security Management	Application Support
		Operations Management
Metrics Administration	Service Level Acheivements	Role Based Scorecards
Tables	Business System 1	CIO
Input Metric Values	Business System 2	IT Service Manager
Edit Metric Attributes		
Changes/Revisions		

©itSMF International 2008. All rights reserved. No part of this application may be reproduced in any form by electronic copying, print, photo print, microfilm or any other means without written permission by the publisher. Although this application has been composed with much care, neither author, nor editor, nor publisher can accept any liability for damage caused by possible errors and/or incompleteness in this application.

This itSMF International application was based on my KPI Designer© 2008, a real-life product, with the approval of the owner of the product, Micromation Canada (www.micromationinc.com). The itSMF application can be used independently by the buyer, as long as copyrights are respected. The Intellectual Property of the application was and is with Micromation. Version 1.553.2

Figure 7.1   Sample console

itSMF KPI Scorecard© - Change Management Sample

S	T	P	ID	KPM Name	Actual	Polarity
	↓	B	CM001	Percentage of failed changes	45	L
	↑	W	CM002	Percentage of rejected RFCs	45	L
	↑	W	CM003	Number of unauthorized changes	15	L
	↓	B	CM004	Change backlog	15	L
	↑	W	CM005	Outages during changes	15	L
	↑	W	CM006	Number of failed changes with no back-out plan	15	L
	↓	W	CM007	Percentage of changes on time	45	M
	↑	W	CM008	Percentage of changes causing incidents	45	L
	↑	W	CM009	Number of CAB items not actioned on time	15	L
	↑	W	CM010	Number of Emergency Changes	3	L
	↑	W	CM011	Number of changes that do not deliver the expected results	15	L
	↓	W	CM012	Customer Satisfaction	2	M
	↔	S	CM013	Avg. labour hours/change - all changes	45	L
	↔	S	CM014	Avg. labour hours/change - standard changes	2	L
	↔	S	CM015	Avg. labour hours/change - basic changes	4	L
	↔	S	CM016	Avg. labour hours/change - emergency changes	5	L
	↓	B	CM017	Avg. cycle days/change - all changes	95	L
	↔	S	CM018	Avg. cycle days/change standard changes	6	L
	↔	S	CM019	Avg. cycle days/change - basic changes	7	L
	↔	S	CM020	Avg. cycle days/change - emergency changes	8	L
	↔	S	CM021	Number of logged RFCs	9	L
	↔	S	CM022	Number of rejected RFCs - initial filtering	11	L
	↔	S	CM023	Number of accepted RFCs	12	L
	↔	S	CM024	Number of unsuccessful changes - failed or timed-out	13	L

Scorecards
Dashboard
Process Map
Root Cause
Initiatives

Metrics Administration
Home
Tables
Input Metric Values
Edit Metric Attributes
Changes/Revisions

Legend
Status	Trending	Progress
Red	↑ Up	B Better
Yellow	↔ Same	S Same
Green	↓ Down	W Worse
No data	*Polarity*	
	M more is better	
	L less it better	

©itSMF International 2008. All rights reserved. No part of this application may be reproduced in any form by electronic copying, print, photo print, microfilm or any other means without written permission by the publisher. Although this application has been composed with much care, neither author, nor editor, nor publisher can accept any liability for damage caused by possible errors and/or incompleteness in this application.

This itSMF International application was based on my KPI Designer© 2008, a real-life product, with the approval of the owner of the product, Micromation Canada (www.micromationinc.com). The itSMF application can be used independently by the buyer, as long as copyrights are respected. The Intellectual Property of the application was and is with Micromation.Version 1.553.2

Figure 7.2   Sample change management metrics

Process ID	ITSM Process	Service Desk	Incident Management	Problem Management	Configuration Management	Change Management	Release Management	Process Owner E-mail
SD	Service Desk	A	C	C	I	I	I	
IM	Incident Management	C	A	C	I	I	I	
PM	Problem Management	C		A	I	I	I	
CFM	Configuration Management	I	I	I	A	C	C	joe.smith@xyz.com
CM	Change Management	C	C	C	I	A	R	john.doe@xyz.com
RM	Release Management	I	I	I	C	C	A	tom.petz@xyz.com

Figure 7.3 Sample R.A.C.I. matrix

Using data from existing change management systems, the implementation team used the average run-rate values from the previous three months to determine a baseline. The baseline was then used to set the thresholds for the metrics to help achieve the goals, objectives and metric targets. Figure 7.4 shows sample metrics thresholds that were set for individual metrics.

ID	KPM Name	DangerValue	TargetValue	LowLimit	HighLimit
CM001	Percentage of failed changes	>10	<5	0	100
CM002	Percentage of rejected RFCs	>20	<10	0	100
CM003	Number of unauthorized changes	>30	<15	0	999999
CM004	Change backlog	>15	<5	0	999999
CM005	Outages during changes	>6	<1	0	999999
CM006	Number of failed changes with no back-out plan	>2	<1	0	999999
CM007	Percentage of changes on time	<90	>95	0	100
CM008	Percentage of changes causing incidents	>10	<5	0	100
CM009	Number of CAB items not actioned on time	>3	<1	0	999999
CM010	Number of Emergency Changes	>3	<2	0	999999
CM011	Number of changes that do not deliver the expected results	>3	<2	0	999999
CM012	Customer Satisfaction	<3	>4	0	5

Figure 7.4 Sample metrics thresholds

7.4 Monitoring

Beginning at the start of the calendar year, the metrics were monitored, recorded and reported on a monthly basis. Figure 7.5 show sample metrics values that were collected by month. The "Report Period" can be set to report on any month.

Input				Home	Report Period		Reporting Year - 2007	
	ITSM Metrics Data Entry Page				Feb-07		Quarter 1	
ID	KPM Name			Format	Jan-	Feb-	Mar-
CM001	Percentage of failed changes			%	50.0	45.0	4.0
CM002	Percentage of rejected RFCs			%	10.0	45.0	3.0
CM003	Number of unauthorized changes			#	3.0	15.0	3.0
CM004	Change backlog			#	30.0	15.0	2.0
CM005	Outages during changes			#	1.0	15.0	4.0
CM006	Number of failed changes with no back-out plan			#	10.0	15.0	2.0
CM007	Percentage of changes on time			%	100.0	45.0	3.0
CM008	Percentage of changes causing incidents			%	30.0	45.0	56.0
CM009	Number of CAB items not actioned on time			#	5.0	15.0	23.0
CM010	Number of Emergency Changes			#	2.0	3.0	1.0
CM011	Number of changes that do not deliver the expected results			#	2.0	15.0	23.0
CM012	Customer Satisfaction			#	4.0	2.0	1.0

Figure 7.5 Sample metrics values

After two months of monitoring, the metrics started to reveal that the processes were not improving, many were degrading further. Figure 7.6 shows a sample change management metrics trending summary by metric including status, trend, identification number, KPM description, actual value and polarity for the reporting period. Many indicators are "Red" status and progressing "Worse".

The dashboards told the implementation team that the current performance of the processes was not going to help them achieve their goals or the anticipated benefits. Figure 7.7 shows a sample change management dashboard which indicates that many of the performance, key goal, benefit and improvement indicators are in a "Red" condition.

By looking in more detail at the individual scorecards, it was possible to see where the deficiencies were coming from based on the color coded statuses of individual metrics. Figure 7.8 shows a sample change management set of performance scorecards which provide the underlying details for the dashboard and highlight problem areas in "Red" condition.

itSMF KPI Scorecard© - Change Management Sample

Metrics Trending

S	T	P	ID	KPM Name	Actual	Polarity
	↓	B	CM001	Percentage of failed changes	45	L
	↑	W	CM002	Percentage of rejected RFCs	45	L
	↑	W	CM003	Number of unauthorized changes	15	L
	↓	B	CM004	Change backlog	15	L
	↑	W	CM005	Outages during changes	15	L
	↑	W	CM006	Number of failed changes with no back-out plan	15	L
	↓	W	CM007	Percentage of changes on time	45	M
	↑	W	CM008	Percentage of changes causing incidents	45	L
	↑	W	CM009	Number of CAB items not actioned on time	15	L
	↑	W	CM010	Number of Emergency Changes	3	L
	↑	W	CM011	Number of changes that do not deliver the expected results	15	L
	↔	S	CM012	Customer Satisfaction	3	M

Scorecards
Dashboard
Process Map
Root Cause
Initiatives

Metrics Administration
Home
Tables
Input Metric Values
Edit Metric Attributes
Changes/Revisions

Legend
S tatus   T rending   P rogress
Red   ↑ Up   B Better
Yellow   ↔ Same   S Same
Green   ↓ Down   W Worse
No data

Polarity
M more is better
L less it better

©itSMF International 2008. All rights reserved. No part of this application may be reproduced in any form by electronic copying, print, photo print, microfilm or any other means without written permission by the publisher. Although this application has been composed with much care, neither author, nor editor, nor publisher can accept any liability for damage caused by possible errors and/or incompleteness in this application.

This itSMF International application was based on my KPI Designer© 2008, a real-life product, with the approval of the owner of the product, Micromation Canada (www.micromationinc.com). The itSMF application can be used independently by the buyer, as long as copyrights are respected. The Intellectual Property of the application was and is with Micromation.Version 1.553.2

Figure 7.6   Sample change management metrics trending

Based on the critical success factors identified in the planning process, it was apparent that the ITIL processes were not tracking to plan. Key goal indicators for Activity, Process and IT goals for the change management process were not being met. Figure 7.9 shows a sample change management KGI scorecards for activity, process and IT goal alignment indicating underlying problem areas.

7.5 Analysis

The Implementation team reviewed the root cause scorecard for "Red Status" indicators; a quick method for determining where the issues were. This scorecard's red status indicators suggested that the change management process was not effective and had quality issues which may be preventing the anticipated benefits from being realized. Figure 7.10 shows a sample change management causal scorecard which depicts cause and effect relationships. The effectiveness and quality metrics indicated many "Red" status conditions suggesting underlying problem areas. The anticipated benefits outcome indicators confirmed that the process was in trouble and not driving value.

The implementation team then reviewed the process scorecard to see where the change management process was experiencing difficulty. They observed problems with the initial filter activity where changes were evaluated for risk, effort and complexity. They also noticed a number of issues around the plan, build, test activities. Figure 7.11 shows a sample change management process scorecard which had process sensors placed to indicate inputs, workload activity and outputs. The process sensors indicate problem areas throughout the process.

ITSM metrics – case study example

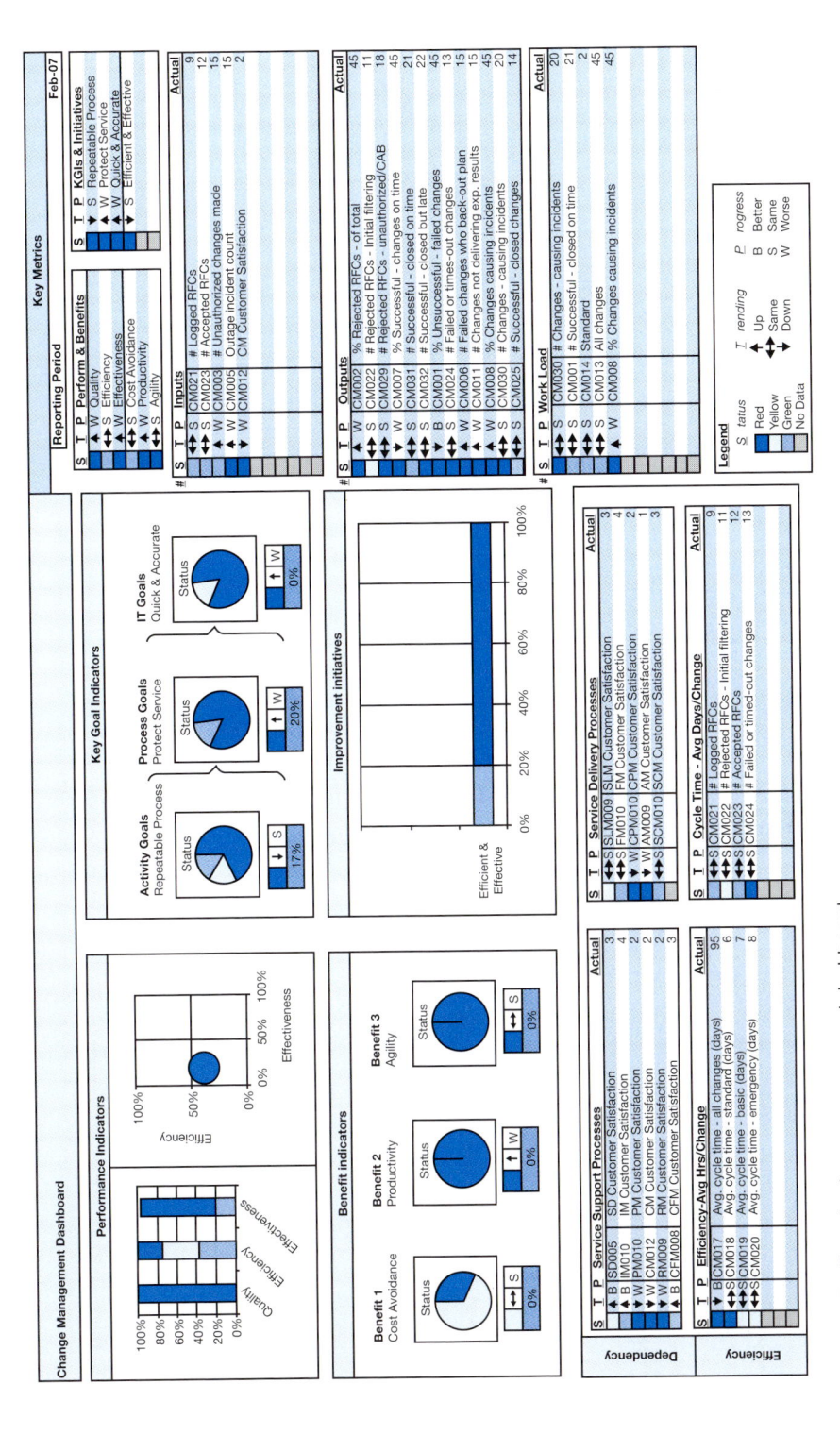

Figure 7.7 Sample change management dashboard

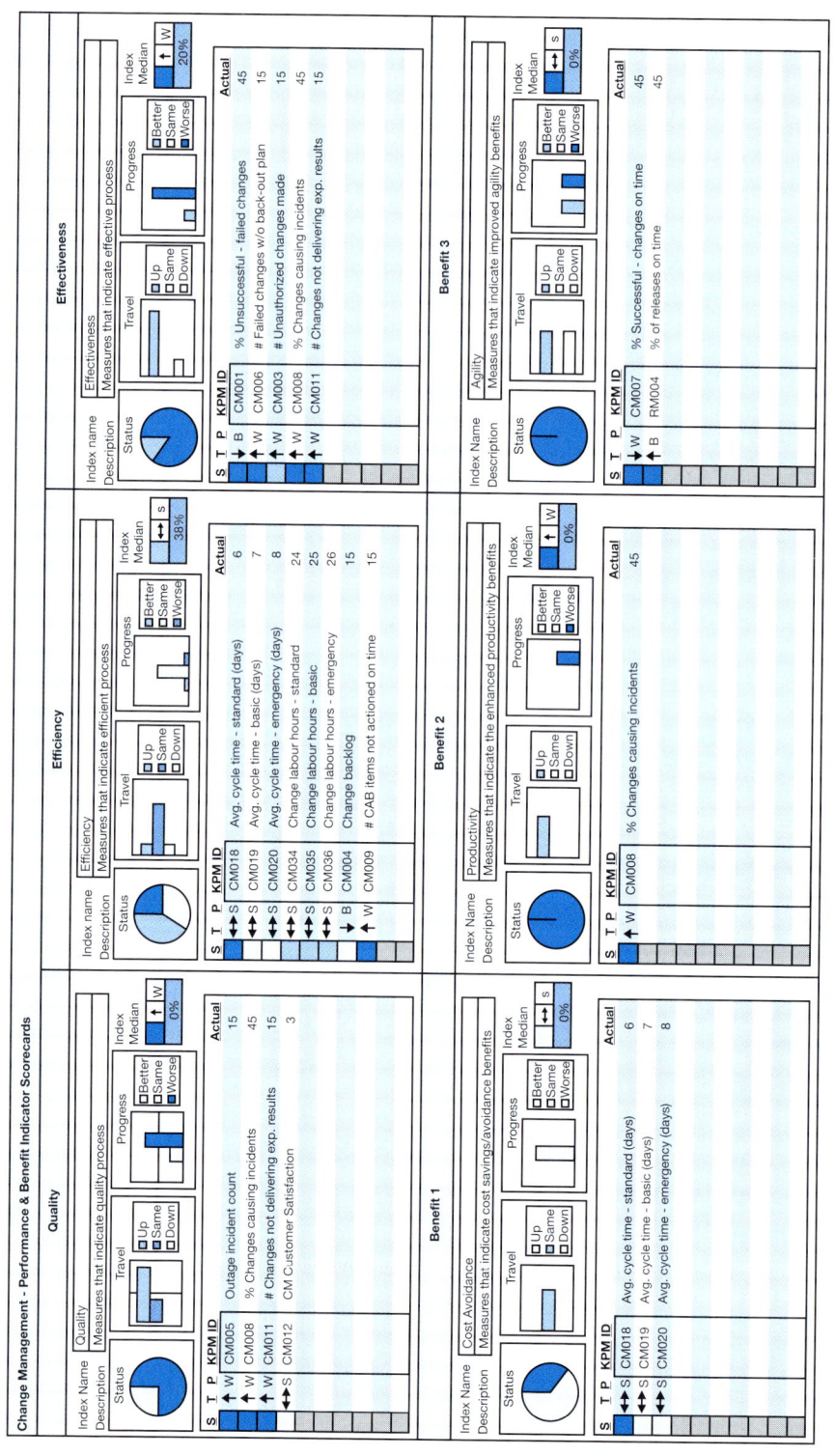

Figure 7.8 Sample change management performance scorecards

ITSM metrics – case study example

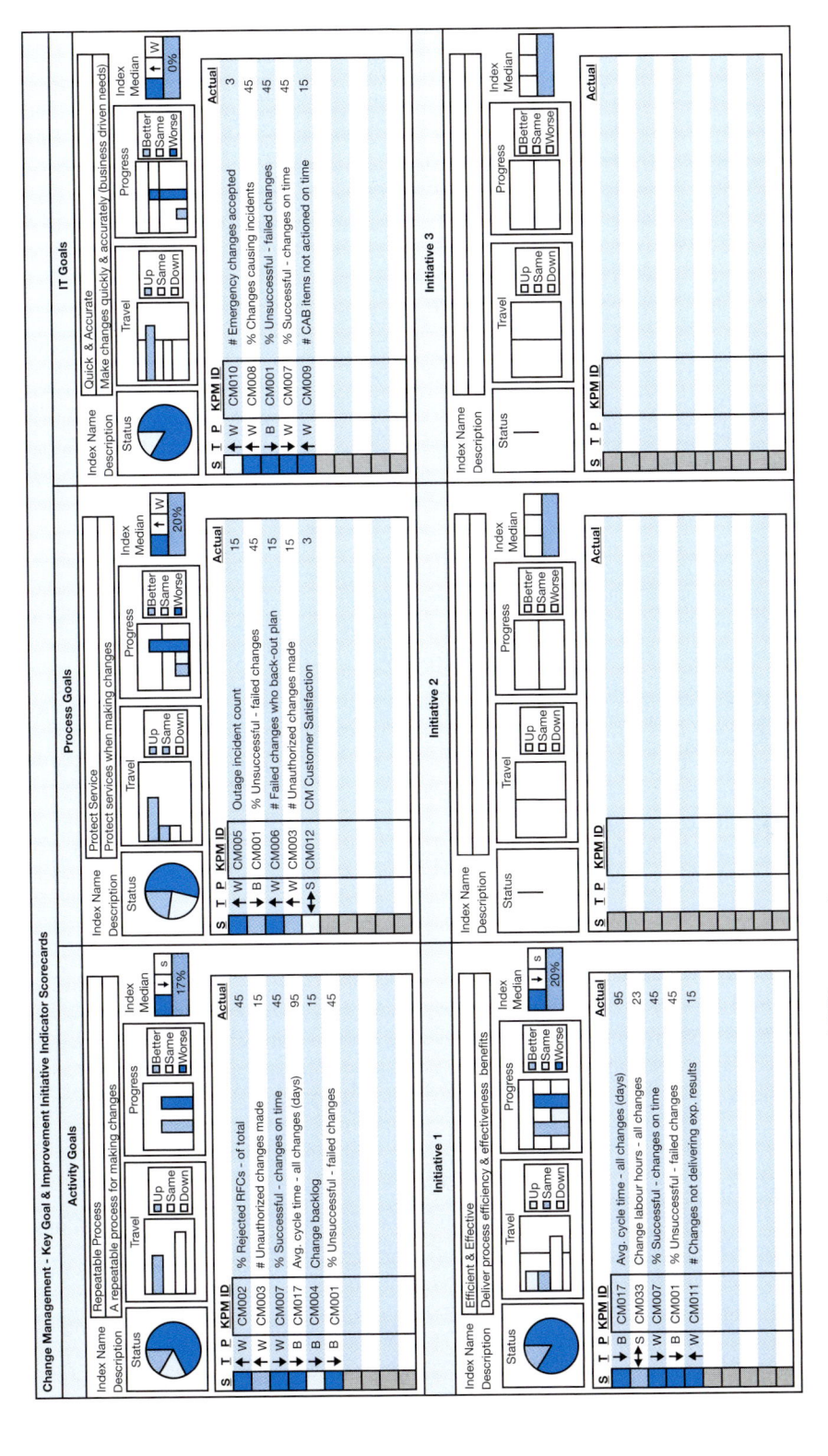

Figure 7.9 Sample change management KGI scorecards

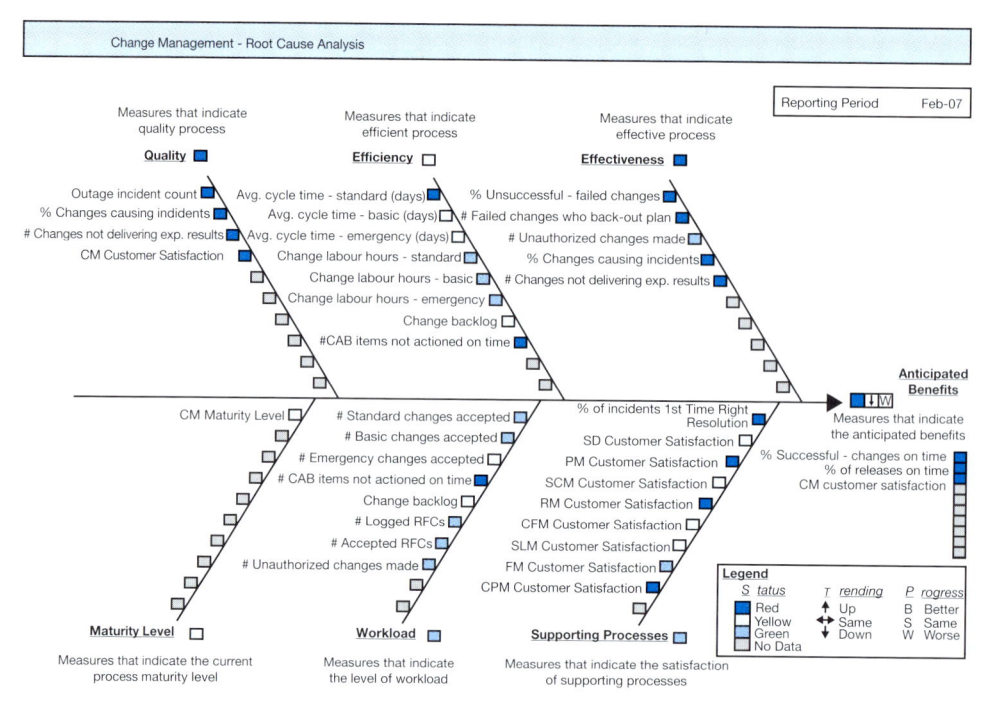

Figure 7.10 Sample change management causal scorecard

7.6 Tuning

After reviewing the symptoms and eliminating suspect causes, the implementation team focused on what they believed to be the root cause: "poor requirements definition & screening activities". The rationale was that requirements were not documented very well and that acceptance criteria not well defined. This left too much room for interpretation; resulting in expectations not being met; and not being able to develop proper testing plans with acceptance criteria.

7.7 Implementation

They implemented an initiative to improve the Requirements Definition Activity and included a training program and communications strategy. They also identified five existing metrics which would help to track the effectiveness of the initiative. Figure 7.12 a sample list of change management initiatives.

7.8 Results

A few months later the change management dashboard revealed that the initiative was working and that the small changes made to the process had a considerable impact on the results. Figure 7.13 shows the same sample change management dashboard which was updated a few months later indicating the process had improved from the previous reporting period by showing more "Green" conditions.

ITSM metrics – case study example

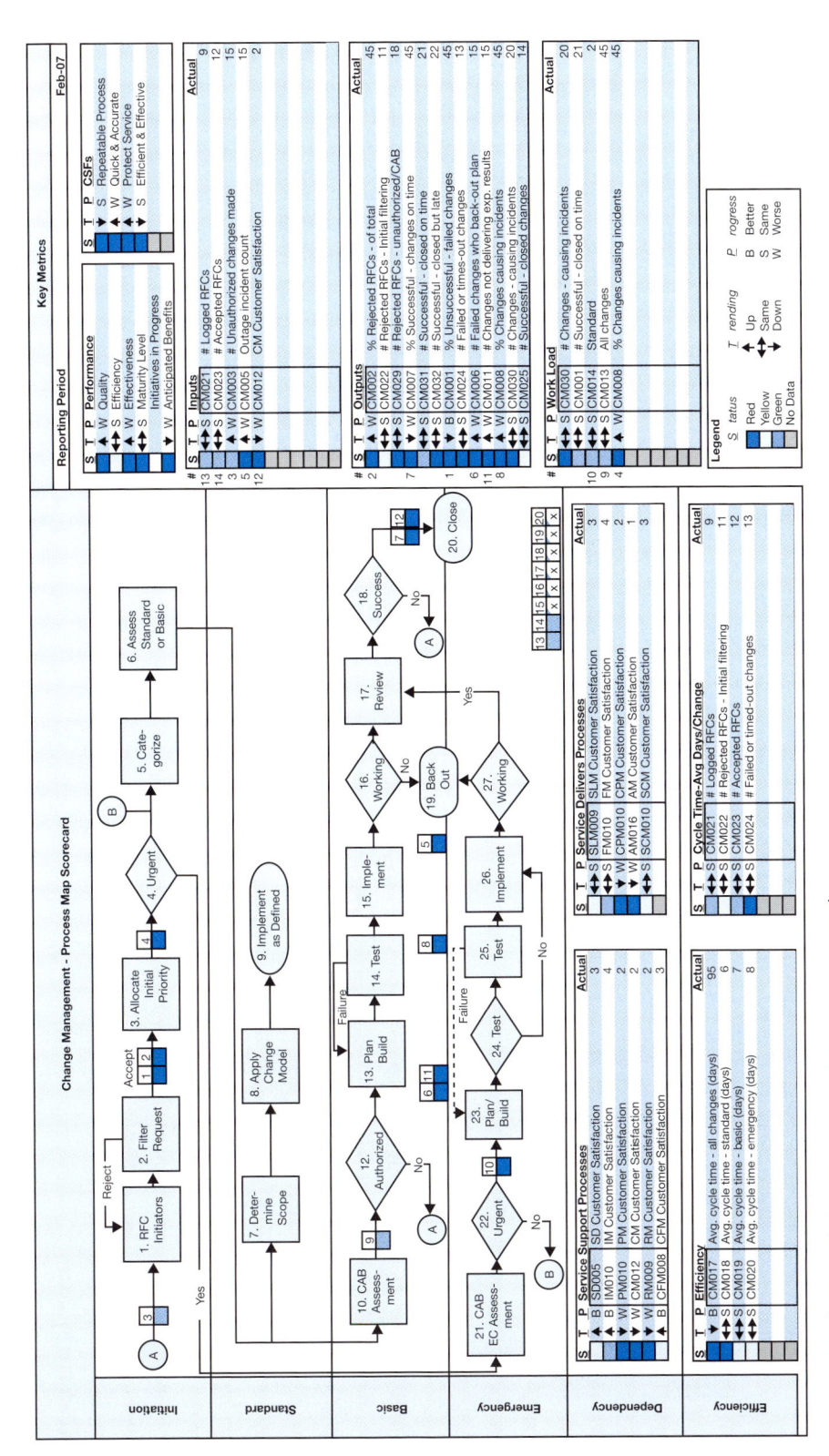

Figure 7.11 Sample change management process scorecard

114 Implementing Metrics for IT Service Management

Date	Process	Initiative Name	Requested by	Completed By	KPM ID	Date Completed	ID #
2-Apr-07	Change Mgmt	Deliver process efficiency and effectiveness benefits	JJ		CM017	In progress	1
		(Note: use exsiting metrics to monitor improvement initiative)			CM033		2
					CM007		3
					CM001		4
					CM011		5
5-Jun-07	Incident Mgmt	Improve 1st call resolution time (Note: used reserved Service Improvement Initiative metric for tracking)	DS		SII001	Not started	6
							7
							8
							9
							10
							11
							12
							13
							14

Figure 7.12   Sample change management initiative

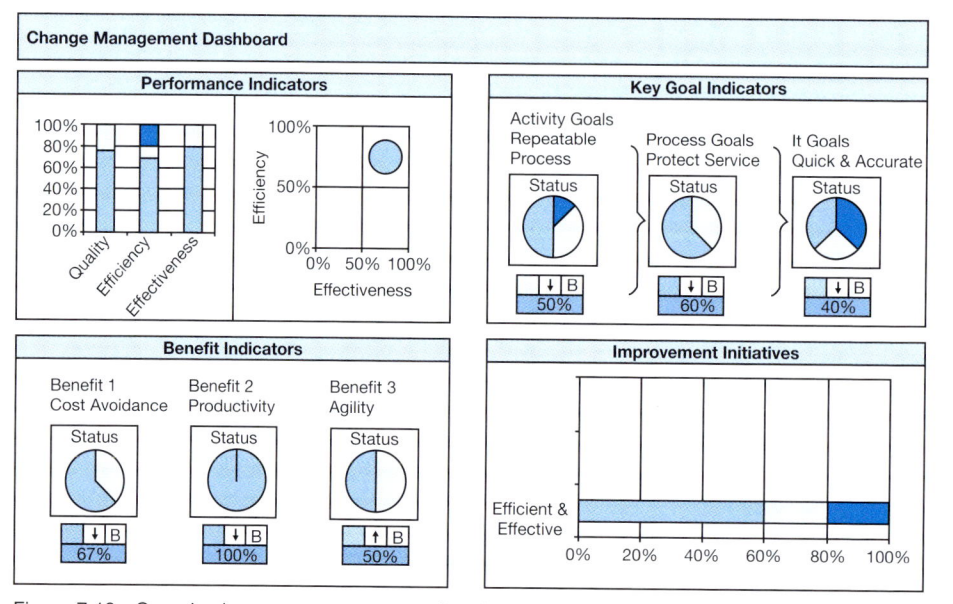

Figure 7.13   Sample change management updated dashboard

Chapter 8
Implementing a measurement program

Implementing a measurement program requires consideration of where to start; why do it; who to involve; what are the steps; when to expect results; and how to make it happen. The following sections provide general guidelines, ideas and best practices to help answer some of these questions. In most cases, the planning and implementation approach must be tailored and fit-for-purpose.

8.1 Planning and implementation overview

Planning and implementing a measurement program is similar to implementing any new IT service management process. Some of the principles and techniques presented here are taken from the ITIL V3 CSI "Continual Service Improvement" book[27], which provides an excellent reference model for implementing the measurement program.

The major steps involved in this model are summarized as:
1. Review the business and IT vision, goals, mission and business objectives
2. Assess the current situation, that is, where you are now
3. Determine reasonable targets, that is, where you want to be
4. Plan what needs to change, that is, how to get there
5. Measure your progress, that is, did you get there
6. Keep the program moving, that is, communicate your successes

Careful consideration of the softer issues is important to affect organizational change including gaining commitment, empowering, motivating, involving and communicating. Many change initiatives and projects are well planned, organized and executed from a technical aspect but fail to deliver; often due to over-looking the people aspect. Using an approach such as John P. Kotter's[28] eight steps outlined in the ITIL® V3 CSI "Continual Service Improvement" book to transform your organization provides a useful check list:
- Creating a 'sense of urgency', that is, 75% of the management should be convinced of the need.

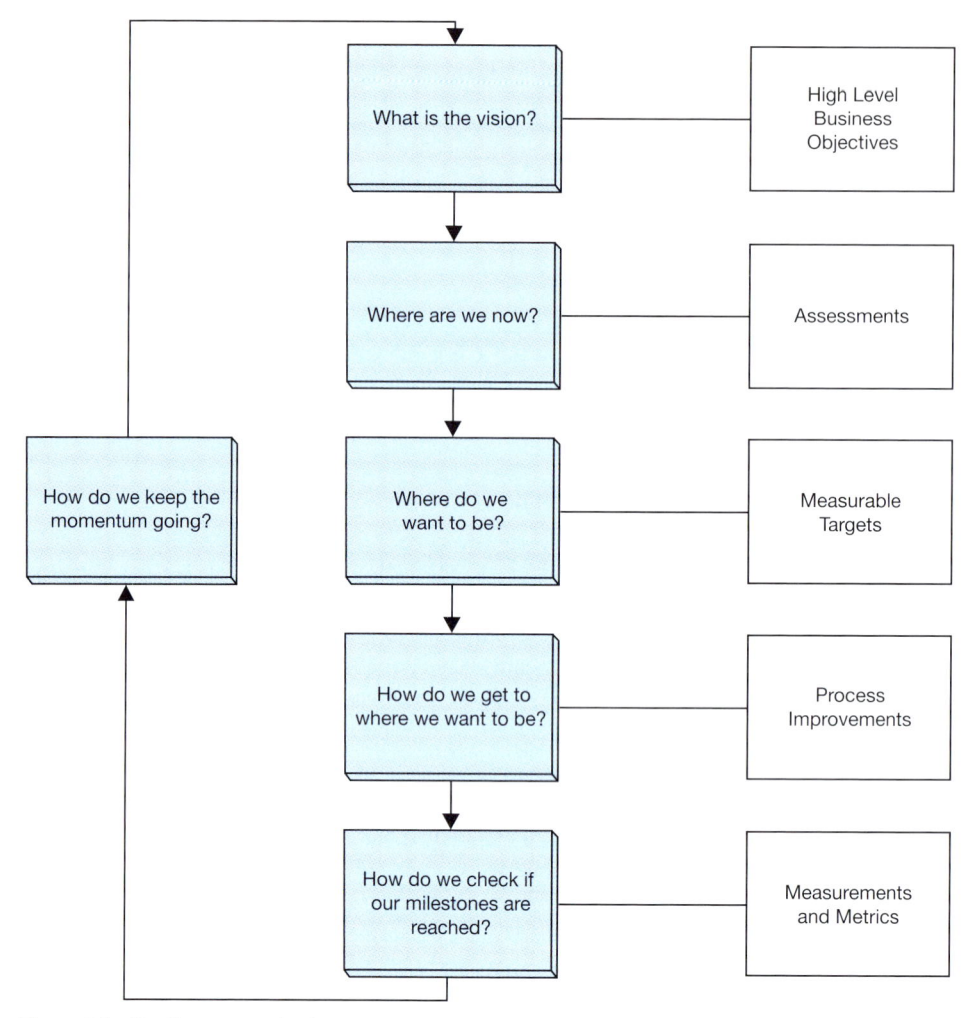

Figure 8.1 Continuous service improvement program

- Forming a 'guiding coalition', that is, effective and strong leadership to overcome any opposition.
- Creating a vision', that is, a short but visual explanation to help keep the understanding and interest focused.
- 'Communicating' the vision, that is, the hearts and minds of the people must be captured through credible and continual communications.
- 'Empowering' people to act the vision, that is, the structures to underpin the vision and the authorities to overcome obstacles.
- Planning for and creating 'quick win', that is, actively looking for small performance improvements and communicating them frequently.
- Consolidating improvements & 'Implement more change', that is, building confidence, credibility and keeping the momentum to tackle the larger issues.
- 'Institutionalizing' the changes, that is, reinforce how new approaches, behaviour and attitude have made performance improvements creating the new normal.

8.2 The 7-Step improvement process

The very first step is a review of what already exists to identify business and IT requirements for alignment. This involves some research to determine the vision, strategy, tactical and operational goals for the business and IT. The output is a clear understanding of the vision and high level business objectives. Use the following 7-step improvement process from the ITIL V3 CSI "Continual Service Improvement" book[29], as a guideline for implementing the measurement framework and metrics:

1. **Define what should be measured**
   The next step is to define what should be measured. This may involve some external assessments and/or internal review sessions to gather information. This helps determine the objectives and critical success factors required to create the ideal situation for both the business and IT. The output of this step is an assessment of "where you are now".

2. **Defined what can be measured**
   This step requires three activities to define what can be measured. This first requires some planning sessions to determination of "where you want to be" by identifying new service levels or process improvement areas. The second part requires gap analysis to identify a prioritized list of actionable items and quick wins. The third part requires breaking the critical success factors down into performance metrics with targets. The output is a vetted list of performance metrics that are specific, measurable, actionable, relevant and timely (SMART) to answer the question "how will we get there".

3. **Gather the data**
   In order to answer the question "did we get there" question, data must be gathered. This step involves identifying the data sources for extracting the raw data. Data sources will include Service Operations and possible other internal of external groups. Determine when the data is required and how it will be validated for accuracy. The output is the provision of raw data and key fact metrics.

4. **Process the data**
   The next step is to process the data and transform it into the required and specified KPMs, KPIs and KGIs. This includes verifying the integrity of the data, ensuring it is properly time-bound, performing any calculations, and rationalizing it into a consistent format. The output is a list of metrics that are loaded into the MDB.

5. **Analyze the data**
   This step reviews the performance metrics and compares the results to the target (desired) performance. This helps to identify service or process gaps, trends and any impact on the business. Gaps should be further analyzed to determine root causes and recommendations. The output from this step is a list of gaps, their root causes and appropriate recommendations for tuning and corrective action.

6. **Present and use the information**
   Presenting and using the information provides the answer to the "did we get there" question. The information must be communicated to the key stakeholders identifying performance results, issues and recommendations. The information can then be used for decision analysis for determining the next steps. The output is a list of initiatives and corrective actions for implementation.

7. Implement corrective actions

The final step is to implement the initiatives and corrective actions. The actions will be assigned to the appropriate service and processes owners/managers and will require addition reporting of progress status to be communicated to the stakeholders periodically. This step may also generate new metrics to monitor the progress and/or involve readjusting the baselines. The output is periodic status reporting of the initiatives and correctives actions.

At this point the 7-steps of measurement are repeated. Figure 8.2 illustrates the 7-step improvement process for measurements taken from the ITIL V3 CSI "Continual Service Improvement" book[27].

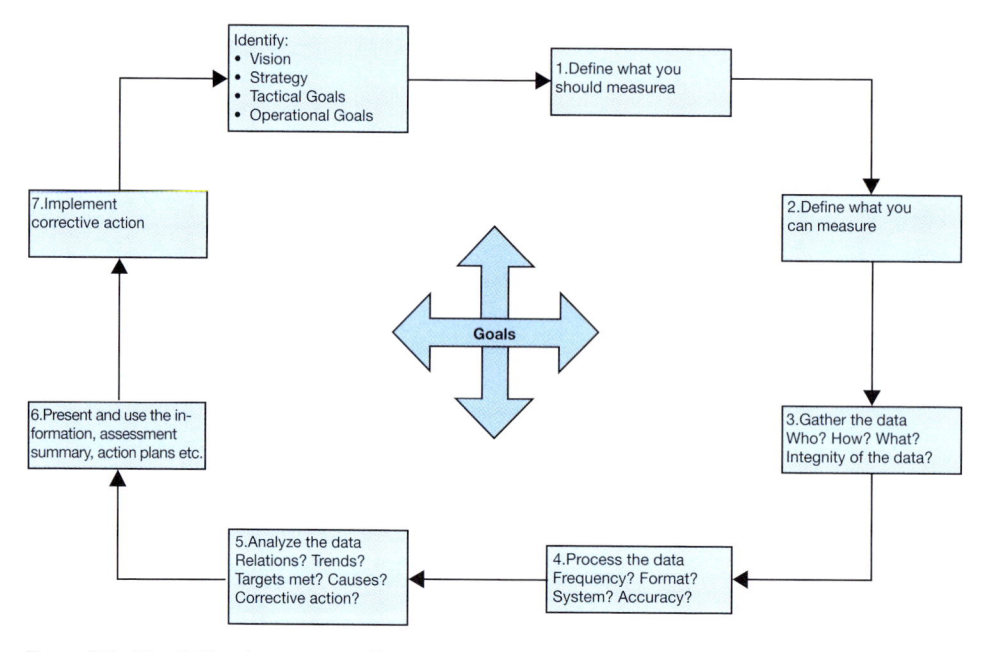

Figure 8.2 The 7-Step Improvement Process

Planning and implementing the measurement program has three phases which are detailed in the following sections:
- planning the process and approach
- implementation of the process
- review and optimization of the process

8.3 Planning the process

To develop the plan for the measurement program, start with the following planning activities:
- review what already exists
- identify roles and responsibilities
- plan the approach
- select the measurements

Review what already exists
Establish a baseline of existing information to work from. To review what already exists, conduct assessments, interviews or workshop meetings to answer the following questions:
- What is the business vision, mission and strategy?
- What is IT strategy?
- What are the current tactical and operational goals?
- What are the current service level requirements and targets?
- Is there senior management commitment to support the program?
- Who is the implementation champion?
- Has a business case or justification been developed; approved?
- Does a budget exist; are resources available?
- Are the skills & knowledge in place?
- What is the culture and organization structure?
- Are performance measurement tools and technology already in place?
- Are there demands for "business as usual"?
- Which processes or services are in scope?
- What the current and desired requirements of each process (scope/ goals/ objectives)?
- Which processes would most benefit from this program?
- Who are the ITSM process owners and key stakeholders?
- Who is the proposed measurement process owner?
- What is the current maturity level of people/process/tools?
- What metrics and targets are in use?
- What are the potential roadblocks?
- Have any benchmarking studies been performed recently?

Identify roles & responsibilities
Identify the measurement program owner/manager and support roles. Planning the roles and responsibilities of the measurement program need to address the following questions:
- Who is accountable for the program, that is, ownership of quality and end results of the program?
- Who is responsible for the process, that is, correct execution of the process and activities?
- Who needs to be consulted, that is, involvement through input of knowledge and information?
- Who needs to be informed, that is, receiving information about the process execution and quality?

Planning the role and responsibilities of the measurement program owner/manager could use the following guidelines:

Role
The measurement program owner/manager is accountable and responsible for the measurement process. The goal of the measurement program owner/manager is to implement and manage an effective measurement framework to enable IT alignment with the business objectives and create value through continuous improvements. The specific intent of the measurement framework is to help the IT organization:
- validate the strategy and vision
- provide direction with targets and metrics

- justify with a means to gauge value realized
- intervene and provide corrective actions

The measurement program owner/manager's objectives are to help:
- help align IT with business objectives and verify results
- maintain compliance requirements for business operations
- drive operational efficiencies, effectiveness and quality

Responsibilities

The measurement program owner/manager has the overall responsibility of implementing, managing and improving a measurement process. Specific responsibilities include measuring performance and working with each of the IT stakeholders to monitor, analyze, tune and implement improvements. The detailed responsibilities of the measurement program owner/manager include:
- implementation, management and optimization of an effective measurement framework
- ensures that appropriate levels of performance measurements are in place to provide an effective measurement framework, that is to validate, direct, justify and intervene
- establishes and maintains policies and procedures guides
- develops and maintains a communications strategy and plan
- produce and maintain measurements that help align IT, maintain compliance and drive operational efficiencies
- maintain a measurement database and document trends over time
- monitor the status of the metrics, targets and thresholds
- assisting with analysis, interpretation, prediction and assessment of key findings and trends with the process and/or service owners
- providing performance reporting against targets and notifications where required
- assisting with identifying metrics to monitor new service improvement initiatives
- tracking the status of service improvement initiatives
- working with key stakeholders to improve the measurement program in terms of quality, efficiency and effectiveness, i.e. automation, timeliness, accuracy, prediction, reporting, et cetera

Key Skills

The key skill required of the measurement program owner/manager:
- sound analytical skills
- ability to interact successfully with all key stakeholder levels
- thorough approach to documentation and measurement framework
- good communication skills
- good presentational skills

Tips for selecting a measurement program owner/manager:
- The measurement programs owner/manager goals, objectives, roles and responsibilities are compatible with and are in alignment with the continual service improvement management and service level management.
- Many of the role, responsibility and activity elements are similar to capacity management and configuration management.

- Some measurement responsibilities can be assigned to existing process/service owner/manager. For example, "determining metrics", "setting targets", "collecting data", "analysis of results", "tuning", "implementing."

Establish policies and procedures

The measurement program owner/manager is responsible for establishing and maintaining polices and procedures guides. High level policies and procedures need established in the planning stage, be implemented and enforced. Some examples of policies and procedures could include:

- Policies
  - Accuracy and confidence levels
  - Classification, themes and naming conventions
  - Target & threshold level setting
  - Reporting cycles, dates and detail level
  - Hierarchical and process based escalations.
- Procedures
  - Monitoring
  - Analysis
  - Tuning
  - Implementation
  - Administration
  - Reporting

Tips for establishing policies and procedures:

- Review existing IT policies. Make sure any new policies are in alignment with existing policies.
- Learn from experience. Initial policies may not be that obvious, make sure there is a method to capture "lessons learned" and review them against current policies for possible insertions or amendments to the policies.
- Where possible, use existing procedures templates. Using existing procedures templates will reduce time and effort to document the processes and will be more familiar to staff for knowledge transfer. If templates are not available, develop them so they are easily repeatable.

Develop a communication strategy and plan

The measurement program owner/manager is responsible for developing and maintaining a communications strategy and plan. Planning the measurement program communications strategy should consider an approach for the following:

- Key stakeholders:
  - Identification of and how to engage the individuals
  - Perceived and real impact of changes
  - Appropriate and required messages to receive, or send
  - Most effective tools for communication by stakeholder group.
- Common components:
  - Messaging, that is, value proposition by stakeholder group
  - Delivery approach or medium, that is, electronic, print, voice
  - Target audiences, that is, stakeholder group

- Message content, that is, who, what, where, when, why, how, et cetera
- Timing, that is, when, how often, follow-up
- Methodology, that is, top-down, bottom-up, and middle-out.

Tips for developing a communications strategy and plan:
- Use a balanced communications approach. Ensure there is a "top-down", "bottom-up and middle-out" approach to the communication strategy.
- Craft the right message to the right audience. Different information about the measurement program needs to be appealing and targeted by stakeholder groups. It needs to answer recipient's question "what's in it for me?" For example, business customers may not be interested in the type of database used for metrics storage.
- Use the right medium for the audience. Keep messages short, to the point, benefits/outcome oriented, at the right frequency using the medium that works best for the company.

Plan the approach

Planning the approach helps determine where and how to get started. Determining the right approach for the organization depends on many variables like internal and external business drivers; volume of change already taking place; the readiness of the organization; senior management involvement; resistance to change; current workload; skills and capability, et cetera. Information from the initial review session can be used to gauge the best implementation approach to use given the circumstances at hand. There are three general approach variations to consider:
- single process/service
- multi process/service
- all processes/service

Single process

The single process/service based approach can be a useful place to start the measurement program as a simple pilot program. This can work well as a 'proof-of-concept' approach for establishing the measurement program and demonstrating value to management. Table 8.1 provides general pros and cons for the single-process/service approach:

Pros – Works best when:	Cons – Potential problems/risks:
• Scepticism exists • Resistance to change • High change volumes • High workloads • Service level breaches • Low Sr. Mgmt. commitment	• Longer implementation cycle for other processes • High start-up costs versus benefits of single process

Table 8.1   Single process pros vs. cons

Examples of the single process/service approach could include:
- Problem management
  - Most pain & disruption to internal IT process
  - Most pain & disruption to business caused by IT process
- Service desk & incident management

- Significant gains
- Quick wins
- Customer facing
- Change management
  - Reduce unplanned work, that is failed changes > incidents > problems > more changes
  - Starter process, that is MAC (Move, Add, Change)
- Release
  - Improve testing, reduce number of change related incidents
- Service Levels
  - Improved availability, reliability, performance
  - Increased customer satisfaction

Multiple processes/service

Multiple process/service based approaches can be a useful place to start your measurement program when high motivation for improvement exists. Due to the high interdependencies and relationships among some of the processes, clustering processes together provides the best opportunity for optimization. For example, the following processes are often clustered or grouped for maximum impact:

- **Support & restore** – Service Desk, Incident and Problem Management
- **Release & control** – Release, Change and Configuration Management
- **Agree & define** – Financial and Service Level Management
- **Plan & improve** – Availability, Capacity and Continuity Management

Table 8.2 provides general pros and cons for the multi-process approach:

Pros – Works best when:	Cons – Potential problems/risks:
• High motivation • Stable operations • Medium change volumes • Medium workloads • Medium service level breaches • High Sr. Mgmt. commitment • Strong project office	• Longer benefits realization cycle • Processes not mature enough or non-existent • Skills and capability

Table 8.2   Multi process pros versus cons

Examples of high motivational drivers for the multi-process approach could include:
- Compliance requirements, that is Regulatory SOX/ C198
- Service Improvement Program (SIP)
- Customer Satisfaction Surveys (CSS) results
- Business Impact Assessment indicating risks or exposures
- Strength/ Weakness/ Opportunity/ Threat (SWOT) assessments results
- Maturity Level assessment results
- External TCO Benchmarking results
- Service Level Target requirements:
  - Service availability
  - Service responsiveness

- Change scheduling
- Incident resolution
- Service performance

All processes/service

All processes/service based approach can be a useful place to start your measurement program provided the right drivers exist to support it. This is one of the more demanding approaches and requires very strong management commitment and support. Table 8.3 provides general pros and cons for the all-process approach:

Pros – Works best when:	Cons – Potential problems/risks:
• High motivation • Stable operations • Manageable change volumes • Manageable workloads • Low occurrences of service level breaches • Very high Sr. Mgmt. commitment • Strong project office	• Longer benefits realization cycle • Processes not uniformly mature • Too much change - resistance • Organization not ready • Skills and capability

Table 8.3   All processes/service pros versus cons

Examples of high motivational drivers and considerations for the all-process approach could include:
- drivers
  - business IT strategy & vision
  - Service Improvement Program (SIP) benchmark
  - ISO/IEC 20000 certification.
- considerations
  - small steps
  - big bag or phased
  - single ITSM owner
  - coordination
  - uniform maturity

Planning considerations

A number of planning considerations need to be taken into account to design your detailed implementation plan. Each of the following considerations should be vetted and documented to determine the right fit for the measurement program:
- management commitment, sponsorship, leadership
- integrating with other process owners – buy-in
- structure of the measurement process, goals, CSFs, objectives
- documenting the measurement process
- reporting cycle/ frequency
- roles & responsibilities
- establishing policies, processes & procedures
- communications strategy

- determining effective metrics/targets/thresholds
- establishing baselines
- determining sources of KFM and KPM data
- data collection methods
- storage of data in metrics database (MDB)
- monitoring by processes
- performance analysis
- production of the reports by stakeholder
- performance tuning
- service improvement initiatives
- measurement review process
- project planning details

Select the measurements

To select the measurements the program, the planning process needs to consider the business goals and objectives and how the IT goals, objectives and activities are to be aligned to support them. Taking this top-down approach helps classify and determine the key goal indicators, critical success factors, key performance indicators, key performance metrics and key fact metrics required. For example, answer the following questions to help determine the structure and scope of the measurement process:

- What are the business goals to support the company mission and vision?
- What are the business objectives to achieve the business goals, that is short term, long term?
- What are the IT goals to support each of the identified business objectives?
- What are the IT objectives to achieve the IT goals, that is short term, long term?
- What are the critical success factors in order to meet each of the objectives?
- What key performance indicators will determine if the critical success factors are being achieved?
- What key performance metrics are required to produce the key performance indicators and/or manage the inputs, outputs and activities of the required processes?
- What facts need to be measured to produce the key performance metrics and/or manage the inputs, outputs and activities of the required processes and activities?
- Who are the stakeholders involved and what are their needs, roles and responsibilities? "Executive", "Owner", "Manager", "Team member", "Customer"
- Which processes or services are in scope? "Short term," "Longer term"
- What metrics reporting tools will be used to manage the measurement lifecycle? "MDB", "Dashboards", "Scorecards", "Metrics", "Trends", "Cause and effect"
- What is the frequency of measurement lifecycle? "Daily", "Weekly", "Monthly", "Quarterly", "Semi-annual or annual"
- Which source transactional systems will provide what source data?

Define the goals

Conduct a brainstorming session with key business stakeholders, identify two to three goals that, if achieved, would best enable IT to contribute to the business's strategic direction, solve urgent business problems, reduce IT service management defects or serve end users better. Ask questions like:

- What are the business goals to support the company mission and vision?
- What are the business objectives to achieve the business goals, that is short term, long term?

- What does IT need to do to best support each of the identified business objectives?
- What would be a good indicator (measure) that the goal has been achieved?
- What are the main benefits or outcomes expected by achieving this goal?

Express your goals in short phrases that start with a verb – for example, "Respond to business requirements in alignment with the business strategy", "Create IT agility", or "Account for and protect all IT assets." State the indicator or measure of goal accomplishment.

Tips for defining goals:
- Review the companies annual report if one exists, business strategy documents and IT strategy documents.
- Interview business stakeholders and senior IT management to determine what business or IT problems/challenges need to be solved.
- Brainstorm effectively with colleagues to gain their views, participation and buy-in to the goals and measurement process.
- Verify the effectiveness of each goal by asking "benefit" or "outcome" oriented questions: "by achieving this goal, will it help meet the defined business or IT strategy it supports and derive the desired benefits or outcomes?"
- Define a key goal indicator by asking: "how will we know that we have accomplished this goal?"

Define the objectives

The IT objectives represent what IT wants to accomplish in order to meet the goals and improve various aspects of IT group's performance. To brainstorm ideas for objectives, meet with IT management, colleagues and direct reports and ask the following questions:
- What are the IT objectives to achieve the IT goals, that is short term, long term?
- What activities, processes or services must IT improve to help meet the identified IT goals?
- How might IT improve its work processes?
- How might IT better serve its customers?
- What are the action verbs that best describe the required improvement?
- What would be the key indicator(s) that this objective has been achieved?

Identify three to five objectives for each goal that, if achieved, would best enable IT to achieve them. Express your objectives in short phrases that start with a verb—for example, "Manage changes", "Ensure continuous service", "Meet service level objectives." or "Manage the IT investment."

Tips for defining objectives:
- Brainstorm with colleagues to gain their input, involvement and buy-in with defining the objectives.
- Begin each objective with an action verb such as "Increase", "Reduce", "Initiate", "Develop", "Lower", "Higher" "Improve", "Become", "Achieve", "Provide", "Manage", "Ensure" "Meet".
- Don't worry about making the objectives quantitative, the metrics will provide this.
- Verify the alignment effectiveness of each objective by asking "benefit" or "outcome" related questions: "by achieving this objective, will it help meet the defined goal it supports?"

- Verify that there is agreement and shared understanding of the meaning of the objective and the expected benefits or outcomes.
- Verify that each objective is SMART, that is, specific, measurable, actionable, relevant and timely. Confirmation will require input from the "Determine the performance metrics" step.
- Define a key performance indicator by asking: "how will we know that we have met this objective?"

Define the critical success factors for each objective

For each objective, list two or three essential elements, features or actions that are necessary to achieve the objective. These are the critical success factors (CSFs). To illustrate, for the objective "Manage changes", a CSFs might be "A repeatable process for making changes", "Make changes quickly and accurately", and "Protect services when making changes." To brainstorm ideas for CSFs, meet with IT management, colleagues and direct reports and ask the following questions:
- If this is a process, ask: "What are the key or major elements, features or actions necessary to make this process successful?"
- If this is a service, ask: "What are the necessary utility functions, features or actions required to make this service successful?"

Tips for defining critical success factors:
- Brainstorm with colleagues to gain their input, involvement and buy-in with listing and defining the critical success factors.
- If the CSFs are process oriented, generate and prioritize a list of CSFs by exploring themes such as "Efficiency", "Cost effectiveness", "Effectiveness", "Quality", "Workload", "Utilization", "Performance", "Compliance", "Improvement", "Value".
- If the CSFs are service oriented, generate and prioritize a list of CSFs by exploring utility (function or feature) themes such as "Availability", "Performance", "Reliability", "Cost effectiveness", "Quality", "Workload", "Utilization", "Maintenance", "Security".
- Using decision analysis tools. Choose only the "Must have", "Most critical", or "Most important factors."
- Don't worry about making the CSFs quantitative, the metrics will provide this.
- Verify the alignment effectiveness of each CSF by asking "benefit" or "outcome" oriented questions: "by achieving this CSF, will it help meet the defined objective it supports?"
- Verify that there is agreement and shared understanding of the meaning of the identified CSF and that it will help direct, steer, manage and control organizational effort.

Determine the performance metrics

Break down critical success factors into one or more metrics, describing them in language that reflects how to measure performance for the factor. For example, one measurement for the critical success factor "A repeatable process for making changes" could be "Percentage fewer rejected RFCs." For the CSF "Make changes quickly and accurately", you might choose these two metrics: "Percentage reduction in the number of urgent changes", and "Percentage reduction of urgent changes causing incidents."

To brainstorm ideas for metrics, meet with IT management, colleagues and direct reports and ask the following questions:

- What is the perspective to be measured? "Process", "Service", "Financial", "Business", "User"
- What is the theme of the measurement? "Efficiency", "Cost effectiveness", "Effectiveness", "Quality", "Workload", "Utilization", "Performance", "Compliance", "Improvement", "Value", "Availability", "Performance", "Reliability", "Maintenance", "Security"
- What is the object that needs to be measured? "Changes", "Service level", "Incidents", "Calls", "Satisfaction", "Problems", "Maturity", "SLA breaches"
- What is the purpose of measuring the object? "Controlling", "Improving" "Maintaining"
- What is the focus of the measure? "Cycle-time", "Cost" "Effort", "Volume"
- What are the units of measure? "Percent", "Count", "Cost", "Time"
- What is the environment in which the measurement takes place? "National Service Desk", "Division 1 - IT department"
- What is the desired polarity of the measure? "Increasing (+) is better", "Decreasing (-) is better"

Use the answers to these questions to start building the metadata data elements for the required metrics.

Tips for defining the performance metrics:
- Translate each CSF into one or more performance metrics. Key performance metrics may require key fact metrics for calculations. For example, "% Rejected RFCs" would require "Count of rejected RFCs this period" divided by "Count of Logged RFCs for this period."
- Consider availability, validity, and reliability of data. For each metric, ask whether data (key fact metrics) exist to track performance on that metric, and whether it will be reliable. A performance metric is useless without the required data or if the data is not up-to-date and accurate.
- Use clear and concise descriptions. Phrase your performance metrics in specific, concrete, and easy-to-understand language - such as "% Successful - changes on time" instead of "Successful changes."
- Examine the set of metrics for cause-and-effect relationships. For example, how will good performance on the metric "% Unsuccessful - failed changes" affect performance on the metric "Customer satisfaction"? What is the strength of these relationships? For instance, will a small improvement in failed changes generate a large improvement in customer satisfaction? Use affinity and relation diagrams and techniques to identify cause-and-effect linkages. Use the Ishikawa diagrams and techniques to record the cause and effect relationships.
- The set of metrics should contain both lagging and leading indicators. Review the set of metrics and examine the lagging/leading mix. Ask whether they show a mix of lagging (backward-looking) and leading (forward-looking) indicators.
- Use decision analysis tools to select metrics. Decision analysis tools can be configured and used to determine which metrics provide the best results for their intended purpose.
- Use the process mapping and scorecard techniques to record the cause and effect relationships. Identify and record suspected root causes and prescriptive remedies for the set of key performance metrics. For example, "Insufficient requirements", or "Poor testing" could two suspected root causes for the metric "% Unsuccessful - failed changes". Prescriptive remedies could include "Improve requirements gathering", "Improve test procedures or tools".

Implementing a measurement program 129

Bus Goal	IT Goal	KGI	Benefit	IT Objective	CSF	KPIs	KPMs	KFMs
Agility in responding to changing business requirements (time to market)								
	Respond to business requirements in alignment with the business strategy.							
		All IT objectives are met						
			Improved business competitive advantage					
				Manage changes				
					A repeatable process for making changes			
						Percentage fewer rejected RFCs		
							% Rejected RFCs - of total	
								Count of Logged RFCs for this Period
								Count of Rejected RFCs this Period
						Percentage reduction in unauthorized changes detected		
							# Unauthorized changes made	
								Count of Unauthorized Changes Discovered this period (reported by Incident Mgmt)
								Count of Unauthorized Changes Discovered this period (reported by Problem Mgmt)
								Count of Unauthorized Changes Discovered this period (reported by Config Mgmt)
						Percentage of change requests (business driven need) implemented on time		
							% Successful - changes on time	
								Count of Closed RFCs for this Period - Successful
								Count of Closed RFCs for this Period - Successful, On Time
						Percentage reduction in average time to make changes		
							Avg. cycle time - all changes (days)	
								Avg. Cycle Time of all RFCs Completed/Closed for this Period (Days)
						Percentage reduction in the change backlog		
							Change backlog	
								Count of Open RFCs at End of this Period - Ending Backlog
						Percentage fewer changes 'backed out=' because of testing failures		
							% Unsuccessful - failed changes	
								Count of Closed RFCs for this Period
								Count of Closed RFCs for this Period - Unsuccessful

Figure 8.3   Example process goal alignment with supporting metrics

For a process example, the following figure 8.3 demonstrates the cause and effect linkages of a single business goal down to individual required key fact metrics.

For a service example, the following figure 8.4 demonstrates the cause and effect linkages of a single business goal down to individual required key fact metrics.

Set targets and thresholds

For every performance metric defined, set a target representing the desired performance on that metric. Additionally set the upper and lower threshold for the metrics. Use historical performance data (such as the current period's performance, three month rolling average or the previous year's average) to set a baseline, or starting point, for your targets. If no historical data exists, use industry benchmarks; discussions with the IT staff, and knowledge of the current IT capabilities to determine appropriate targets.

Consider the following questions to help set the targets and thresholds for each of the required measurements:
- Is the polarity increasing or decreasing? "More is better" versus "Less is better."
- Is there a high level of confidence in the availability, validity, and reliability of the baseline?
- Do historical baselines exist for the reported metrics? KPMs, KPIs, KGIs, KPIs, KPMs, KFMs.
- Does the existing source data have three consecutive periods from which a running average could be calculated?
- Can the IT management team determine the baselines from experience?
- Does benchmark data exist and can it be obtained?
- What target settings do IT staff think are attainable?
- What is the current IT capability or maturity level?
- What is the lowest possible setting for the metric, that is, low limit?
- What is the highest possible setting for the metric, that is, high limit?
- What is the danger value setting for the metric, that is, condition red?
- What is the optimal or target setting for the measurement, that is, condition green?

Tips for setting targets and thresholds:
- Set realistic and achievable targets. If the answers to the previous questions suggest a low level of confidence in the baselines, set the danger value and optimal target value for the thresholds to an easy to obtain level. Readjust the targets and thresholds when better baseline data becomes available. For example, the average of three consecutive measurement periods could be used to form a baseline from which the targets and thresholds could be calculated.
- Set thresholds to provide early warning indication. All thresholds should be set below the level at which the resource is over-utilized or below the target SLA. If the threshold level is reached, there will opportunity to take corrective action before breaching a service level agreement SLA or experiencing a process failure.
- Involve IT Operations Staff and Management. Operational staff are closest to the action and in the best position to provide information on what's possible. Involve them in setting targets—it will help gain their buy-in as they feel a sense of ownership in the process or service.
- Consider past performance as a target baseline. If past data exist for performance on a particular metric, examine that data for trends that can serve as a baseline for setting targets for future performance.

Implementing a measurement program

Bus Goal	IT Goal	KGI	Benefit	IT Objective	CSF	KPIs	KPMs	KFMs
Improve customer orientation and service								
	Ensure the satisfaction of end users with service offerings and service levels							
		All IT service level objective targets are met						
			Higher User productivity & satisfaction					
				Meet Email service level objectives				
					Email service availability - end to end			
						Percentage Network availability during agreed service time		
							% available - in agreed service time	
								MTTR (Mean Time To Repair/Restore "downtime")
								Agreed service time
						Percentage Exchange Server availability during agreed service time		
							% available - in agreed service time	
								MTTR (Mean Time To Repair/Restore "downtime")
								Agreed service time
						Percentage Replication Server availability during agreed service time		
							% available - in agreed service time	
								MTTR (Mean Time To Repair/Restore "downtime")
								Agreed service time
					Email service reliability - end to end			
						Percentage improvement Network reliability		
							% change - MTBSI (Mean Time Between System Incidents)	
								MTBSI (Mean Time Between System Incidents) - Days
						Percentage improvement Exchange Server reliability		
							% change - MTBSI (Mean Time Between System Incidents)	
								MTBSI (Mean Time Between System Incidents) - Days
						Percentage improvement Replication Server reliability		
							% change - MTBSI (Mean Time Between System Incidents)	
								MTBSI (Mean Time Between System Incidents) - Days

Figure 8.4 Example service goal alignment with supporting metrics

- Use capability or process maturity assessments and SWOT analysis techniques. Consider the IT group's current maturity level before setting targets. Consider the IT group's internal strengths and weaknesses, as well as its external opportunities and threats. Ask what targets would enable the IT group to build on its strengths and leverage opportunities, as well as minimize weaknesses and threats.
- Use internal and external customer surveys. Gather feedback from customers and other stakeholders. Expectations from these groups might yield insights that can be used to set targets.
- Consider peer benchmarks or industry averages. Numerous IT benchmarking agencies monitor IT performance. External benchmarking can compare and assess current effectiveness, level of maturity, compliance status, cost effectiveness and satisfaction levels.

8.4 Implementation of the measurement process

Implementing the measurement process is best treated as a project and should complete at least one process lifecycle before being transferred to operations. The high level phases and steps are outlined as follows which should be adapted to meet organizational requirements:

- Phase I - Planning
  - assign roles and responsibilities
  - conduct the initial planning phase
  - initiate communications plan
  - select the metrics
- Phase II - Implementation
  - create/install MDB
  - design/configure dashboards, scorecards, KGIs, CSFs, KPIs, KPMs and KFMs
  - establish monitoring and collect
  - analyze results
  - produce reports
  - process tuning
  - initiate service improvements
- Phase III - Optimization
  - transfer control to operational staff
  - audit/review for compliance, effectiveness, efficiency and quality

Tips for implementing the measurement process:
- Engage subject-matter experts. Identify internal or external subject-matter experts who may have insights into the aspects of the IT group's performance that is being measured.
- Consult with existing performance management groups. If performance management system exists, ask the system manager or administrator for advice on how they monitor, analyze, tune and implement performance improvements.
- Organize a SWAT team. Assemble a group of peer managers and IT Staff who can help brainstorm ideas for objectives, metrics, targets, and so forth.
- Consider external data sources and resources. Use industry benchmarking data and other external information sources to define objectives, metrics, and targets.
- Identify quick wins. Choose areas that can generate quick wins to gain momentum.

Implementing a measurement program 133

- Analyze results and take action. Measuring for the sake of measuring does not produce results. Action must be taken to make improvements.

Data collection and monitoring

Gather data on actual performance for the defined metrics. Data sources might include existing IT systems, data warehouse, Users (for example, IT may survey customer satisfaction), IT staff, and third-party organizations (such as outsourcers) that keep records needed. Many industry research firms and consultants also conduct proprietary baseline and benchmarking surveys; ask if IT or the company participates in such surveys.

To help plan for data collection and monitoring, consider the following questions:
- What metrics need to be reported? KGIs, KPIs, CSFs, KPMs and KFMs
- What is the frequency of data collection? Hourly, Daily, Weekly, Monthly, Quarterly, Semi-annual, Annual
- What core elements are required? Mandatory, Optional, Meta-data
- Where is the source data for extraction? Sub-systems, Databases, Reports, Spreadsheets
- Who are the source data owners and what is their expected involvement?
- What data calculations are required to transform the metrics?
- When will the data be available for extraction?
- How will the data be validated for reliability and accuracy?
- Who to report or escalate quality and accuracy issues from the source data?
- How will the data be loaded into the MDB?
- How will the data collection process be documented?
- What actions to take if the quality or accuracy is up to acceptable standards?
- What predefined actions to take if important KPIs trigger alerts, that is, red condition?
- What dashboards/scorecards/metrics need to be configured, published and to whom?
- What trending reports need to be published and to whom?

Tips for data collection and monitoring:
- Automate the data collection. Where possible automate the extract, transform and load activities.
- Validate the data. Automate the data validation process by using filters, scripts or formulas to test the validity of data. For example, data is expected to be "Within an expected range", "Not higher than", "Not less than", "Not equal to."
- Report delays. It may be necessary to report reason for delays and escalate where appropriate to avoid holding up the monitoring cycle.

Storage of Metrics Data (MDB)

There should be short-term and longer-term planning considerations for the storage, administration and reporting of the metrics data in a Measurement Database (MDB) and whether to buy or build. In the short-term, spreadsheet solutions are ideal for the design and development of measurement program. Spreadsheet solutions are low cost, low risk, familiar and easy to work with. In the longer-term, dimensional database applications provide better reporting capabilities, more storage, better interfaces and have more versatility in the types of data that can be stored, that is documents, pictures, et cetera.

Some general points that should be considered when designing or evaluating the functionality of an MDB solution include:
- data structure, data handling and integration
- integration with other applications and source transactional systems
- modeling capabilities
- conformity to open standards
- dimension conformance
- flexibility in implementation, usage and data sharing
- ease of use
- distributed client for information sharing, that is web interface
- data integrity and validation capability
- conversion requirements for previously tracked data
- data backup, control and security
- support options provided by the tool vendor
- organizational constraints:
  - impact on organization
  - staff availability, experience and skill sets
- implementation complexity
- costs:
  - software/hardware – purchase, and installation and upgrades
  - licenses, training, development and customization
  - consulting

Some specific points that should be considered when designing or evaluating the functionality of an MDB solution include:
- the inputs to the MDB:
  - metrics data
  - core elements
  - business data
  - technical data
  - financial data
  - performance data
  - survey data
  - initiatives data
- the outputs from the MDB:
  - performance based reports
  - trend analysis
  - exception reporting
  - process initiative status
  - benefits realized
  - Ad-hoc reporting
  - production of the measurement reports

Performance analysis

Compare the actual data gathered to the target (desired) performance. Identify the performance gaps, analyze the root cause and determine potential corrective actions.

Implementing a measurement program

To help plan the implementation for the analysis process, consider the following questions:
- What "People", "Process", "Tools" and "Techniques" are required to assess and prioritise improvements, degradations and exceptions?
- What "People", "Process", "Tools" and "Techniques" are required to assess process improvement recommendations.
- What are the training or skills gaps and how will they be overcome?
- Who will approve initiatives and how will their status be reported?
- How to assess the anticipated outcomes/benefits and report the value realized?
- How to report the findings, observations, problems & predictions and to whom?

Tips for performance analysis:
- Use compare and contrast techniques. Determine where the performance gaps are. Large gaps between actual and target may suggest improvement initiatives are required. They could also indicate the target is overly aggressive and needs to be adjusted.
- Pre-configure root cause analysis tools. Use tools and techniques like process flowcharting, affinity diagrams, Ishikawa diagrams and relations diagrams to pre-configure analysis scorecards. Pre-configured analysis tools will reduce troubleshooting effort and improve effectiveness.
- Assess possible recommendations. Use problem analysis tools to assess recommended improvement initiatives. Problem analysis tools will help select the best choices for improvement.
- Use trending to determine if action is required. Use trending to verify is a process/service is improving or degrading. Do not launch a major improvement initiative if the process/service data is trending in the right direction.

Production of the reports by stakeholder

Measurement reports need to be tailored to the audience. Reporting will generally have five types of information "Executive Summary", "Scope", "Summary Findings", "Initiative Status", and "Recommendations." Create a performance reporting matrix of performance measurement reports and mapped to stakeholder groups. See figure 8.5 for and example of a performance reporting matrix.

Performance Reporting Matrix	Client	IT Manager	Process Owner	Service Owner	Team Members	CSI Owner	External Service Provider
Performance Measurement Reports							
1.0 Executive Summary	X	X	X	X	X	X	
2.0 Scope of Measurements	X	X	X	X	X	X	
3.0 Findings Summary		X	X	X	X	X	X
3.1 Performance Achievements			X		X	X	X
3.2 Performance Gap Analysis			X		X	X	X
3.3 Root Cause Analysis			X		X	X	X
3.4 Predictive Analysis			X		X	X	X
4.0 Initiative Status		X	X	X	X	X	X
5.0 Recommendations		X	X	X	X	X	X

Figure 8.5 Example Performance Reporting Matrix

To help plan for the reporting process, consider the following questions:
- Who are the key stakeholders? "Business Client", "Sr. IT Management", "Process Owners", "Service Owners", "Team Members", "Continual Service Improvement Owner", "Third Party Suppliers"
- What types of reports need to be produced and for whom? "Executive Summary", "Scope of Measurements", "Performance Achievements", "Performance Gap Analysis", "Root Cause Analysis", "Predictive Analysis", "Key Findings", "Recommendations"
- What level of detail is required by each stakeholder group? "Summary", "Achievements", "Deficiencies", "Alerts", "Conclusions", "Recommendations"
- What is the reporting frequency? "Daily", "Weekly", "Monthly", "Quarterly", "Semi-annual or annual"
- How will the reports be distributed? "Hard Copy", "Email", "Intranet", "Online Dynamic", "News Letter", "Bulletin Boards"
- How will the reports be archived? "Hard Copy Library", "Electronic Library"

Tips for production of reports:
- Create and use templates. Templates will help reduce the time and effort required to produce the reports. Consistent formats will make it easier for production of reports and comprehension of the information with familiar formats.
- Tell a story. Based on the analysis information, summarize the information and tell a store about what has happened (past), what actions are being proposed or taken (present), and what might happen (Future).
- Use visual information. Charts and graphs help convey numerical information very effectively. Use them where possible to transform you data into easy to use and understandable information.
- Use the appropriate level of detail for your audience. Too much detail – your audience may become confused or lose interest. Too little detail – they may not grasp the importance of a performance problem. Gather feedback and adjust your reporting detail accordingly.
- Communicate poor results constructively. The truth must be communicated about poor performance results. Don't single out individuals as the reason for poor performance. Focus on the underlying causes and explore ideas for resolving problematic areas.
- Capture lessons learned. Conduct review sessions to capture lessons learned. Ask questions like: "What worked well?" "What did not work?" "What could be improved?" Use this information to create knowledge and wisdom. Take action through the tuning process to optimize, correct or improve the process or service.

Performance tuning

Performance tuning will require some initial policies and guidelines on initial set up. A decision analysis framework and criteria must be established to effectively assess "Optimization", "Improvement", and "Corrective" recommendations. To help plan for the tuning process, consider the following questions:
- What are the qualification criteria for performance tuning and creation of a service improvement initiative?
- What decision analysis method and/or techniques will be used to evaluate recommendations?
- What are the criteria for documenting a service improvement initiative request?

- What is the level of detail required for documenting a service improvement initiative project plan?
- What is the level of detail required for documenting service improvement initiative activities?
- What "Request for Change" details are required and what method will be used for control and monitoring?
- How will request for project resources be made?
- What is the service improvement initiative approval process?

Tips for performance tuning setup:
- Use decision analysis frameworks and tools. Brainstorm with process/service owners to gain consensus on the decision analysis framework and criteria required for effective and efficient decision making. Use decision analysis tools and methods to make better decisions more quickly and accurately.

Improvement initiatives

Implementing the "Improvement Initiatives" sub-process will require some initial policies and guidelines to be established. Brainstorm with process/service owners to gain consensus on how improvement initiatives will be implemented, tracked and verified. To help plan for the implementation of the improvement initiatives sub-process, consider the following questions:
- How will improvement initiatives be managed in the execution stage?
- What are the criteria for documenting improvement initiative anticipated benefits?
- What are the criteria for documenting improvement initiative tracking metrics? KGIs, CSFs, KPIs, KPMs, KFMs
- What is the service improvement initiative acceptance and review process?
- How will the anticipated benefits be tracked, reviewed and reported?
- When and how often will audit/reviews be conducted and by whom?

Tips for improvement initiative setup:
- Use change control. Implement all improvement initiatives under change control using the change management process.
- Use tracking metrics. Identify tracking metrics the will help confirm and verify the improvement initiatives are progressing and effective.

8.5 Optimizing the measurement process

The measurement process should be reviewed for effectiveness and efficiency at regular intervals to determine areas for improvement and optimization. Some general guidelines should include:
- Review
  - assess/report if measurement program goals, CSFs and objectives are being met
  - assess/report completeness, accuracy, validity, that is quality of information
  - assess/report if benefits have been realized and communicated
  - assess/report the cost effectiveness of measurement program
  - assess/report the satisfaction of the users of the measurement program
  - assess/recommend any service improvement initiatives

- Optimization
  - initiate measurement program improvements
  - add new or improved processes when appropriate
  - update the core elements, targets, thresholds, benchmarks, that is raise the bar
  - automate data collections
  - improve reporting

Some key performance metrics that could be used to assess the effectiveness of the measurement program could include:
- Overall customer satisfaction
- Percentage of processes overdue for measurement
- Number of outstanding approved actions that have not achieved their objective
- Number of outstanding actions in initiative improvement communications plan
- Number of improvements carried out by process owners
- Number of service improvement initiatives on target
- Percentage of overall improvement since last benchmark
- Number of recommendations for improvement received from other process owners
- Number of changes requested for process improvement
- Percent change in the total cost of ownership

Critical success factors

It is important to assess the critical success factors required for the measurement program, the following list although not exhaustive, presents a checklist for consideration:
- clear vision, goals and objectives
- senior management commitment
- organizational buy-in to the program
- stakeholders clearly identified
- metrics aligned to organizational goals and objectives
- frequent and effective communications
- funding and resources availability
- skills and capability
- demonstrate quick-wins
- access to source data
- data collection automation

Updating the measures, targets, thresholds

Business needs are constantly evolving and changing requiring the measurement program to evolve and change over time. It is good practice to periodically review the measures, targets and thresholds to determine if they still support the business requirements. Some areas to consider on where to get input could include:
- annual business planning and budgeting cycle
- regular budget to plan reviews
- service level management reviews
- service improvement program reviews
- poorly performing processes/services highly dependent on other processes/services with targets set too low

Implementing a measurement program

- external regulatory compliance changes
- new or changing business services requiring IT services

8.6 Review and audit

Like all ITSM processes it is good practice to provide an independent review and audit of the measurement process for compliance, effectiveness, efficiency and quality. Audits should be performed by an independent person or group rather than the measurement process owner or manager. The general intent of the review and audit is to determine:
- what was done well – key success, quick wins
- what went wrong – problems areas
- what could be done better next time – suggested improvements
- steps taken to prevent issues from happening again – improvement initiatives
- investigate cause why the issue occurred – root cause analysis
- define how we can learn from it in the future – knowledge capture

Measurement program reviews and audits should be considered at the following times:
- shortly after implementation of a new measurement system
- before and after major changes to the measurement process
- at random intervals
- at regular intervals

Chapter 9
Costs, benefits and possible problems

A well planned and implemented measurement program is one of the better investments an organization can make. Most mature organizations have well established measurement programs in their financial, human resources, sales & marketing and business operations departments where measurements are just common sense and part of the normal operating practices.

Justifying the implementation of a measurement program will require examination of the costs, benefits and risks to determine the right scope and fit-for-purpose.

9.1 Costs
The first step is to estimate the project and ongoing costs required for the measurement program.

Project
- **hardware and software** – metrics database, design & reporting tools
- **project management** - should be treated as a project
- **staff costs** – training and consultancy

Ongoing
- **hardware and software maintenance cost**
- **ongoing staff costs** – salaries, training, ad-hoc consulting
- **storage, upgrades, licenses**

9.2 Benefits
Measurements help improve performance, align goals and realize value. The positive benefits of a measurement program can be weighed against the negative consequences of not having one.

Benefits of a measurement program
- provides the instrumentation necessary to control an organization
- direct focus on specific performance and control objectives
- easier to spot danger in time to correct it
- improves morale in an organization
- stimulates healthy competition between process owners
- helps align IT with the business goals and verify results
- drives efficiency/ effectiveness/ quality
- inspires continual improvements
- helps reduce total cost of ownership (TCO)

Consequences of not having a measurement program
- reduced visibility resulting in loss of control
- focus on noise vs. what's important
- reactive fire-fighting mode
- low morale in organization
- unhealthy political competition
- benefits not apparent or realized
- cost effectiveness not understood
- customer complaints drive improvements
- TCO not optimized
- increasing risk

9.3 Possible Problems

Potential problems can be identified, prepared-for and dealt-with in advance. The following provides a list of potential problems that could be encountered and some suggestions on how to avoid them:

- **An overall lack of commitment from IT staff** - Conduct awareness campaigns to provide general information and clearly publicise the business and personal benefits that will be realized by implementing a Measurement Program. Also involve as many people as possible in the decision-making process to gain their commitment.
- **Insufficient commitment interest from senior business management** - Commitment is more than making funds or resources available. Senior management commitment is about leading by example. Conduct awareness campaigns for IT Customers and senior management stressing the financial and business benefits.
- **Metrics not aligned with organizational goals** - Ensure that the objectives and metrics support the business and IT strategic goals. Too many managers decide to measure aspects of their group's performance that have little connection to higher-level goals.
- **Lack of education and training on measurements and/or process** - It is vitally important that the concepts of measurements are well known and understood. Metrics and performance management training is now widely available. Ensure that everyone has the appropriate skills for the job and have received the correct amount of training. In addition it would be beneficial for IT staff to receive business-related training covering the broader aspects of IT Infrastructure. Far too often IT is accused of not knowing enough about the business and its needs.

- **Lack of understanding – leading to misinterpretation of results** – Conduct awareness campaigns for IT staff explaining the metrics and their interpretation. Keep metrics well documented by populating and updating the metadata.
- **Wrong level of detail – too much or not enough** – Avoid relying on just one metric to measure overall performance. Also resist creating a long list of metrics to measure everything that relates performance. The goal is to identify the activities that will have the greatest direct impact on IT's service and process performance – and develop metrics for those activities. A rule of thumb is six to ten metrics per objective.
- **Difficulty obtaining input data – time and/or resources** – Automating data-gathering systems often linked to a data warehouse and/or IT management systems, offer many benefits. They reduce manual effort, handle huge volumes of data easily and can generate reports showing the data in different formats (such as pie charts, tables, or graphs). In addition, they can aggregate data from different units or groups into one number.
- **Inadequate measurement tool – MDB or source transactional systems lacking** – Verify if company may already be using a formal performance measurement (PM) system – a set of strategic objectives and performance metrics (including KPIs) applied throughout the entire enterprise. It will be easier to get approval use the existing company system than to procure a new one. If not, develop a business case to select and acquire the required tools and systems to support the measurement program.
- **Goals & objectives not clear – non-existent** – Difficulty seeing the overall picture can result in over-focus on isolated or unconnected processes. Ensure the measurement program is set up with high-level objectives as well as detailed low-level objectives. Ensure that emphasis is placed on the end-to-end process.
- **Stakeholders not identified – roles and responsibilities not clear** – Someone should be given the task of managing the overall implementation and this person should be held responsible. Ideally this is not the person who is actually doing the work on a day-to-day basis. Conduct brainstorming sessions with IT management staff to develop the RACI matrix and the beneficiaries of the anticipated benefits.
- **Takes too long to demonstrate benefits – quick wins** – To maintain enthusiasm and commitment quick wins must be realized and expectations managed as to when longer-term results and benefits will be realized. Select processes or services for performance improvement that can generate benefits, with the least amount of effort/cost, and in the shortest amount of time.
- **Overly aggressive targets – or set too low** – Aggressive or unrealistic targets can demoralize employees if they lack the resources to meet the targets and if they view the targets as unreachable and unrealistic. Set targets high enough to inspire staff to reach for better performance—but not so high that employees conclude they can't possibly reach them. Additionally, targets that are set too low can look like superior performance without having to work too hard. Benchmarking data can be useful in setting targets relative to comparable peer groups or industry groups.
- **Manipulation of measurement data** – Measurement systems can change employees' behaviors – sometimes in ways never intended! Ask how staff might alter their behaviors in order to meet targets set for the performance metrics. Consider whether these behavior changes might cause unintended – and unwanted – consequences.
- **Difficulty assessing data accuracy and reliability** – Subjective data can be difficult to validate for accuracy and reliability. It can be easily manipulated by individuals seeking to make their

performance look better than it really is. Avoid relying on just one subjective metric as the indicator for a critical success factor.
- **Drastic reactions from poor performance data** – When actual performance data falls far short from targets, avoid taking drastic actions or reactive target adjustments. Take time to investigate what may have caused the performance shortfall and to consider a range of possible solutions to the problem.
- **Not regularly reassessing objectives and metrics** – The business priorities change but the objectives and metrics are not updated. This may cause the organization to continue focus on measuring metrics which are no longer important. Use the tuning process to continually reassess objectives, anticipated benefits and metrics.

9.4 Reduce total cost of ownership

A measurement program can help reduce the total cost of ownership (TCO). TCO was developed by Gartner[30] and has become a key performance measurement for efficiency and effectiveness. TCO is the total cost of computer assets throughout their lifecycle, from acquisition to disposal and includes vendor, staff, management and hidden User costs. Gartner's TCO studies revealed that the TCO for an average PC could range from $6,000 to $12,000 per user per year. TCO is a measure of efficiency which can be reduced through improved performance by implementing better IT practices.

Total cost of ownership is the combined hard and soft costs of owning networked information assets throughout their lifecycle. Direct costs include items such as capital, operations and management costs. These costs are considered 'hard costs' because they are tangible and easily accounted for. However, even more significant in many IT environments are the indirect or 'hidden costs' related to user peer support, training and downtime. Because they don't occur at acquisition time, they are often overlooked in budgets. Ineffective performance causes a transfer of management and support responsibility to end users resulting in higher hidden costs and dissatisfaction.

Figure 9.1 illustrates the TCO of technology assets throughout their lifecycle.

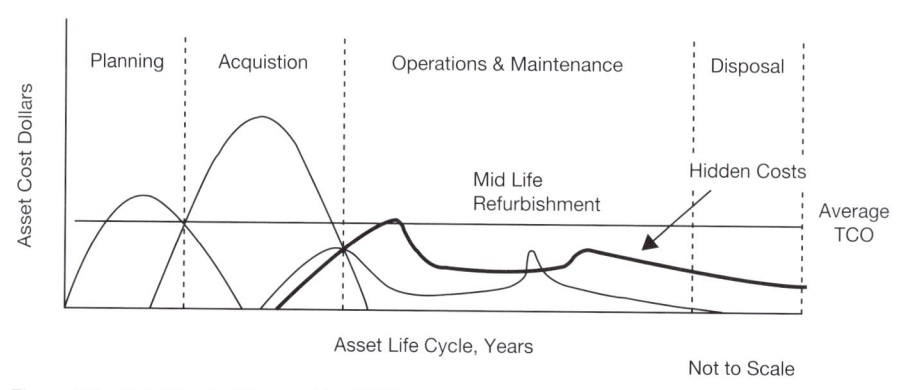

Figure 9.1   Total Cost of Ownership (TCO)

Costs, benefits and possible problems

For example, a hypothetical worst-performer organization could have an annual TCO per user as high as $12,000 where a best-performer peer organization could have an annual TCO as low as $6,000, a 50% improvement in US dollars.

Figure 9.2 provides an extrapolation table and indication of the size and range of TCO savings opportunities possible for organizations that measure and improve performance through the implementation of best practices. The table demonstrates how much a company could save by reducing their TCO by 5% through 30% in US dollars.

User Base	Hypothetical TCO Savings Opportunity			
	5.0%	10.0%	20.0%	30.0%
500	200,000	400,000	800,000	1,200,000
1,000	400,000	800,000	1,600,000	2,400,000
1,500	600,000	1,200,000	2,400,000	3,600,000
2,000	800,000	1,600,000	3,200,000	4,800,000
2,500	1,000,000	2,000,000	4,000,000	6,000,000
3,000	1,200,000	2,400,000	4,800,000	7,200,000
5,000	2,000,000	4,000,000	8,000,000	12,000,000
7,500	3,000,000	6,000,000	12,000,000	18,000,000
10,000	4,000,000	8,000,000	16,000,000	24,000,000
20,000	8,000,000	16,000,000	32,000,000	48,000,000

Rule of Thumb
1% TCO Improvement = $80-$100 per User/Yr

Figure 9.2 Hypothetical TCO Savings Opportunity

Assumptions
- average TCO is between $8,000 and $10,000 per User/Year
- Rule of Thumb calculation = 1% TCO improvement would range from $80 to $100 per User/Year [.01 x $8,000] = $80 or [.01 x $10,000] = $100
- distributed computing environment only
- U.S. dollars.

Chapter 10
Conclusions

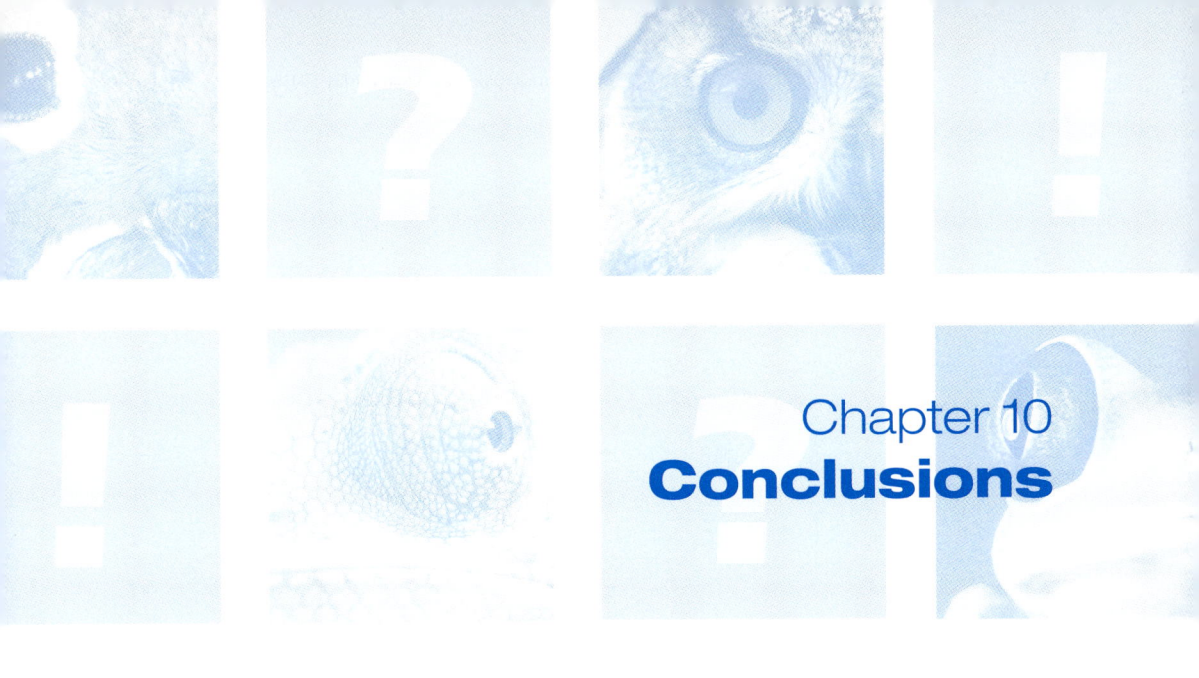

Even though we are often too busy to ask for directions, implementing a measurement framework should help align IT with the business objectives and create value through continuous improvements because it helps us create a roadmap and keeps us from getting lost.

The measurement framework acts as the map, meeting the business goals and objectives are the destination, the critical success factors provide the directions and the metrics provide the sign posts to keep you on course.

This book "Implementing Metrics for IT Service Management" provides a measurement framework which is based on a continual improvement lifecycle. The objectives of the measurement framework are to help the reader determine ways to:
- help align IT with business objectives and verify results
- maintain compliance requirements for business operations
- drive operational efficiencies, effectiveness and quality

The measurement framework can be implemented as a comprehensive measurement program for all processes and services or selectively for individual process or services.

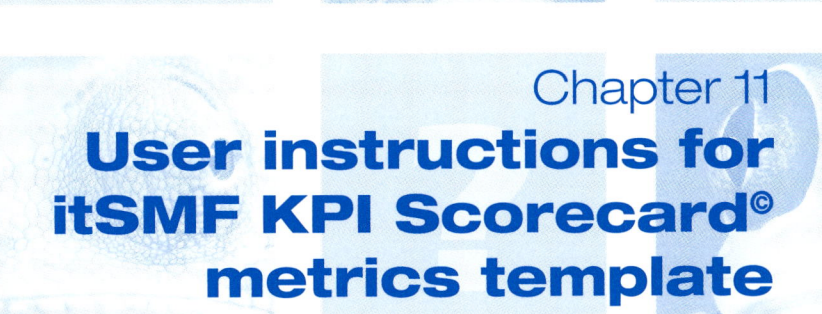

Chapter 11
User instructions for itSMF KPI Scorecard© metrics template

11.1 Overview

Included with this book is a CD with a copy of the itSMF KPI Scorecard© metrics templates. The itSMF KPI Scorecard© is pre-populated with over 300 key performance metrics and scorecards for IT Service Management (ITSM). The itSMF KPI Scorecard© is a series of Microsoft Excel® 2003[31] templates which helps to quickly enter and report metrics, scorecards and dashboards, demonstrating many of the principles described in this book.

The itSMF KPI Scorecard© is protected under copyright by itSMF-International 2007. All rights reserved. No part of this application may be reproduced in any form by electronic copying, print, photo print, microfilm or any other means without written permission by the publisher. Although this application has been composed with much care, neither author, nor editor, nor publisher can accept any liability for damage caused by possible errors and/or incompleteness in this application.

This itSMF International application was based on myKPI Designer© 2007, a real-life product, with the approval of the owner of the product, Micromation Canada (ww.micromationinc.com). The itSMF application can be used independently by the buyer, as long copyrights are respected. The intellectual property of the application was and is with Micromation.

Table 11.1 provides an overview of the features included in the itSMF KPI Scorecard© metrics template:

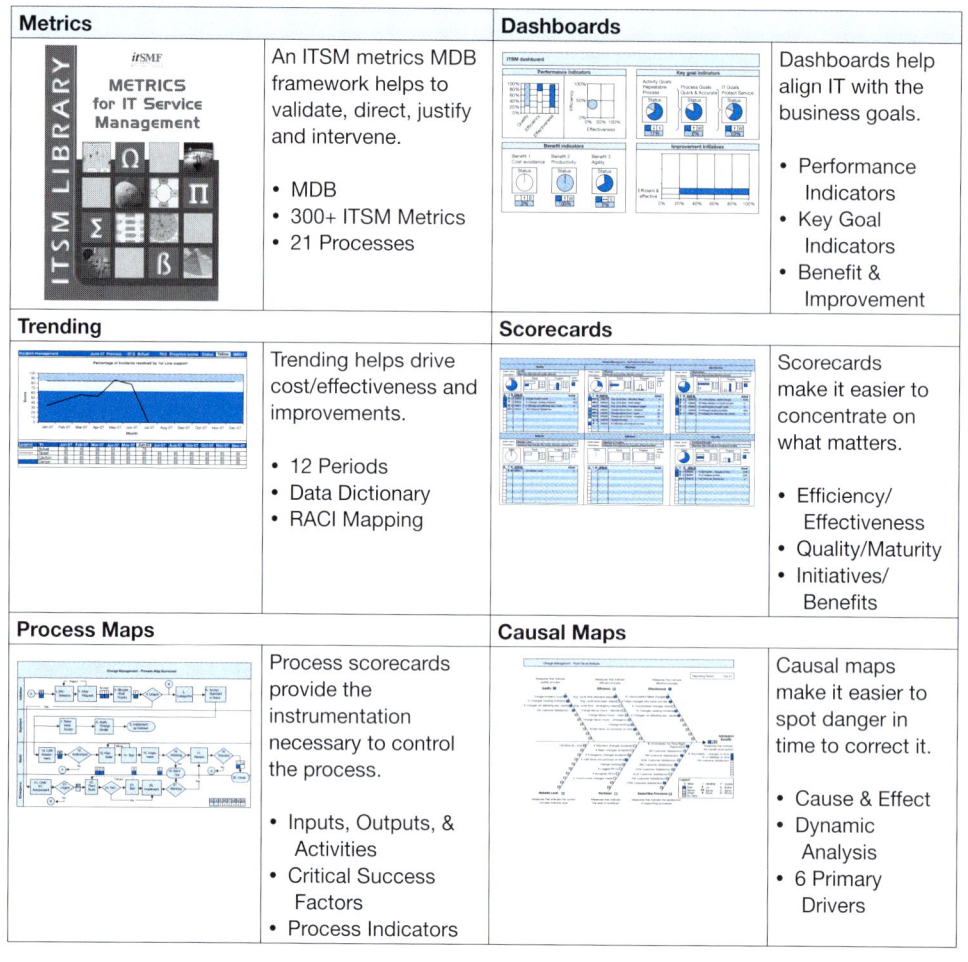

Metrics		Dashboards	
itSMF METRICS for IT Service Management	An ITSM metrics MDB framework helps to validate, direct, justify and intervene. • MDB • 300+ ITSM Metrics • 21 Processes		Dashboards help align IT with the business goals. • Performance Indicators • Key Goal Indicators • Benefit & Improvement
Trending		**Scorecards**	
	Trending helps drive cost/effectiveness and improvements. • 12 Periods • Data Dictionary • RACI Mapping		Scorecards make it easier to concentrate on what matters. • Efficiency/ Effectiveness • Quality/Maturity • Initiatives/ Benefits
Process Maps		**Causal Maps**	
	Process scorecards provide the instrumentation necessary to control the process. • Inputs, Outputs, & Activities • Critical Success Factors • Process Indicators		Causal maps make it easier to spot danger in time to correct it. • Cause & Effect • Dynamic Analysis • 6 Primary Drivers

Table 11.1   itSMF KPI Scorecard© features

11.2 System requirements

The itSMF KPI Scorecard© requires at least 35MB of disk space and a copy of Microsoft Excel® 2003 or higher to run.

11.3 Installation instructions

Copy the folder called 'itSMF KPI Scorecard' (this is one of the two buttons on the home page of the CD) to a location on your computer system. Using Excel®, locate and open the template file called 'itSMF KPI Scorecard v1.553 - Metrics MDB'. Links are provided in the [Home] tab which will locate the process scorecard files.

User instructions for itSMF KPI Scorecard© metrics template

Tip

> To see preloaded sample data for the change management process, open the following file and follow the links provided:
>
> "**itSMF KPI Scorecard v1.553 - Metrics MDB Sample**"

Tip "Important"

> It is required that the **Excel Analysis ToolPack** feature be activated to properly calculate and display dates for reporting periods.
> 1. Click **Tools** on the file menu.
> 2. Select **Add-Ins** option.
> 3. Click the **Analysis ToolPack** check box. (toolbar: A bar with buttons and options that you use to carry out commands. To display a toolbar, click **Customize** on the **Tools** menu, and then click the **Toolbars** tab.)

Tip

> It is recommended that the Excel Web tool bar be activated to allow easy navigation between files.
> 4. If the **Web** toolbar (toolbar: A bar with buttons and options that you use to carry out commands. To display a toolbar, click **Customize** on the **Tools** menu, and then click the **Toolbars** tab.) is not displayed, point to **Toolbars** on the **View** menu, and then click **Web**.
> 5. On the **Web** toolbar (toolbar: A bar with buttons and options that you use to carry out commands. To display a toolbar, click **Customize** on the **Tools** menu, and then click the **Toolbars** tab.), click **Show Only Web Toolbar**.

11.4 Navigation & structure

The itSMF KPI Scorecard© metrics template is a series of Microsoft Excel 2003 templates which can be navigated using links found in each of the [Home] tabs in the file 'itSMF KPI Scorecard v 1.533 - Metrics MDB'.

The itSMF KPI Scorecard v 1.533 - Metrics MDB template is a workbook which contains the following tabs:
- Home – navigation links
- Tables – reporting dates, R.A.C.I. matrix
- Input – metrics input data entry
- KPMs – key performance metrics and thresholds
- Changes – record of file changes

The Process templates are a series of workbooks, each of which contains the following tabs:
- Home – navigation links to metrics, scorecards and dashboards
- Dashboard – summary of performance, goals, benefits & initiatives scorecards
- Process – detailed inputs, outputs, activities, performance & CSF scorecards
- Causal – root cause analysis tool
- Initiatives – summary of improvement initiatives
- 001 – 012 – trending and data dictionary

Since the files are linked together, they must reside in the same file directory as a group to maintain their relationships. It is recommended that file directory folder names are kept short and do not exceed seven levels from the root directory to avoid Excel® file structure limitations. The following diagram provides a visual representation of the navigation, file structures and tabs:

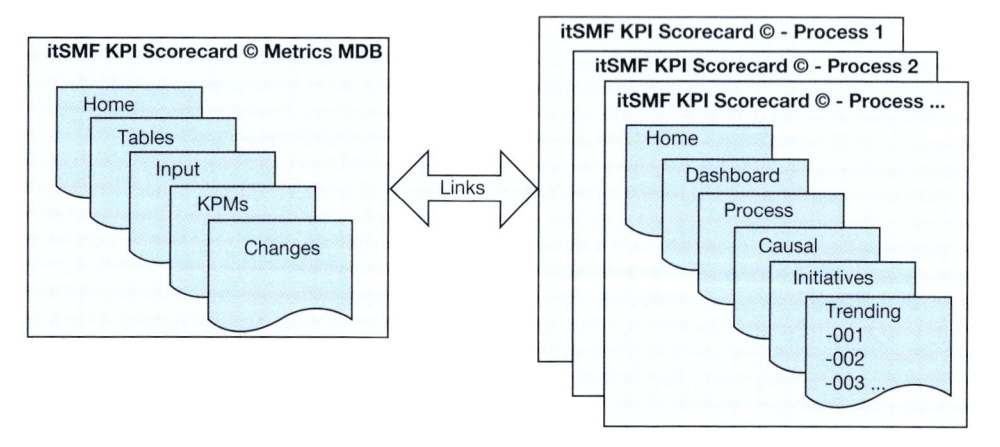

Figure 11.1 itSMF KPI Scorecard© navigation and structure

11.5 itSMF KPI Scorecard v 1.533 - Metrics MDB template

he itSMF KPI Scorecard© Metrics MDB template is used for navigation and administration of the metrics data.

[Home]

The [Home] tab is the main navigation page to all process templates and administrative functions by clicking the appropriate link.

User instructions for itSMF KPI Scorecard© metrics template

itSMF KPI Scorecard© Metrics MDB Sample		Home
Strategic	**Tactical**	**Operational**
Business Perspective Service Improvement Program Risk Management Document Management Competence, Awareness & Training Programme and Project Management	Service Level Management Problem Management Financial Management Availability Management Capacity Management Service Continuity Management	Service Desk Indicent Management Configuration Management Change Management Release Management Application Development Application Support Operations Management
Metrics Administration		
Tables Input Metric Values Edit Metric Attributes Changes/Revisions		

© itSMF-international 2007. All rights reserved. No part of this application may be reproduced in any electronic copying, print, photo print, microfilm or any other means without written permission by the publisher, Although this application has been composed with much care, neither author, nor editor, nor publisher can accept any liability for damage caused by possible errors and/or incompleteness in this application.

This itSMF international application was based on myKPI Designer© 2007, a real-life product, with the approval of the owner of the product, Micromation Canada (www.micromationinc.com). The itSMF application can be used independently by the buyer, as long copyrights are respected. The Intellectual Property of the application was and is with Micromation.

Version 1.553

Figure 11.2   itSMF KPI Scorecard© - ITSM Metrics MDB sample home page

[Tables]

The [Tables] tab is used to set the overall reporting start date and to configure the ITSM process owners and Roles using an R.A.C.I. matrix.

Date

The reporting start date determines the reporting year for all metrics data inputs and trending. For example, if the start date is set to Jan-07, then the 1st data entry and trend reporting period will begin on Jan-07 on the [Input] tab. If the start date is set to Aug-08, then the 1st data entry and trend reporting period will begin on Jan-08 on the [Input] tab.

Date	Reporting State Date - MM/DD/YY	Jan-07

Figure 11.3   itSMF KPI Scorecard© Reporting Start Date

Tip

> Anything highlighted in **Turquoise** is a User data entry field. Use these fields to enter customized data.

ITSM process owners and roles

The ITSM Process Owners and Roles table is used to determine who are Accountable, Responsible, Consulted (R.A.C.I.) and Informed for each of the processes.

Process ID	ITSM Process	Service Desk	Incident Management	Problem Management	Configuration Management	Change Management	Release Management	Process Owner E-mail
SD	Service Desk	R	C	C	I	I	I	
IM	Incident Management	C	R	C	I	I	I	
PM	Problem Management	C		R	I	I	I	
CFM	Configuration Management	I	I	I	R	C	C	joe.smith@xyz.com
CM	Change Management	C	C	C	I	A	R	john.doe@xyz.com
RM	Release Management	I	I	I	C	C	R	tom.petz@xyz.com

Figure 11.4 itSMF KPI Scorecard© Roles Table

R.A.C.I Matrix

RACI ID	Role Responsibility
R	Responsible
A	Accountable
C	Consulted
I	Informed

Figure 11.5 itSMF KPI Scorecard© R.A.C.I. Matrix Table

[Input]

The [Input] tab is used to set the reporting period and to input the metric values for up to 12 reporting periods (months).

Report Period

The report period is a drop down field which selects the reporting period (month) for all dashboard and scorecard metrics. There are 12 reporting periods (months) representing one calendar year. For example, notice in the following table that the report period is set to June-2007 (user entry highlighted in turquoise); all dashboards and scorecards will be adjusted to report only Jun-07 values for each key performance metric.

User instructions for itSMF KPI Scorecard© metrics template

Input	Home			Report Period	Reporting Year - 2007		
	ITSM Metrics Data Entry Page			Jun-07	Quarter 1		
ID	KPM Name	ITSM Process	Format	Jan-	Feb-	Mar-
CM001	Percentage of failed changes	Change Management	%	50.0	45.0	48.0
CM002	Percentage of rejected RFCs	Change Management	%	10.0	45.0	15.0
CM003	Number of unauthorized changes	Change Management	%	3.0	15.0	10.0
CM004	Change backlog	Change Management	#	30.0	15.0	18.0
CM005	Outages during changes	Change Management	#	1.0	15.0	3.0
CM006	Number of failed changes with no back-out plan	Change Management	#	10.0	15.0	11.0
CM007	Percentage of changes on time	Change Management	%	100.0	45.0	75.0
CM008	Percentage of changes causing incidents	Change Management	%	30.0	45.0	56.0

Figure 11.6   itSMF KPI Scorecard© Metrics Data Entry Tab

Metric values

The actual metric values are entered into the appropriate reporting period. For example, the preceding table has Change Management metrics values entered for the Jan-07 through Mar-07 periods.

[KPMs]

The [KPMs] tab is used to adjust the thresholds for each of the key performance metrics. For example, the following table shows the current thresholds set for the change management metrics.

Danger value

The danger value is used to set the metrics danger threshold or Red condition. A greater-than (>) or less-than (<) symbol must precede the value to determine the desired polarity. For example, the danger value for the metric CM007 in the previous table (<90) will cause the CM007 metric to show a red condition in all scorecards if the actual value entered in the [Input] tab is less than 90 percent.

Target value

The target value is used to set the metrics target threshold or Green condition. A greater-than (>) or less-than (<) symbol must precede the value to determine the desired polarity. For example, the target value for the metric CM007 in the previous table (>95) will cause the CM007 metric to show a green condition in all scorecards if the actual value entered in the [Input] tab is greater than 95 percent.

KPMs	Home					
	KPM Attributes Page		General Information		Thresholds	
ID	KPM Name	ITSM Process	Danger Value	Target Value	Low Limit	High Limit
CM001	Percentage of failed changes	Change Management	>10	<5	0	100
CM002	Percentage of rejected RFCs	Change Management	>20	<10	0	100
CM003	Number of unauthorized changes	Change Management	>30	<15	0	999999
CM004	Change backlog	Change Management	>15	<5	0	999999
CM005	Outages during changes	Change Management	>6	<1	0	999999
CM006	Number of failed changes with no back-out plan	Change Management	>2	<1	0	999999
CM007	Percentage of changes on time	Change Management	<90	>95	0	100
CM008	Percentage of changes causing incidents	Change Management	>10	<5	0	100
CM009	Number of CAB items not actioned on time	Change Management	>3	<1	0	999999
CM010	Number of Emergency Changes	Change Management	>3	<2	0	999999
CM011	Number of changes that do not deliver the expected results	Change Management	>3	<2	0	999999

Figure 11.7 itSMF KPI Scorecard© Thresholds Tab

Note that when the metrics actual value falls between the danger value and target value, a Yellow condition will be shown in all scorecards.

Low limit
The low limit value is used to indicate the lowest possible value for the metric. Note that when the metrics actual value falls below the low limit, a White condition will be shown in all scorecards indicating a potential data entry error in the [Input] tab or a wrong threshold value.

High limit
The high limit value is used to indicate the highest possible value for the metric. Note that when the metrics actual value falls above the high limit, a White condition will be shown in all scorecards indicating a potential data entry error in the [Input] tab or a wrong threshold value.

Polarity
The polarity indicates the desired directional change of each metric. For example, "More is better" or "Less is better". Polarity is set automatically by the (>) or (<) symbol used in the danger value threshold and is displayed on most scorecards.

User instructions for itSMF KPI Scorecard© metrics template

[Changes]

The [Changes] tab is used to record requests for change (RFCs) and to document when changes have been completed to the files or tabs. This helps to keep an audit trail of various requests and activities. The following table provides an example of various RFCs, activities and status.

Date	File	Tab	Item	Requested by	Completed by	Version	Variant	RFC #
24-Mar-07	MDB	Table	Enter preliminary ARCI values into Process Owner table	JJ	JJ	1.00		1
2-Apr-07	MDB	KPMs	Updated all thresholds	DS	DS	1.00		2
3-Apr-07	MDB	Input	Entered Mar-07 service desk values	JJ	DS	1.00		3
4-Apr-07	SD	Dashboard	Created performance scorecard entries	JJ	JJ	1.00		4
5-Apr-07	MDB	Table	Revised ARCI Process Owner for Service Desk to new Manager	DS	DS	1.00		5
								6
								7
								8
								9
								10
								11
								12
								13
								14

Figure 11.7   itSMF KPI Scorecard© Change Tab

11.6 Process templates

The individual process templates are used for the design and administration of the dashboards and scorecards. There are several process templates to choose from including:

Strategic
- Business Perspective
- Service Improvement Program
- Risk Management

- Document Management
- Competence, Awareness and Training
- Programme & Project Management

Tactical
- Service Level Management
- Problem Management
- Financial Management
- Availability Management
- Capacity Management
- Service Continuity Management
- Security Management

Operational
- Service Desk
- Incident Management
- Configuration Management
- Change Management
- Release Management
- Application Development
- Application Support
- Operations Management

itSMF KPI Scorecard© Process Home Tab for Change Management						
\multicolumn{6}{c	}{Metrics Trending}	Scorecards
S	T	P	ID	KPM Name	Actual	Polarity
		B	CM001	Percentage of failed changes	5	L
		W	CM002	Percentage of rejected RFCs	15	L
		B	CM003	Number of unauthorized changes	6	L
		B	CM004	Change backlog	5	L
		B	CM005	Outages during changes	6	L
		B	CM006	Number of failed changes with no back-out plan	2	L
		B	CM007	Percentage of changes on time	90	M
		B	CM008	Percentage of changes causing incidents	5	L
		B	CM009	Number of CAB items not actioned on the	6	L
		W	CM010	Number of Emergency Changes	6	L
		B	CM011	Number of changes that do not deliver the expected results	2	L
		B	CM012	Customer Satisfaction	4	M
		S	CM013	Avg. labour hours/change - all changes	45	L
		S	CM014	Avg. labour hours/change - standard changes	2	L
		S	CM015	Avg. labour hours/change - basic changes	4	L
		S	CM016	Avg. labour hours/change - emergency changes	5	L
		B	CM017	Avg. cycle days/change - all changes	95	L
		B	CM018	Avg. cycle days/change - standard changes	1	L
		B	CM019	Avg. cycle days/change - basic changes	4	L
		S	CM020	Avg. cycle days/change - emergency changes	8	L

Scorecards panel:
- Reporting Period: Jun-07
- Dashboard
- Process Map
- Root Cause
- Initiatives

Metrics Administration:
- Home
- Tables
- Input Metric Values
- Edit Metric Attributes
- Changes/Revisions

Legend
- Status: Red, Yellow, Green, No data
- Trending: Up (↑) Same (↔) Down (↓)
- Progress: B Better, S Same, W Worse
- Polarity: M more is better, L less it better

©itSMF International 2008. All rights reserved. No part of this application may be reproduced in any form by electronic copying, print, photo print, microfilm or any other means without written permission by the publisher. Although this application has been composed with much care, neither author, nor editor, nor publisher can accept any liability for damage caused by possible errors and/or incompleteness in this application. This itSMF International application was based on my KPI Designer© 2008, a real-life product, with the approval of the owner of the product, Micromation Canada (www.micromationinc.com). The itSMF application can be used independently by the buyer, as long as copyrights are respected. The Intellectual Property of the application was and is with Micromation. Version 1.553.2

Figure 11.8   itSMF KPI Scorecard© Process Home Tab for Change Management

User instructions for itSMF KPI Scorecard© metrics template

[Home]
The [Home] tab is the main navigation page to all metrics, process tabs and administrative functions by clicking the appropriate link.

Legend
The legend provides a quick reference for the Polarity, **S**tatus, **T**rending and **P**rogress data fields.

Legend			
S tatus		**T rending**	**P rogress**
Red		↑ Up	B Better
Yellow		↔ Same	S Same
Green		↓ Down	W Worse
No data			
		Polarity	
		M more is better	
		L less it better	

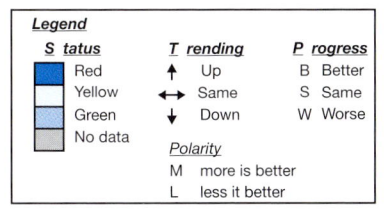

Figure 11.9   itSMF KPI Scorecard© Legend

Status
- Red – metric has exceeded its Danger Value
- Yellow – metric is between Danger and Target Value
- Green – metric has met its Target Value
- White – metric has no data entered or has exceeded low or high limits.

Tip

> A "**White**" status i.e. no colour is present, indicates the metric's actual value has exceeded it's **Low Limit** or **High Limit** value set in the thresholds section of the MDB. This may indicate a potential data entry problem on the [**Inputs**] tab or that the thresholds have not been correctly set on the [**KPMs**] tab.

Metrics trending
The metrics trending table displays the current status of the key performance metrics for the given process. This includes:
- **S**tatus – current colour when actual is compared to threshold values set in the [KPMs] tab of the MDB template
- **T**rending – compared to last period
- **P**rogress – compared to the last period
- ID – the identification number for the metric including link to trending details
- KPM Name – description of the metric
- Actual – metrics current value
- Polarity – metrics desired direction i.e. **M**ore is better or **L**ess is better

Tip

> Clicking the metric **ID** link will open the corresponding trending and data dictionary tab.

Scorecards
Clicking the scorecard navigation links will open the corresponding scorecard tab.

Metrics Administration
Clicking the metrics administration navigation links will open the corresponding process tab in the ITSM Metrics MDB template.

Polarity
The polarity indicates the desired directional change of the actual metric.

L	Less – decreasing is the desired directional change
M	More – increasing is the desired directional change

Trending
The trending indicates the movement of the current metric value compared to the last period and does not take polarity into consideration. That is the metric has increased from the last period but did not improve because "Less is better".

↑	Up – actual metric value is higher than last period
↔	Same – actual metric value is same as last period
↓	Down – actual metric value is lower than last period

Progress
The progress indicates the movement of the current metric value compared to the last period and takes polarity into consideration, that is did an improvement occur.

B	Better – actual metric value is better than last period
S	Same – actual metric value is the same as last period
W	Worse – actual metric value is worse than last period

[Dashboard]
The [Dashboard] tab is used to design, configure and display the summary results in chart panels for the process performance, goals, benefits and initiatives. The dashboard also relies on scorecards to configure and display the inputs, outputs, workload, dependencies, efficiency, performance, benefits, key goals and improvement initiatives of the process.

Performance indicators
The performance indicators panel displays the results of the Performance Scorecards located on the same tab below the dashboard. Performance is based on the aggregated quality, efficiency and effectiveness metrics.

Benefit indicators
The benefit indicators panel displays the results of the benefit Scorecards located on the same tab below the dashboard. Benefits are based on the aggregated metrics provided by three user-defined scorecards i.e. benefit 1, benefit 2 and benefit 3. For example, benefit 1 could be cost avoidance, benefit 2 could be productivity improvements, benefit 3 could be agility et cetera.

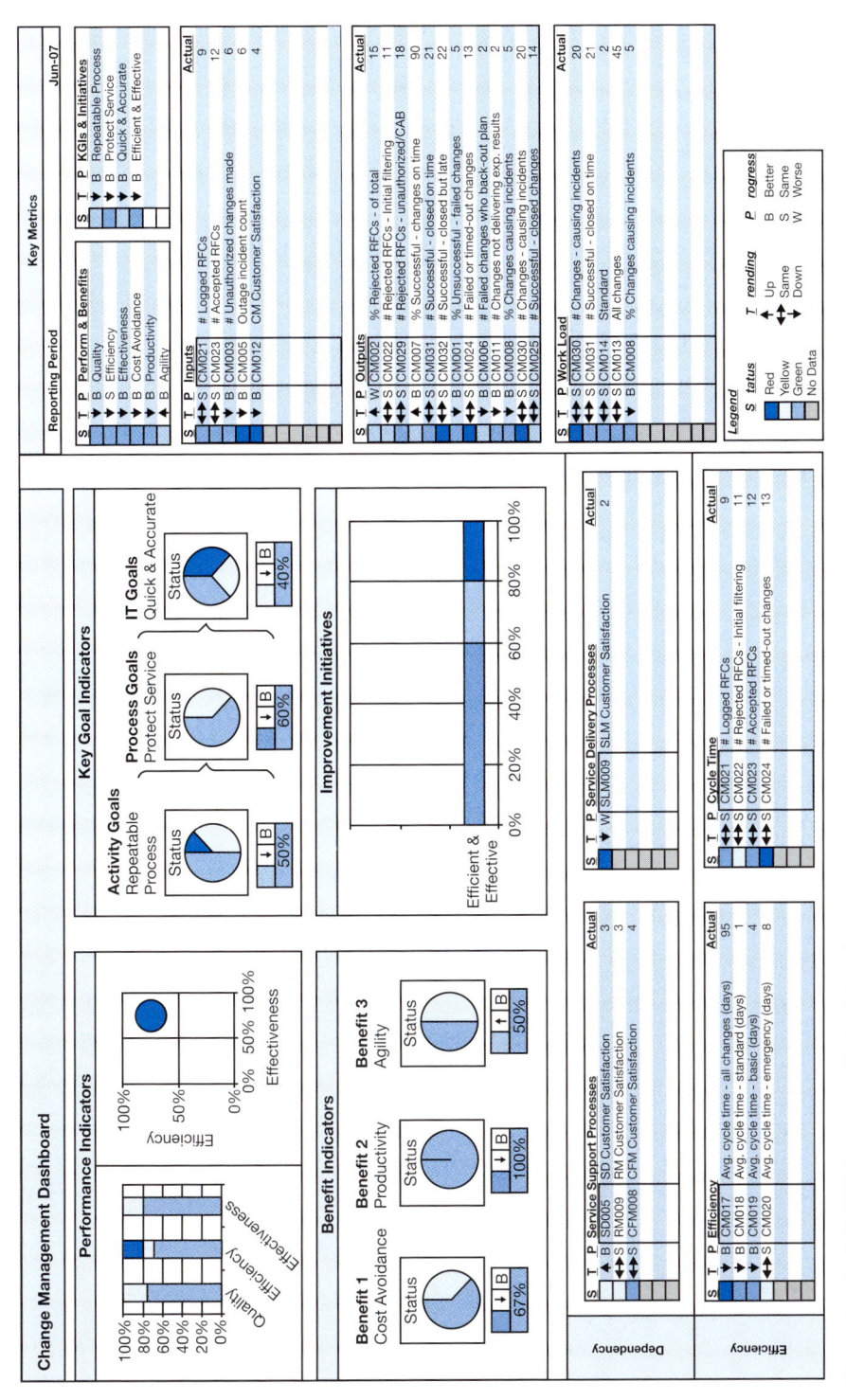

User instructions for itSMF KPI Scorecard© metrics template 161

Figure 11.10   itSMF KPI Scorecard© Dashboard

Key goal indicators

The key goal indicators panel displays the results of the Key goal scorecards located on the same tab below the dashboard. Key goals are based on the aggregated activity, process and IT goal metrics.

Improvement initiatives

The improvement initiative indicators panel displays the results of the improvement initiative Scorecards located on the same tab below the dashboard. Improvement initiatives are based on the aggregated metrics provided by three user-defined scorecards, that is initiative 1, initiative 2 and initiative 3. For example, initiative 1 could be a service improve plan to improve effectiveness, benefit 2 could be a service improve plan to improve efficiency, benefit 3 could be a service improve plan to improve quality, et cetera.

Tip

> See [Initiatives] tab instructions for the creation of initiative metrics.

Performance & benefits

The performance & benefits panel displays the details of the Performance & Benefits Scorecards located on the same tab below the dashboard.

KGIs & initiatives

The Key Goal Indicators (KGIs) & initiatives panel displays the details of the KGIs & Initiatives Scorecards located on the same tab below the dashboard.

Inputs

The inputs panel is a mini scorecard which displays User-defined input metrics for the process by entering the metric ID in the Input column. For example, entering CM021 in the input column will automatically display the details for the "# of logged RFCs" metric.

S	T	P	Inputs		Actual
	⇔	S	CM021	# Logged RFCs	9
	⇔	S	CM023	# Accepted RFCs	12
	▼	B	CM003	# Unauthorized changes made	6
	▼	B	CM005	Outage incident count	6
	▲	B	CM012	CM Customer Satisfaction	4

Figure 11.11   itSMF KPI Scorecard© Inputs Table

Outputs

The outputs panel is a mini scorecard which displays user-defined output metrics for the process by entering the metric ID in the Output column.

User instructions for itSMF KPI Scorecard© metrics template

Workload

The workload panel is a mini scorecard which displays user-defined workload metrics for the process by entering the metric ID in the Workload column.

Dependency

The dependency panel is a mini scorecard which displays user-defined dependency metrics for the process by entering the metric ID in the Service Support or Service delivery columns. For example, the change management process is heavily dependent on the success and well-being of the service desk, release & deployment management, configuration management and service level management processes. By entering SD005, RM009 and CFM008; and by entering SLM009 'Customer Satisfaction' metrics into the respective data entry columns, their current process satisfaction levels are displayed. Figure11.13 reveals some dependant processes of change management with poor to mediocre satisfaction levels resulting in strain on the change management process.

S	T	P	Service Support Processes	Actual		S	T	P	Service Delivery Processes	Actual
	▲	B	SD005	SD Customer Satisfaction	3		▼	W	SLM009	SLM Customer Satisfaction	2
	↔	S	RM009	RM Customer Satisfaction	3						
	↔	S	CFM008	CFM Customer Satisfaction	4						

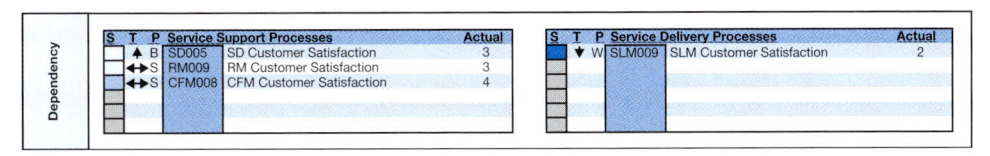

Figure 11.12   itSMF KPI Scorecard© Dependency Table

Efficiency

The Efficiency panel is a mini scorecard which displays user-defined efficiency metrics for the process by entering the metric ID in the Efficiency or Cycle-time columns. For example, entering CM019 in the 'Cycle Time – Avg. Hrs/Change' column will automatically display the details for the 'Avg. cycle time – basic (days)' metric.

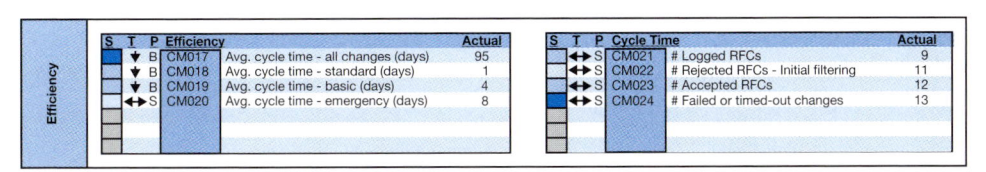

S	T	P	Efficiency		Actual		S	T	P	Cycle Time		Actual
	▼	B	CM017	Avg. cycle time - all changes (days)	95		↔	S	CM021	# Logged RFCs	9
	▼	B	CM018	Avg. cycle time - standard (days)	1		↔	S	CM022	# Rejected RFCs - Initial filtering	11
	▼	B	CM019	Avg. cycle time - basic (days)	4		↔	S	CM023	# Accepted RFCs	12
	↔	S	CM020	Avg. cycle time - emergency (days)	8		↔	S	CM024	# Failed or timed-out changes	13

Figure 11.13   itSMF KPI Scorecard© Efficiency Table

Tip

> It is permissible to change the headings for the Efficiency scorecards. Click on the heading and type in new entry.

Performance and Benefit Indicator scorecards

A series of scorecards are used to aggregate metrics for the Performance and Benefit Indicators used in the dashboard. For example, the Performance Indicators panel is based on the aggregated metrics in the quality, efficiency and effectiveness scorecards. Another example, the Benefits Indicator panel is based on the aggregated metrics provided by three user-defined scorecards, that is benefit 1, benefit 2 and benefit 3.

Key Goal & Improvement Indicator Scorecards

A series of scorecards are used to aggregate metrics for the Key Goal & Improvement Indicators used in the dashboard. For example, the Key Goal Indicators panel is based on the aggregated metrics in the activity, process and IT goals scorecards. Another example, the Improvement Initiative Indicators panel is based on the aggregated metrics provided by three user-defined scorecards, that is initiative 1, initiative 2 and initiative 3.

Dashboard scorecards

Dashboard scorecards are used to aggregate up to 10 key performance metrics and to assess them collectively as an index or group. Scorecards also allow user-defined index names and descriptions to be customized. For example, the following quality scorecard for the change management process is comprised of four key performance metrics i.e. CM005, CM008, CM011 and CM012.

Collectively this group of metrics is aggregated into a series of status indicators which display the Status, Trend, Progress and Index Median of the metrics group.

[Process]

The [Process] tab is used to design, configure and display the summary results in a generic process scorecard allowing the placement of key performance metric sensors throughout the process to identify potential hot-spots. The process scorecard also provides scorecards to configure and display the inputs, outputs, workload, dependencies, efficiency, performance and critical success factors of the process.

Process scorecards

The process scorecard provides a visual representation of a generic process. The process scorecard allows up to 20 user-defined 'Process Sensors' to be configured and placed throughout the process to identify potential hot-spots. For example, in the preceding diagram process step '1 RFC Initiators' has process sensor number 3 placed before it. Process sensor 3 has been mapped to 'CM003 - # of unauthorized changes made' and has been placed at the beginning of the process to indicate if the process is being used. For another example, in the preceding diagram process step '19 Back Out' has a process sensor number 5 placed beside it. Process sensor 5 has been mapped to 'CM005 - # outage incident count' and has been placed by the back out step to indicate a potential hot-spot with the back out procedure.

There are three steps involved in the configuring the process scorecard with the process sensors:

1. Determine which metrics are useful and map them to an Input, Output or Workload metric by entering the sensor # to the left of the metric. For example, the following diagram shows process sensor # 3 mapped to 'CM003 - # of unauthorized changes made'.

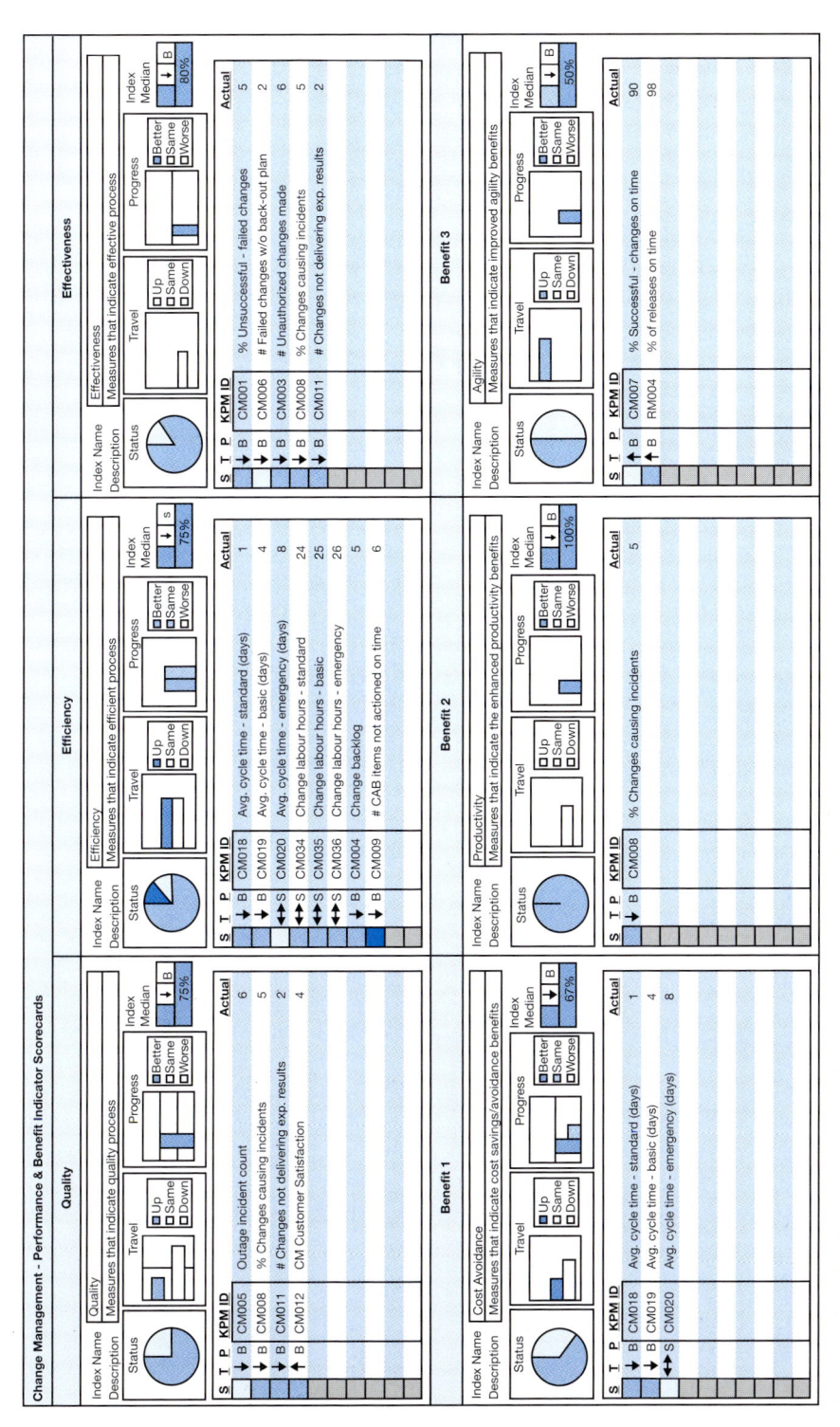

User instructions for itSMF KPI Scorecard© metrics template 165

Figure 11.14   SMF KPI Scorecard© Performance & Benefits Scorecards

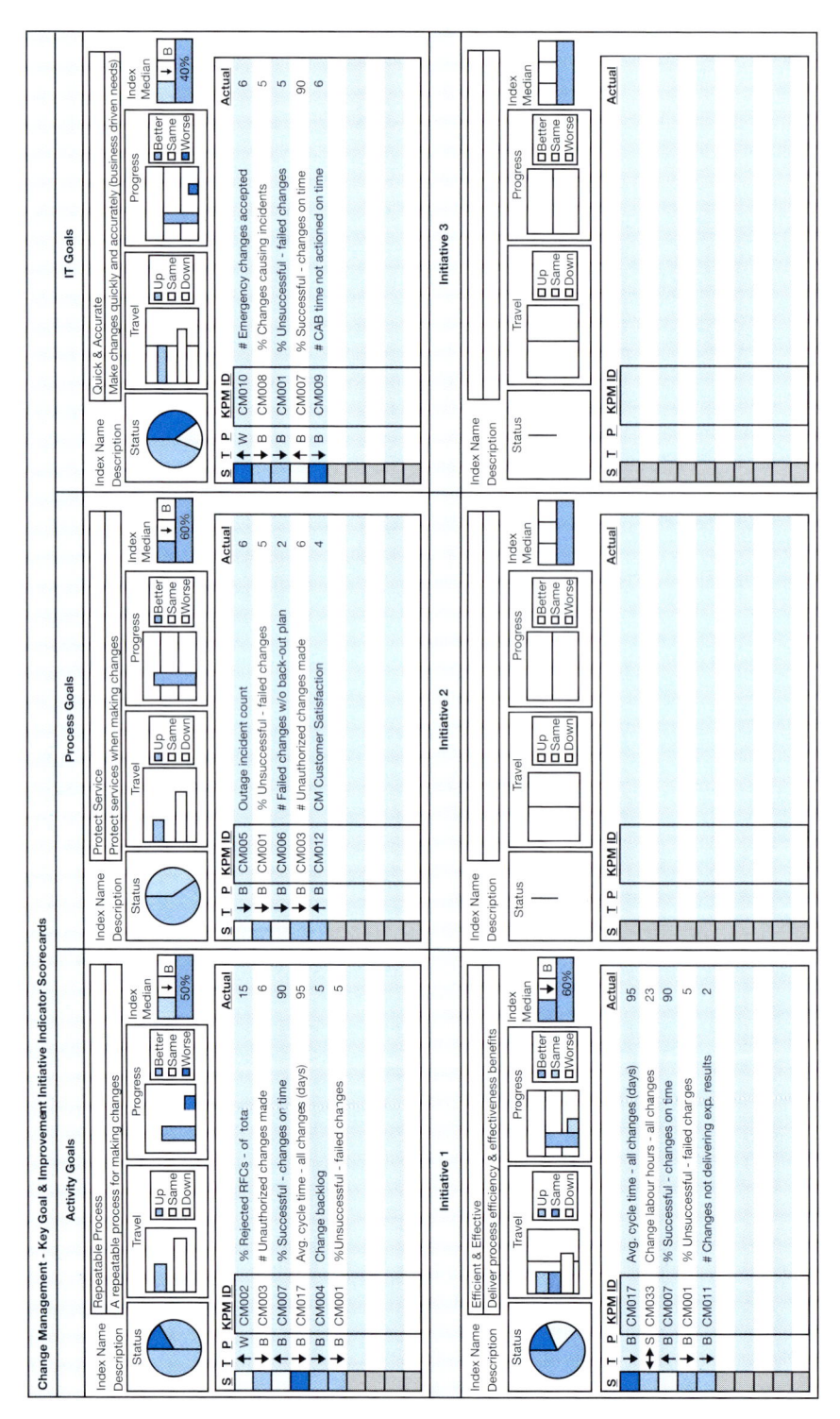

Figure 11.15   SMF KPI Scorecard© KGIs & Initiatives Scorecards

User instructions for itSMF KPI Scorecard© metrics template   167

Quality				
Index Name	Quality			
Description	Measures that indicate quality process			

Status	Travel	Progress	Index Median
(pie chart)	☐ Up ☐ Same ☐ Down	☐ Better ☐ Same ☐ Worse	↓ B 75%

S	T	P	KPM ID		Actual
	↓	B	CM005	Outage incedent count	6
	↓	B	CM008	% Changes causing incidents	5
	↓	B	CM011	# Changes not delivering exp. results	2
	↑	B	CM012	CM Customer Satisfaction	4

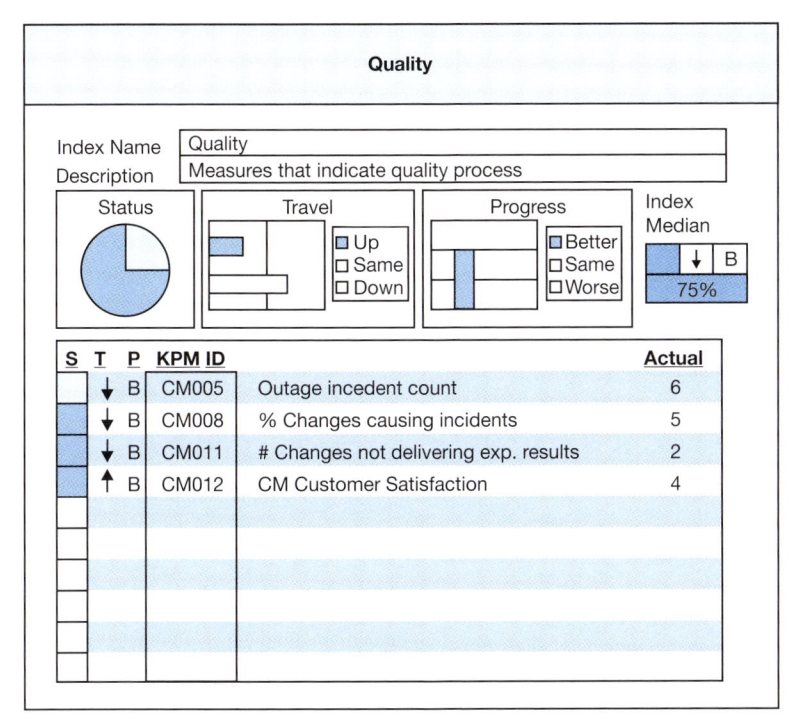

Figure 11.16   itSMF KPI Scorecard© Dashboard Scorecards

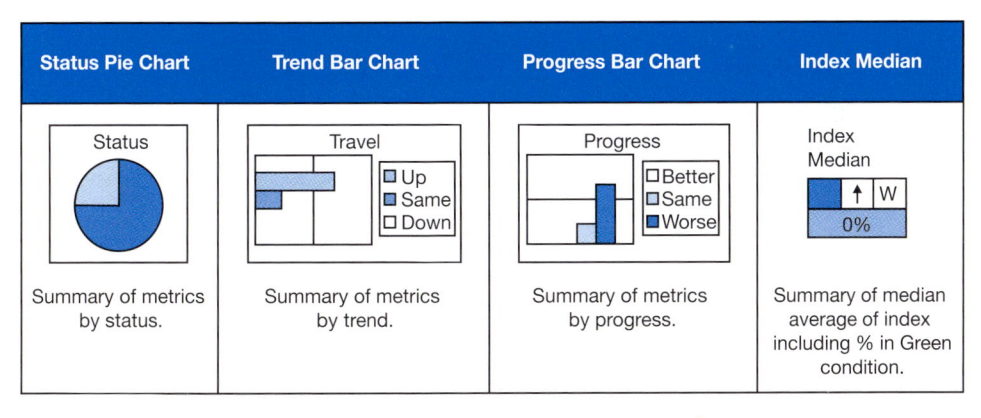

Status Pie Chart	Trend Bar Chart	Progress Bar Chart	Index Median
Status (pie chart)	Travel ☐ Up ☐ Same ☐ Down	Progress ☐ Better ☐ Same ■ Worse	Index Median ↑ W 0%
Summary of metrics by status.	Summary of metrics by trend.	Summary of metrics by progress.	Summary of median average of index including % in Green condition.

Figure 11.17   itSMF KPI Scorecard© Scorecard Status Indicators

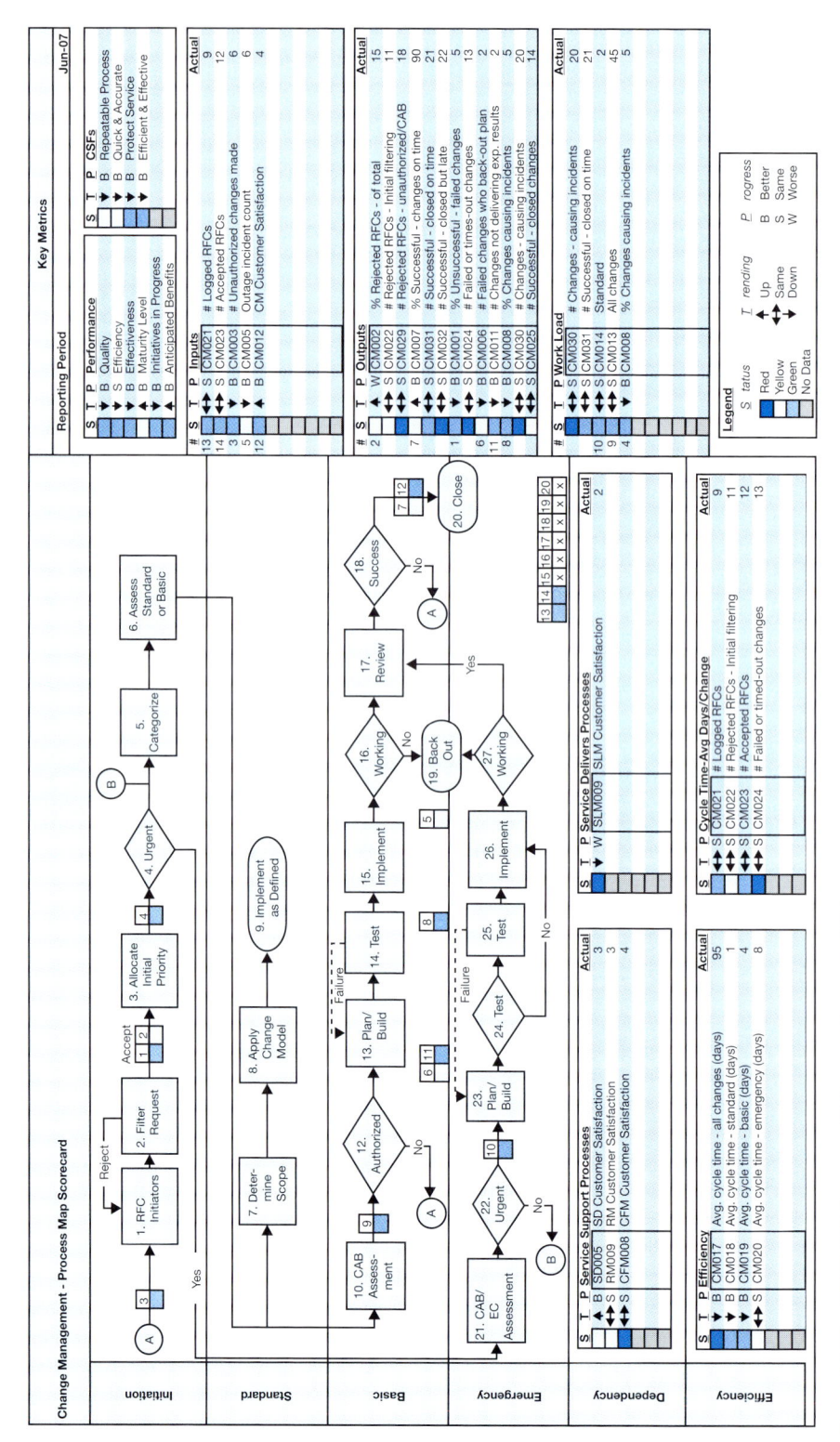

Figure 11.18 itSMF KPI Scorecard© Process Scorecard Tab

User instructions for itSMF KPI Scorecard© metrics template

#	S	T	P	Inputs		Actual
13		↔	S	CM021	# Logged RFCs	9
14		↔	S	CM023	# Accepted RFCs	12
3		▼	B	CM003	# Unauthorized changes made	6
5		▼	B	CM005	Outage incident count	6
12		▲	B	CM012	CM Customer Satisfaction	4

Figure 11.19   itSMF KPI Scorecard© Process Sensor Mapping

Tip

> Where possible, it is good practice to **number the Process Sensors to match the Metric ID number**. For example, Process Sensor #5 matched to Metric ID CM005.

2. Select the entire process sensor (ID number and process state colour box) and drag it to the appropriate position on the process scorecard. For example, process sensor # 5 has been selected in the following diagram and is being dragged to the new location beside the '19 Back Out' step.

Tip

> Some basic instructions for placing the sensors throughout the process include:
>
> - **Select Process Sensor** – click and select the process number and colour status box together to form a group
> - **Drag Process Sensor to position** – click on the outer edge of the process sensor group selection and drag to the desired location

3. Document the process sensor diagnostic reasoning located at the bottom of the worksheet. Diagnostic reasoning should include 'Suspect Root Causes' and 'Prescriptive Remedies' information for each process sensor. This will help optimize the trouble-shooting process when things go wrong.

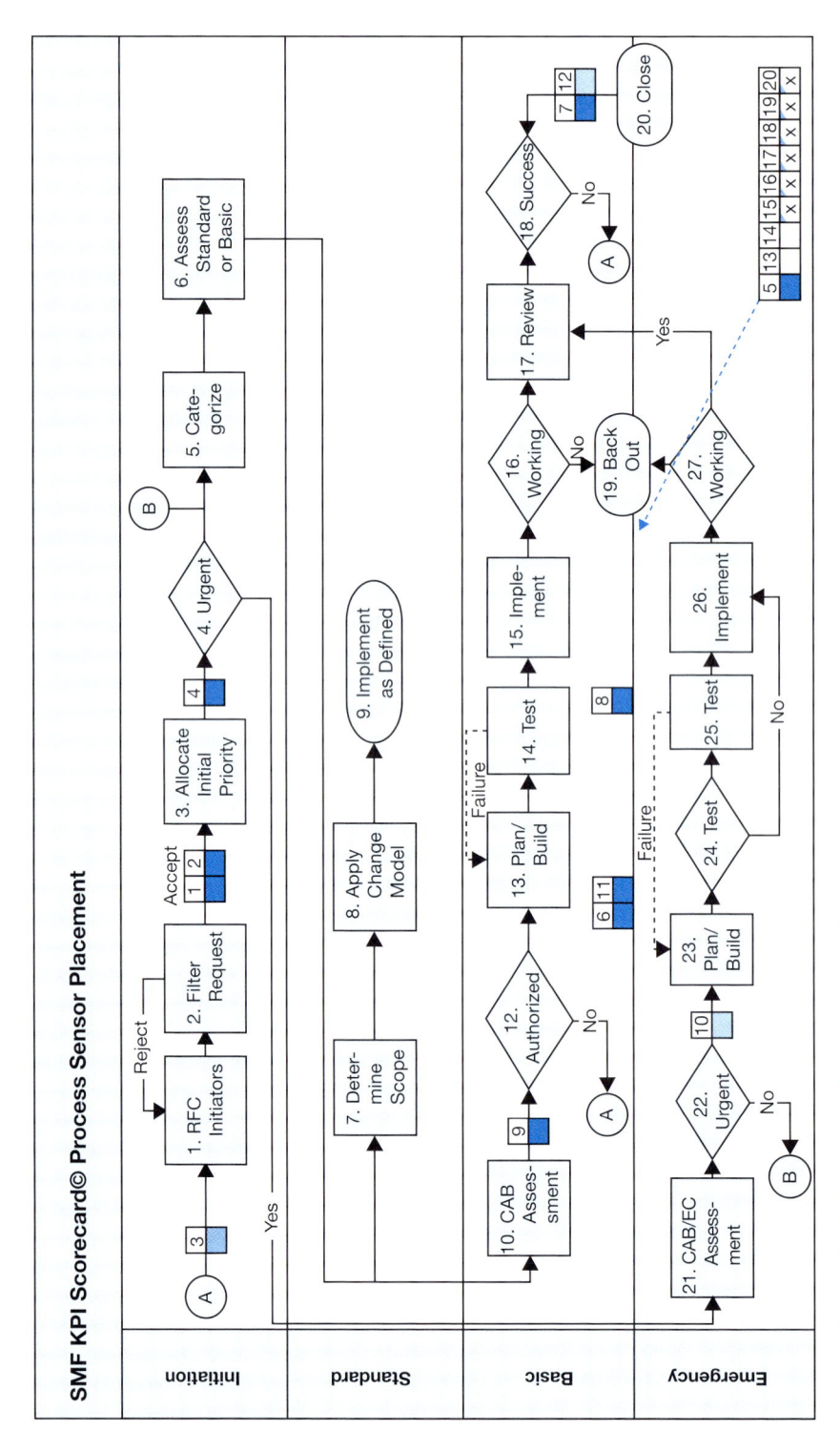

Figure 11.20 SMF KPI Scorecard© Process Sensor Placement

User instructions for itSMF KPI Scorecard© metrics template

Change Management - Process Sensor Documentation - Diagnostic Reasoning

#	S	T	P	KPM ID	Description	Actual	Suspect "Root Causes"	Prescriptive Remedies
1		→	B	CM001	% Unsuccessful - failed changes	5	a) insufficient requirements b) poor testing	a) improve requirements gathering b) improve test procedures or tools
2		←	W	CM002	% Rejected RFCs - of total	15	a) User education b) filter process too stringent	a) better communications b) revise filter process
3		→	B	CM003	# Unauthorized changes made	8	a) insufficient education b) compliance policy too lax	a) training b) revisit policy
4		→	B	CM008	% Changed causing incidents	5	a) too many emergencies b) poor testing	a) improve requirements filtering b) improve test procedures or tools
5		→	B	CM005	Outage incident count	6	a) failed backouts b) poor testing	a) improve backout planning b) improve test procedures or tools
6		→	B	CM006	# Failed changes w/c back-out plan	2	a) poor RM planning b) weak compliance policy c) risk assessments	a) improve planning b) revisit policy c) improve risk assessments
7		←	B	CM007	% Successful - changes on time	90	a) workload b) poor prioritization	a) add resouces b) revise prioritization methods
8		→	S	CM008	% Changes causing incidents	5	a) too many emergencies b) poor testing	a) improve requirements filtering b) improve test procedures or tools
9		↔	S	CM013	All changes	45	a) workload b) unstable infrastructure	a) add resouces b) problem management required
10		↔	S	CM014	Standard	2	a) workload	a) add resources
11		→	B	CM011	# Changes not delivering exp. results	2	a) insufficient requirements b) poor testing	a) improve requirements gathering b) improve test procedures or tools
12		←	B	CM012	CM Customer Satisfaction	4		
13								
14								
15								
16								
17								
18								
19								
20								

Figure 11.21 itSMF KPI Scorecard© Documenting Diagnostic Reasoning

> **Tip**
>
> Some basic rule-of-thumb guidelines for placing the sensors throughout the process include:
> - **Keep it simple** – too many sensors will congest the process and make interpretation difficult and confusing
> - **Inputs** – generally placed at the beginning of the process as leading indicators
> - **Activities** – generally placed throughout the process as leading indicators
> - **Outputs** – generally placed at the end of the process as leading indicators
> - **Root-cause approach** – place sensors close to activities which may be the source or potential cause of problem areas
> - **Documentation** – good record keeping of the diagnostic reasoning behind sensor placement.

Note the inputs, outputs, workload, dependencies and efficiency scorecards are the same as and are described in the Dashboard section.

> **Tip**
>
> See [**Dashboard**] tab instructions for the creation of inputs, outputs, workload, dependencies and efficiency scorecards.

Performance scorecards

Similar to the [Dashboard] tab, a series of scorecards are used to aggregate metrics for the Performance Indicators used in the process scorecard. For example, the Performance Indicators are based on the aggregated metrics in the quality, efficiency, effectiveness, maturity, initiatives and benefits scorecards.

Critical Success Factor scorecards

Similar to the [Dashboard] tab, a series of scorecards are used to aggregate metrics for the Critical Success Factor Indicators used in the process scorecard. For example, the Critical Success Factor Indicators are based on the aggregated metrics in the CSF1 through CSF6 scorecards.

Note that configuring and interpreting the scorecards is the same as and is described in the Dashboard section.

User instructions for itSMF KPI Scorecard© metrics template

Change Management - Performance Scorecards

Quality
Measures that indicate quality process

KPM ID	Description	Actual
CM005	Outage incident count	6
CM008	% Changes causing incidents	5
CM011	# Changes not delivering exp. results	2
CM012	CM Customer Satisfaction	4

Index Median: 75%

Efficiency
Measures that indicate efficient process

KPM ID	Description	Actual
CM018	Avg. cycle time - standard (days)	1
CM019	Avg. cycle time - basic (days)	4
CM020	Avg. cycle time - emergency (days)	8
CM034	Change labour hours - standard	24
CM035	Change labour hours - basic	25
CM036	Change labour hours - emergency	26
CM004	Change backlog	5
CM009	# CAB items not actioned on time	6

Index Median: 75%

Effectiveness
Measures that indicate effective process

KPM ID	Description	Actual
CM001	% Unsuccessful - failed changes	5
CM006	# Failed changes w/o back-out plan	2
CM003	# Unauthorized changes made	6
CM008	% Changes causing incidents	5
CM011	# Changes not delivering exp. results	2

Index Median: 80%

Maturity
Cost Avoidance - Measures that indicate cost savings/avoidance benefits

KPM ID	Description	Actual
CM037	CM Maturity Level	2

Index Median: 0%

Initiatives
Initiatives in Progress - Measures that indicate the progress of improvements

KPM ID	Description	Actual
CM017	Avg. cycle time - all changes (days)	95
CM033	Change labour hours - all changes	23
CM007	% Successful - changes on time	90
CM001	% Unsuccessful - failed changes	5
CM011	# Changes not delivering exp. results	2

Index Median: 100%

Benefits
Anticipated Benefits - Measures that indicate the anticipated benefits

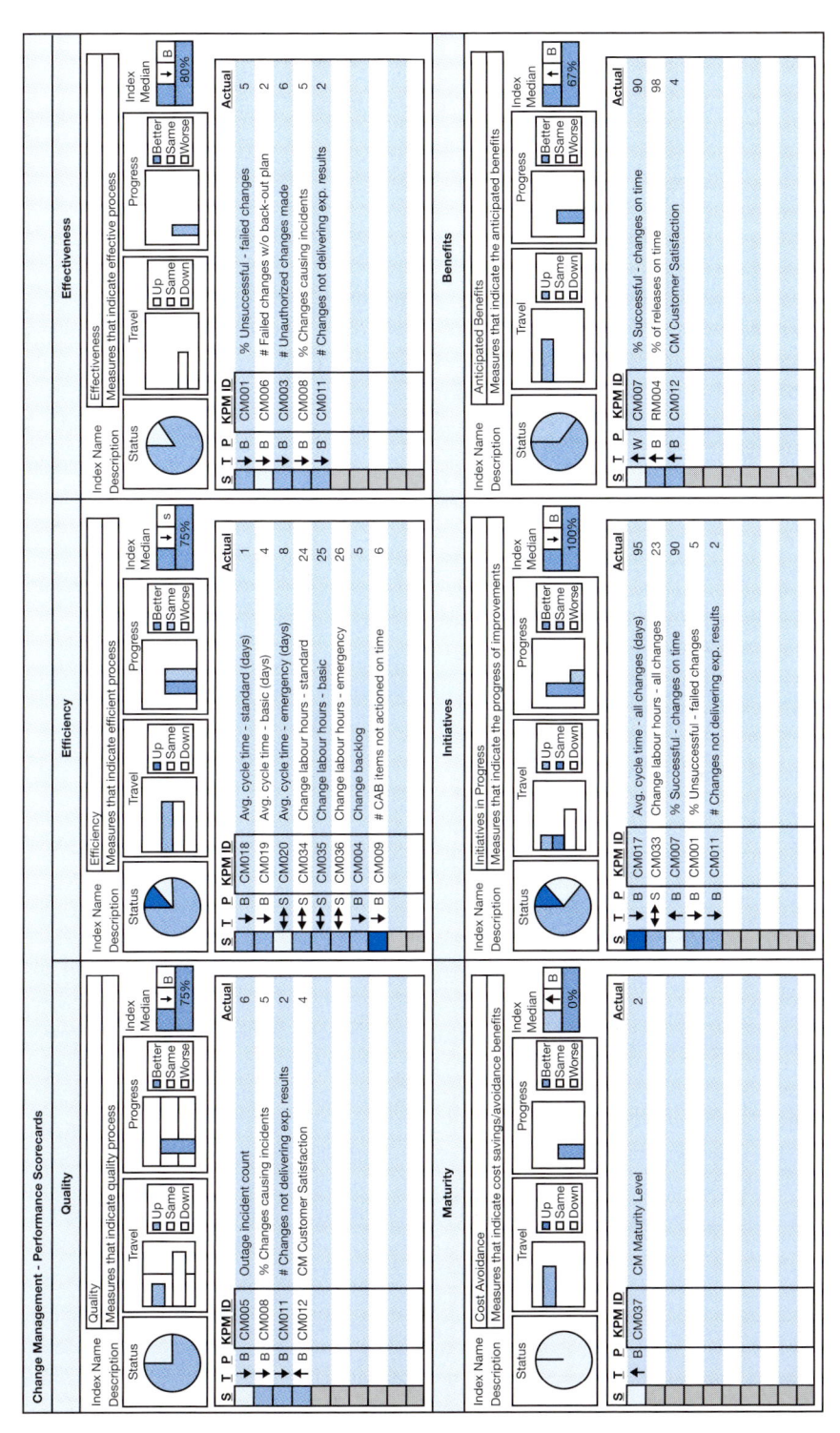

KPM ID	Description	Actual
CM007	% Successful - changes on time	90
RM004	% of releases on time	98
CM012	CM Customer Satisfaction	4

Index Median: 67%

Figure 11.22 itSMF KPI Scorecard© Process Performance scorecards

> 💡 Tip
>
> See [**Dashboard**] tab instructions for the creation, configuration and interpretation of scorecards.

[Causal]

The [Causal] tab is used to design, configure and display the summary results of a root-cause analysis map to identify potential cause and effect relationships. The causal map also provides scorecards to configure and display the quality, efficiency, effectiveness, maturity, workload, supporting processes and anticipated benefits of the process.

Note the causal map could be configured for either a theme or process based classification type.

> 💡 Tip
>
> See section **"Cause-and-Effect Diagram (Ishikawa)"** for examples of Theme vs. Process classification types.

Causal scorecards

Similar to the [Dashboard] tab, a series of causal scorecards are used to aggregate metrics for the Root Cause Analysis Indicators used in the causal map. For example, the Root Cause Analysis Indicators are based on the aggregated metrics in the quality, efficiency, effectiveness, maturity, workload, supporting process and anticipated benefits scorecards.

Note that configuring and interpreting the scorecards is the same as and is described in the Dashboard section.

> 💡 Tip
>
> See [**Dashboard**] tab instructions for the creation, configuration and interpretation of scorecards.

[Initiatives]

The [Initiatives] tab is used to record Service Improvement Initiatives (SIIs) and to document when SIIs have been completed and what if any new metrics are being used to track the progress. This helps to keep an audit trail of various SII requests and activities. The following table found on the [Initiatives] tab, provides an example of various SIIs, activities and status.

User instructions for itSMF KPI Scorecard© metrics template

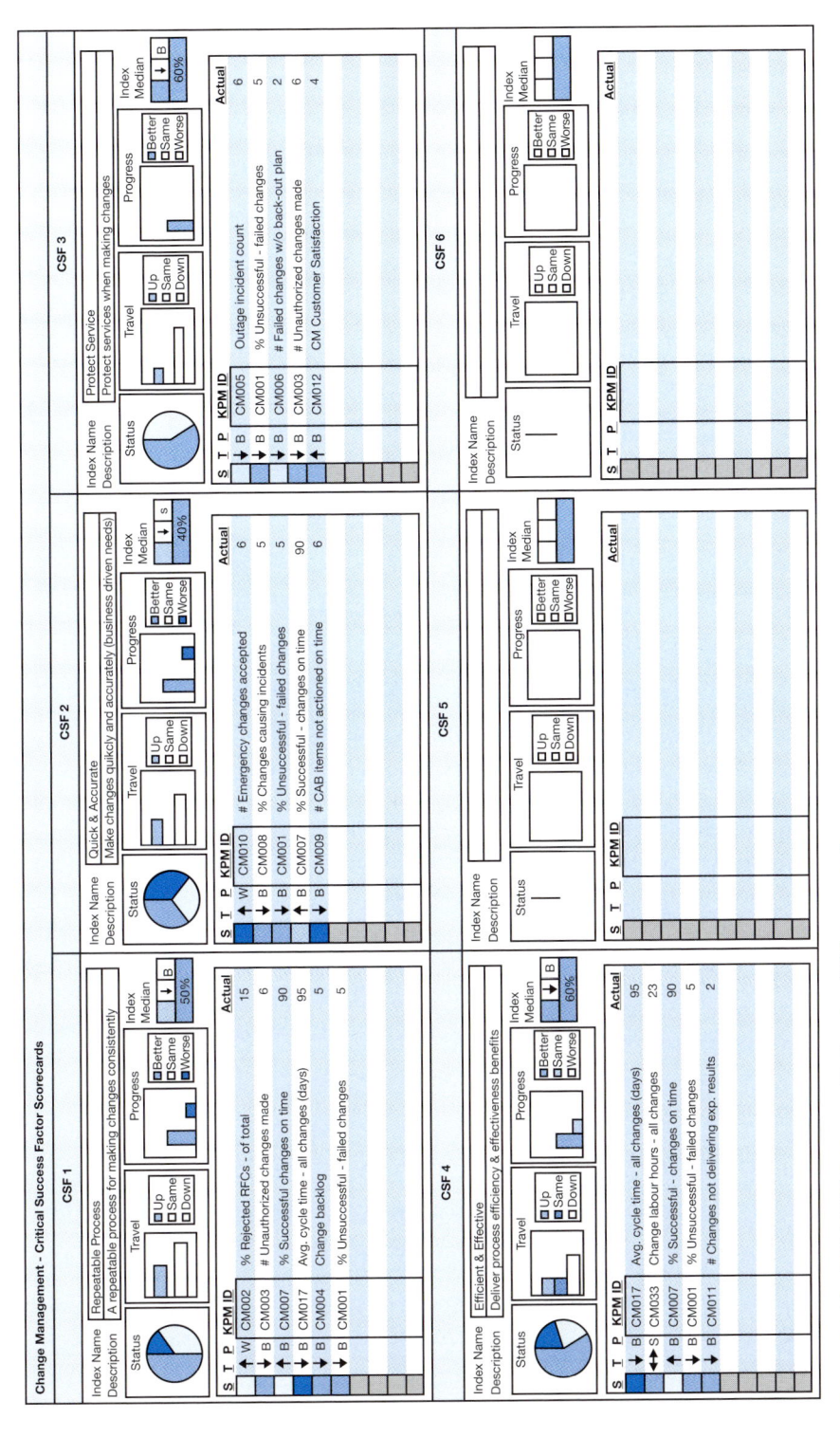

Figure 11.23   itSMF KPI Scorecard© Process CSF scorecards

Change Management - Root Cause Analysis

Reporting Period: Feb-07

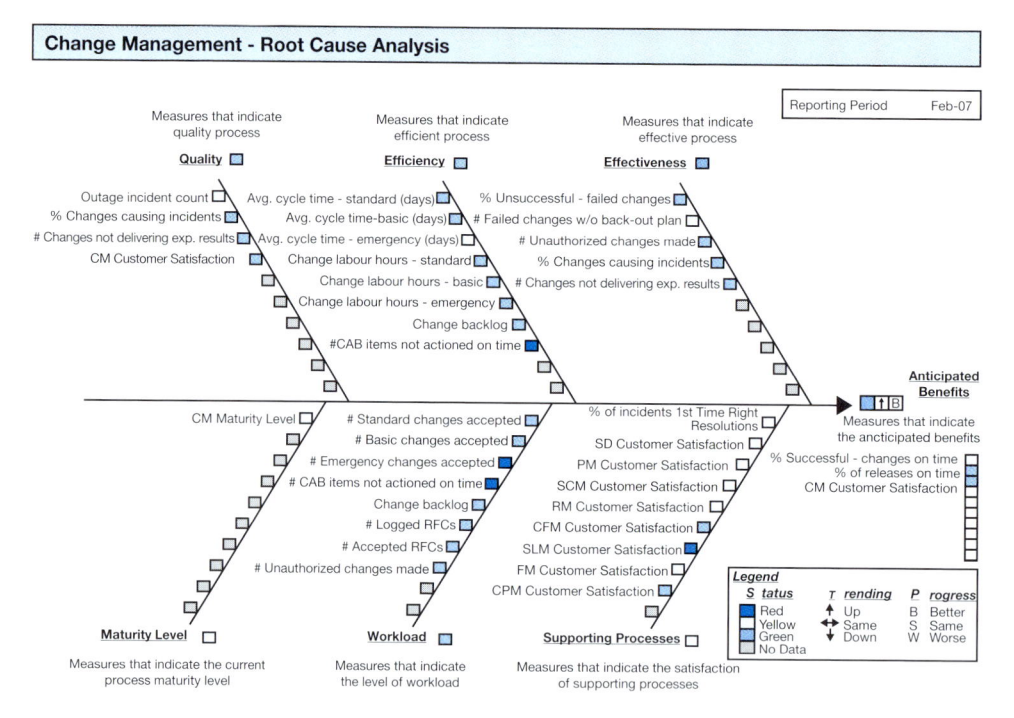

Measures that indicate quality process — Quality
- Outage incident count
- % Changes causing incidents
- # Changes not delivering exp. results
- CM Customer Satisfaction

Measures that indicate efficient process — Efficiency
- Avg. cycle time - standard (days)
- Avg. cycle time-basic (days)
- Avg. cycle time - emergency (days)
- Change labour hours - standard
- Change labour hours - basic
- Change labour hours - emergency
- Change backlog
- #CAB items not actioned on time

Measures that indicate effective process — Effectiveness
- % Unsuccessful - failed changes
- # Failed changes w/o back-out plan
- # Unauthorized changes made
- % Changes causing incidents
- # Changes not delivering exp. results

Anticipated Benefits — Measures that indicate the anticipated benefits
- % Successful - changes on time
- % of releases on time
- CM Customer Satisfaction

Maturity Level — Measures that indicate the current process maturity level
- CM Maturity Level

Workload — Measures that indicate the level of workload
- # Standard changes accepted
- # Basic changes accepted
- # Emergency changes accepted
- # CAB items not actioned on time
- Change backlog
- # Logged RFCs
- # Accepted RFCs
- # Unauthorized changes made

Supporting Processes — Measures that indicate the satisfaction of supporting processes
- % of incidents 1st Time Right Resolutions
- SD Customer Satisfaction
- PM Customer Satisfaction
- SCM Customer Satisfaction
- RM Customer Satisfaction
- CFM Customer Satisfaction
- SLM Customer Satisfaction
- FM Customer Satisfaction
- CPM Customer Satisfaction

Legend
- Status: Red / Yellow / Green / No Data
- Trending: Up / Same / Down
- Progress: B Better / S Same / W Worse

Figure 11.24   itSMF KPI Scorecard© Causal Tab

Note there are 30 Service Improvement Initiative metrics (SII001 – SII030) reserved as placeholders for tracking improvement initiatives. These Improvement Initiative metrics are used to track the status of improvement initiatives and are configured and updated using the [KPMs] and [Input] tab respectively. For example, in the preceding table on 5-Jun-07 a service improvement initiative was raised for incident management to improve 1st call resolution where the user chose KPM 'SII001' as the progress tracking metric.

[001 – 012]

The [001 – 012] tabs are used to display trending and data dictionary information for specific metrics. For example, the following diagram trending data is displayed up to Jun-07 however the period being summarized in the title bar is for Feb-07.

Tip

> Make sure the Reporting Period is set to the correct date. The report period is a drop down field which selects the reporting period (month) for all dashboard and scorecard metrics found on the [**Input**] tab. See **Report Period** in the [**Input**] tab instructions for more details.

User instructions for itSMF KPI Scorecard© metrics template

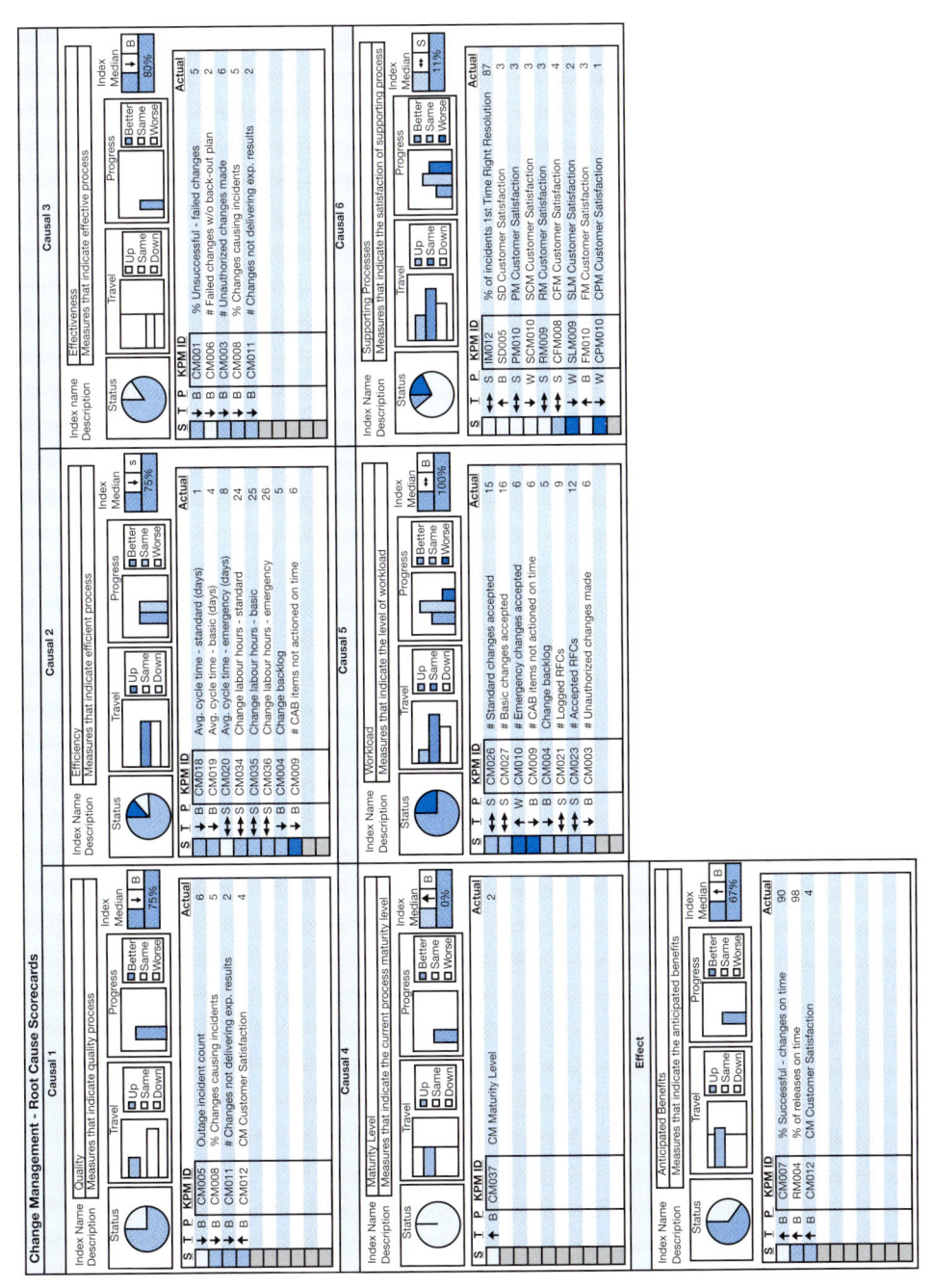

Figure 11.25 itSMF KPI Scorecard© Causal scorecards

Date	Process	Initiative Name	Requested by	Completed By	KPM ID	Date Completed	ID #
2-Apr-07	Change Mgmt	Deliver process efficiency and effectiveness benefits (Note: use exsiting metrics to monitor improvement initiative)	JJ		CM017	In progress	1
					CM033		2
					CM007		3
					CM001		4
					CM011		5
5-Jun-07	Incident Mgmt	Improve 1st call resolution time (Note: used reserved Service Improvement Initiative metric for tracking)	DS		SII001	Not started	6
							7
							8
							9
							10
							11
							12
							13
							14

Figure 11.26   itSMF KPI Scorecard© Initiatives Table

Comments or actions

A user-defined space has been provided to record temporary comments or actions for the specific key performance metric.

11.7 Getting Started

To get started, use the following steps as a general guideline to implementing a basic metrics framework pilot using the itSMF KPI Scorecard© metrics template:

Administration of the Metrics
1. Familiarise yourself the concepts presented in this book.
2. Copy metrics templates to a working directory, remember to make frequent saves and backups
3. Enter the Reporting Start Date in the [Tables] tab.
4. Enter the ITSM process owners and roles in the [Tables] tab.

User instructions for itSMF KPI Scorecard© metrics template

Change Management			Feb 07	Previous	100.0	Actual	45.0	Progress	Worse	Status	Red	CM007

Percentage of Changes on Time

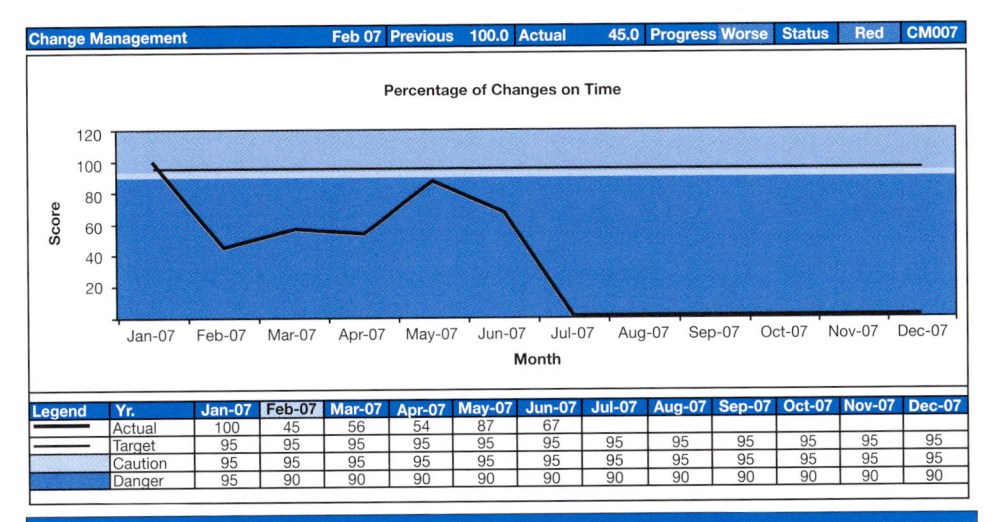

Legend	Yr.	Jan-07	Feb-07	Mar-07	Apr-07	May-07	Jun-07	Jul-07	Aug-07	Sep-07	Oct-07	Nov-07	Dec-07
	Actual	100	45	56	54	87	67						
	Target	95	95	95	95	95	95	95	95	95	95	95	95
	Caution	95	95	95	95	95	95	95	95	95	95	95	95
	Danger	95	90	90	90	90	90	90	90	90	90	90	90

Change Management	Percentage of changes on time
Goal	The goal of the Change Management process is to ensure that standardized methods and procedures are used for efficient and prompt handling of all changes, in order to minimize the impact of change-related incidents upon service quality, and consequently to improve the day-to-day operation of the organization.
Mission	To manage all changes that could impact on IT's ability to deliver services through a formal, centralized process of approval, scheduling and control to ensure that the IT infrastructure stays aligned to business requirements with a minimum of risk.
Objective	To be an effective process for implementing changes required by the organization
Description	All changes have a completion time. If they are still open after this time they count towards this metric.
Specification	Delays can be caused by good reasons - if Percentage of Failed Changes is low then a high value here might be OK, so it should be a lower priority.
Justification	If changes are consistently late then it shows poor change control and an increased risk of business disruption.
Audience	Process Owner, IT Management, SLA Process Owner, Business Customer, Team Members, SIP Process Owner
Constraints	None
Polarity	More is Better
Process Owner Email	john.doe@micromationinc.com
Comments or Actions	

Figure 11.27   itSMF KPI Scorecard© Metrics Trending Tabs

5. Enter the thresholds including Danger Value, Target Value, Low Limit and High Limit for the desired metrics in the [KPMs] tab.
6. Configure the Dashboard scorecards to align the metrics and scorecards to best meet your organizational needs on the [Dashboard] tab.

7. Configure the Process scorecards to align the metrics and scorecards to best meet your organizational needs on the [Process] tab.
8. Configure the Causal scorecards to align the metrics and scorecards to best meet your organizational needs on the [Causal] tab.

Monitoring the Metrics – Check

9. Set the Report Period in the [Input] tab.
10. Enter the actual Metric Values in the appropriate Reporting Period column for the desired metrics in the [Input] tab.
11. Validate the Metric Values by looking for 'White' statuses on the [Home] tab of the applicable process for the desired metrics.

Analysis of the Metrics – Act

12. Analyse the [Dashboard], [Process] and [Causal] tabs to determine if improvement initiatives are necessary.

Tuning the Process – Plan

13. Log tuning improvement initiatives in the [Initiatives] tab.

Implement Process Initiatives – Do

14. Create Improvement Initiative key performance indicators in the [KPMs] tab.
15. Configure Improvement Initiative scorecards in the [Dashboard] tab.

Measurement Reporting

16. Report progress to key stakeholders and process owners as required.
17. Repeat cycle and verify performance improvements and value realized over time.

11.8 Printing

Each tab can be configured to print using standard Microsoft Excel® 2003 print functions.

List of tables and figures

Table 2.1	Strategic, tactical and operational processes	4
Figure 3.1	Steering towards value realization	8
Figure 3.2	Drivers of change	9
Figure 3.3	Metrics help management, owners & staff	11
Figure 4.1	Measurement framework	14
Figure 4.2	Deming Plan/Do/Check/Act Cycle	15
Figure 4.3	Value to customer themes	16
Figure 4.4	Linking goals and objectives	17
Figure 4.5	Metric thresholds	20
Figure 4.6	Sample data sources	22
Figure 4.7	Sample measurement dictionary	23
Figure 4.8	Sample metric elements – Temperature	24
Figure 5.1	Sample trending report	28
Figure 5.2	Sample aggregation of measures	28
Figure 5.3	Sample classification of measures	30
Figure 5.4	Alignment of key Measures	30
Figure 5.5	Sample dashboard report	31
Figure 5.6	Sample roles-based dashboard hierarchy	31
Figure 5.7	Sample BSC perspectives	32
Figure 5.8	Sample general scorecards by themes	33
Figure 5.9	Cascading of scorecards	34
Figure 5.10	Sample strategy map for IT	35
Figure 5.11	Sample process scorecard	37
Figure 6.1	Measurement process inputs/activities/outputs	42
Figure 6.2	Measurement Process Lifecycle	44
Figure 6.3	Measurement sub-process activities	45
Figure 6.4	Measurement Database MDB	47
Table 6.1	Sample IT service management processes	48
Table 6.2	R.A.C.I authority matrix	52
Figure 6.5	Classification of measurements	55

Figure 6.6	Measurement structures	56
Figure 6.7	Measurement dimensions	57
Figure 6.8	Measurement structure and dimensional breakdown	58
Figure 6.9	Measurement lifecycle states	58
Figure 6.10	Compare and contrast references	69
Figure 6.11	Sample Change Management process flowchart	70
Figure 6.12	Affinity Diagram – likely contributors to high costs	71
Figure 6.13	Theme Classification Type Ishikawa	72
Figure 6.14	Process Classification Type Ishikawa	72
Figure 6.15	Sample Theme Classification Type Ishikawa	73
Figure 6.16	Sample Interrelationship Diagram	74
Figure 6.17	Sample Trending Report	77
Figure 6.18	Sample leading and lagging indicators	79
Figure 6.19	Assessing initiative options	84
Figure 6.20	Sample Decision Analysis Tool	86
Figure 6.21	Stakeholder types	93
Figure 6-22	Stakeholder mapping	93
Figure 6-23	Mapping measurement reporting	95
Figure 6.24	Measurement communications plan	97
Figure 7.1	Sample console	105
Figure 7.2	Sample change management metrics	105
Figure 7.3	Sample R.A.C.I. matrix	106
Figure 7.4	Sample metrics thresholds	106
Figure 7.5	Sample metrics values	107
Figure 7.6	Sample change management metrics trending	108
Figure 7.7	Sample change management dashboard	109
Figure 7.8	Sample change management performance scorecards	110
Figure 7.9	Sample change management KGI scorecards	111
Figure 7.10	Sample change management causal scorecard	112
Figure 7.11	Sample change management process scorecard	113
Figure 7.12	Sample change management initiative	114
Figure 7.13	Sample change management updated dashboard	114
Figure 8.1	Continuous service improvement program	116
Figure 8.2	The 7-Step Improvement Process	118
Table 8.1	Single process pros vs. cons	122
Table 8.2	Multi process pros versus cons	123
Table 8.3	All processes/service pros versus cons	124
Figure 8.3	Example process goal alignment with supporting metrics	129
Figure 8.4	Example service goal alignment with supporting metrics	131
Figure 8.5	Example Performance Reporting Matrix	135
Figure 9.1	Total Cost of Ownership (TCO)	144
Figure 9.2	Hypothetical TCO Savings Opportunity	145
Table 11.1	itSMF KPI Scorecard© features	150
Figure 11.1	itSMF KPI Scorecard© navigation and structure	152
Figure 11.2	itSMF KPI Scorecard© - ITSM Metrics MDB sample home page	153
Figure 11.3	itSMF KPI Scorecard© Reporting Start Date	153

Figure 11.4	itSMF KPI Scorecard© Roles Table	154
Figure 11.5	itSMF KPI Scorecard© R.A.C.I. Matrix Table	154
Figure 11.6	itSMF KPI Scorecard© Metrics Data Entry Tab	155
Figure 11.7	itSMF KPI Scorecard© Thresholds Tab	156
Figure 11.7	itSMF KPI Scorecard© Change Tab	157
Figure 11.8	itSMF KPI Scorecard© Process Home Tab for Change Management	158
Figure 11.9	itSMF KPI Scorecard© Legend	159
Figure 11.10	itSMF KPI Scorecard© Dashboard	161
Figure 11.11	itSMF KPI Scorecard© Inputs Table	162
Figure 11.12	itSMF KPI Scorecard© Dependency Table	163
Figure 11.13	itSMF KPI Scorecard© Efficiency Table	163
Figure 11.14	SMF KPI Scorecard© Performance & Benefits Scorecards	165
Figure 11.15	SMF KPI Scorecard© KGIs & Initiatives Scorecards	166
Figure 11.16	itSMF KPI Scorecard© Dashboard Scorecards	167
Figure 11.17	itSMF KPI Scorecard© Scorecard Status Indicators	167
Figure 11.18	itSMF KPI Scorecard© Process Scorecard Tab	168
Figure 11.19	itSMF KPI Scorecard© Process Sensor Mapping	169
Figure 11.20	SMF KPI Scorecard© Process Sensor Placement	170
Figure 11.21	itSMF KPI Scorecard© Documenting Diagnostic Reasoning	171
Figure 11.22	itSMF KPI Scorecard© Process Performance scorecards	173
Figure 11.23	itSMF KPI Scorecard© Process CSF scorecards	175
Figure 11.24	itSMF KPI Scorecard© Causal Tab	176
Figure 11.25	itSMF KPI Scorecard© Causal scorecards	177
Figure 11.26	itSMF KPI Scorecard© Initiatives Table	178
Figure 11.27	itSMF KPI Scorecard© Metrics Trending Tabs	179

References

1. ITIL® is a Registered Trade Mark, and a Registered Community Trade Mark of the Office of Government Commerce, and is Registered in the U.S. Patent and Trade Mark Office
2. Control Objectives for Information Technology CobiT® 2005 is a Registered Trade Mark of The IT Governance Institute, ISBN 1933284374, www.itgi.org
3. BS ISO/IEC 20000-1:2005, International Standard for Information Technology – Service Management, ISBN 0580475298, www.iso.org
4. Brooks, P. (2006). *Metrics for IT Service Management*, ISBN 9077212698, Van Haren Publishing, Zaltbommel, www.vanharen.net
5. Brooks, P. (2006) *Metrics for IT Service Management*, ISBN 9077212698, Van Haren Publishing, Zaltbommel, www.vanharen.net, 15
6. ITIL® V3 CSI Book, Office of Government Commerce (2007). Continual Service Improvement, ISBN 9780113310494, The Stationary Office, www.tso.co.uk/bookshop, 30
7. ITIL® V3 CSI Book, Office of Government Commerce (2007). Continual Service Improvement, ISBN 9780113310494, The Stationary Office, www.tso.co.uk/bookshop, 31
8. Deming, W. Edwards, Plan/Do/Check/Act cycle, www.deming.org
9. ITIL® V3 SD Book, Office of Government Commerce (2007). Service Design, ISBN 9780113310470, The Stationary Office, www.tso.co.uk/bookshop, 173
10. Basili, V. R., *GQM Paradigm*, University of Maryland, ftp://ftp.cs.umd.edu/pub/sel/papers/gqm.pdf
11. Kaplan, R. S. & D. P. Norton (1996). *The Balanced Scorecard*, Boston: Harvard Business School Press
12. Brooks, P. (2006). *Metrics for IT Service Management*, ISBN 9077212698, Van Haren Publishing, Zaltbommel, www.vanharen.net, 20 - 21
13. Ishikawa, Kaoru (1990), (Translator: J. H. Loftus), *Introduction to Quality Control*; 448 p; ISBN 4-906224-61-X OCLC 61341428
14. Charles Kepner and Benjamin Tregoe, Kepner-Tregoe, KT Problem Analysis Techniques, www.kepner-tregoe.com

15. ITIL® V3 SD Book, Office of Government Commerce (2007). Service Design, ISBN 9780113310470, The Stationary Office, www.tso.co.uk/bookshop, 79 - 97
16. ITIL® V3 SO Book, Office of Government Commerce (2007). Service Operations, ISBN 9780113310463, The Stationary Office, www.tso.co.uk/bookshop, 35 - 46
17. William H. Inmon, Richard D. Hackathorn: Using the Data Warehouse, ISBN 0-471-05966-8, John Wiley & Son's,
18. Ralph Kimball, Margy Ross: The Data Warehouse Toolkit: The Complete Guide to Dimensional Modeling (Second Edition), ISBN 0-471-20024-7, John Wiley & Sons
19. ITIL® V3 ST Book, Office of Government Commerce (2007). Service Transition, ISBN 9780113310487, The Stationary Office, www.tso.co.uk/bookshop, 145 - 154
20. The Data Management Association www.dama.org
21. ITIL® V3 SO Book, Office of Government Commerce (2007). Service Operations, ISBN 9780113310463, The Stationary Office, www.tso.co.uk/bookshop, 35 - 46
22. ITIL® V3 SO Book, Office of Government Commerce (2007). Service Operations, ISBN 9780113310463, The Stationary Office, www.tso.co.uk/bookshop, 58 - 68
23. ITIL® V3 SO Book, Office of Government Commerce (2007). Service Operations, ISBN 9780113310463, The Stationary Office, www.tso.co.uk/bookshop, 58 - 68
24. Brassard M. & D. Ritter (1994). *The Memory Jogger II*, ISBN 1879364441, Goal/QPC, www.goalqpc.com
25. ITIL® V3 CSI Book, Office of Government Commerce (2007). Continual Service Improvement, ISBN 9780113310494, The Stationary Office, www.tso.co.uk/bookshop, 157 - 160
26. ITIL® V3 CSI Book, Office of Government Commerce (2007). Continual Service Improvement, ISBN 9780113310494, The Stationary Office, www.tso.co.uk/bookshop, 137
27. ITIL® V3 CSI Book, Office of Government Commerce (2007). Continual Service Improvement, ISBN 9780113310494, The Stationary Office, www.tso.co.uk/bookshop, 30
28. John P. Kotter, (1996). *Leading Change* ISBN 0875847472 Harvard Business School Press
29. ITIL® V3 CSI Book, Office of Government Commerce (2007). Continual Service Improvement, ISBN 9780113310494, The Stationary Office, www.tso.co.uk/bookshop, 31 - 32
30. TCO Total Cost of Ownership, Gartner www.gartner.com
31. Microsoft Excel® 2003 is a Registered Trade Mark of Microsoft, www.microsoft.com

ITIL Books
The Official Books from itSMF

Foundations of IT Service Management Based on ITIL®V3
Now updated to encompass all of the implications of the V3 refresh of ITIL, the new V3 Foundations book looks at Best Practices, focusing on the Lifecycle approach, and covering the ITIL Service Lifecycle, processes and functions for Service Strategy, Service Design, Service Operation, Service Transition and Continual Service Improvement.
ISBN: 978 908753057 0 (ENGLISH EDITION)
PRICE €39.95 EXCL TAX

Foundations of IT Service Management Based on ITIL®
The bestselling ITIL® V2 edition of this popular guide is available as usual, with 13 language options to give you the widest possible global perspective on this important subject.
ISBN: 978 907721258 5 (ENGLISH EDITION)
PRICE €39.95 EXCL TAX

IT Service Management Based on ITIL®V3: A Pocket Guide
A concise summary for ITIL®V3, providing a quick and portable reference tool to this leading set of best practices for IT Service Management.
ISBN: 978 908753102 7 (ENGLISH EDITION)
PRICE €14.95 EXCL TAX

Van Haren Publishing (VHP) is a leading international publisher, specializing in best practice titles for IT management and business management. VHP publishes in 14 languages, and has sales and distribution agents in over 40 countries worldwide: www.vanharen.net

ISO/IEC 20000
The Official Books from itSMF

ISO/IEC 20000: An Introduction
Promoting awareness of the certification for organizations within the IT Service Management environment.
ISBN: 978 908753081 5 (ENGLISH EDITION)
PRICE €49.95 EXCL TAX

Implementing ISO/IEC 20000 Certification: The Roadmap
Practical advice, to assist readers through the requirements of the standard, the scoping, the project approach, the certification procedure and management of the certification.
ISBN: 978 908753082 2
PRICE €39.95 EXCL TAX

ISO/IEC 20000: A Pocket Guide
A quick and accessible guide to the fundamental requirements for corporate certification.
ISBN: 978 907721279 0 (ENGLISH EDITION)
PRICE €14.95 EXCL TAX

Other leading ITSM Books from itSMF

Metrics for IT Service Management
A general guide to the use of metrics as a mechanism to control and steer IT service organizations, with consideration of the design and implementation of metrics in service organizations using industry standard frameworks.
ISBN: 978 907721269 1
PRICE €39.95 EXCL TAX

Six Sigma for IT Management
The first book to provide a coherent view and guidance for using the Six Sigma approach successfully in IT Service Management, whilst aiming to merge both Six Sigma and ITIL® into a single unified approach to continuous improvement. Six Sigma for IT Management: A Pocket Guide is also available.
ISBN: 978 907721230 1 (ENGLISH EDITION)
PRICE €39.95 EXCL TAX

Frameworks for IT Management
An unparalleled guide to the myriad of IT management instruments currently available to IT and business managers. Frameworks for IT Management: A Pocket Guide is also available.
ISBN: 978 907721290 5 (ENGLISH EDITION)
PRICE €39.95 EXCL TAX

IT Governance based on CobiT 4.1: A Management Guide
Detailed information on the overall process model as well as the theory behind it.
ISBN: 978 90 8753116 4 (ENGLISH EDITION)
PRICE €20,75 EXCL TAX

Contact your local chapter for ITSM Library titles ...please see www.itsmfbooks.com for details.